APPRECIATING POETRY

APPRECIATING POETRY

SADLER – HAYLLAR – POWELL

M

First published 1986 by
THE MACMILLAN COMPANY OF AUSTRALIA PTY LTD
107 Moray Street, South Melbourne 3205
6 Clarke Street, Crows Nest 2065
Reprinted 1987 (twice), 1988, 1989 (twice)

Associated companies and representatives
throughout the world

National Library of Australia
cataloguing in publication data

Sadler, R. K. (Rex Kevin).
  Appreciating poetry.

  Includes index.
  ISBN 0 333 43014 X.

  1. English poetry.   I. Hayllar, T. A. S. (Thomas Albert
S.).   II. Powell, C. J. (Chris J.).   III. Title.

821'.008

Typeset in Century Schoolbook by
Graphicraft Typesetters Ltd, Hong Kong
Printed in Hong Kong

Contents

9   Rhyme and Rhythm 82

—— **Rhyme** —— **Rhyme Pattern Variations** —— **Blank Verse** —— **Rhythm** ——

10   Modern Living 90

11   Sonnets 101

—— **Classical or Petrarchan Sonnets** —— **English Sonnets** ——
**Shakespearean Sonnets — Other Classical English Sonnets — Modern
Sonnets** ——

12   Sport 109

Contents

13 Symbols

—— **Identifying Symbolism** ——

14 The Poetry of War

—— **World War I** —— **Poems from World War II** —— **Poems about the Vietnam War**

15 Satire

—— **Satirizing Sport** —— **Satirizing the Media** ——

16 Fun with Poetry

17 Odes and Elegies 164

—— The Ode —— Elegies —— Modern Elegies ——

18 Comparing Poems 176

—— Work —— Sharks —— The Bomb —— School Days —— Trains ——
Winter ——

19 Parody 189

20 Relationships 199

Preface

Appreciating Poetry offers an outstanding selection of poems suitable for high school students in the middle to upper years. While the book includes representative 'classics' from Shakespeare, Milton, Donne, Marvell, the Romantics, Hopkins, Eliot, Frost, and many more, there are also many poems from contemporary writers. There are numerous poems not previously collected into a school resource book. The criteria for selection included high-interest for students and literary merit.

The book is, unashamedly, a 'teaching' book. We have included chapters of instruction on such diverse areas as: appreciating a poem, rhyme and rhythm, sonnets, elegies and odes, 'sound' in poetry, personification, simile and metaphor, hyperbole, ballads, parodies, and others. Students are encouraged not only to experience a poem but to ask: Why and how? They are encouraged to analyse, to question, to try to understand why a poem achieves its particular effect and how the poet has crafted such a work.

This analytical approach has received some bad press in recent years. We have read and heard from some learned people that such an approach 'kills off' true appreciation of poetry. No concrete evidence has been produced; indeed, the task of designing a piece of research that would provide any such evidence is well-nigh impossible. In the absence of any compelling evidence, then, we returned to sober reflection upon our common experience. Each of us recalled occasions when via an expository lecture, a class discussion, or written questions, our eyes were opened and our hearts warmed as we encountered a previously meaningless poem. For each of us poems have come to life through detailed analysis. We seek to share that experience through the approach used in *Appreciating Poetry*.

So there are questions in this book–plenty of them. Their purpose is to guide students in their encounter with each poem, to direct their attention to specific aspects. The teacher who wishes to adopt a totally different approach can certainly do so. Our desire is not to prescribe, but to offer possibilities.

R. K. Sadler
T. A. S. Hayllar
C. J. Powell

1 Appreciating a Poem

Many people are a little afraid of poetry. Perhaps they have been 'tested' by having to answer difficult questions about a poem they didn't fully understand, and so they felt inadequate. Perhaps they have had someone (such as a teacher!) praise a particular poem, only to find that they didn't understand it, or enjoy it, at all. Experiences like these can cause people to be a little unsure about poetry, so that when they are asked to analyse, understand and appreciate a poem, the task can easily seem overwhelming. Because of this, we need clear guidelines to help us approach the task.

Some people believe that the requisite skills for appreciating a poem cannot be taught. They voice concern that attempts to teach the skills useful in analysing a poem, will make the whole process mechanical and lifeless, and end up reducing works of art to clockwork gadgetry. They are concerned that, in the long run, students will thus come to dislike poetry. They argue that a person's response to a poem should be individual, personal and spontaneous, and that any attempt to learn methods of analysis risks destroying this personal response. And yet, almost every adult lover of poetry can recall a time when a teacher, lecturer, poet, or someone analysed the technique and language used by a poet in a specific poem and, suddenly, the poem came alive for them! The impact of the poem was immeasurably enhanced, not diminished. Thus, while learning and using the skills involved in analysing a poem probably does involve some risk, it also involves considerable potential benefit. We would hold strongly to the view that the ability to analyse a poem, as a means of more finely appreciating the work of art, is a gift, a blessing. When we have these skills we are the better able to resonate with the message and achievement of a poem.

Poetry is an art form. At its best, a poem will bring forth from a reader (or, better still, a listener!) both an emotional, and an intellectual, response. Our ability to respond to poetry is enhanced when we understand more of the more delicate nuances of the artist's achievement.

The purpose of this chapter, then, is to provide you with a glimpse of some of the guidelines that will help you better appreciate a poem. Like all guidelines these will become more familiar in your hands as you make use of them – applying them to specific poems that you encounter.

Guidelines for Analysing a Poem

To help you remember the important aspects of a poem, so that you can 'see' its achievements with more insight, we have provided the following guidelines.

SUBJECT-MATTER of the poem: The question to ask here is: 'What event, situation, or experience does the poem describe or record?'

PURPOSE or theme, or message of the poet: The question to ask here is: 'What is the poet's purpose in writing this – what message does he or she want to communicate?'

EMOTION, or mood, or feeling: What is the predominant emotion, or mood, of the poem? Does the mood change during the poem? What emotions or feelings does the poet seek to evoke in the reader/hearer?

CRAFTSMANSHIP, or technique: This aspect of the poem deals with specific skills the poet has used in creating his or her work of art. A mnemonic, SLIMS, is provided below to help you remember the important areas to look at here.

SUMMARY: Having analysed the poem, it is important to synthesize (i.e. pull all the information together) into a summary. What is the impact of the whole poem for you? How successful is it as a work of art? Does it successfully achieve the poet's purpose or is it flawed in some serious way?

Looking Closer at Craftsmanship

As we saw above, one of the important aspects of a poem's achievement is the *craftsmanship*, or technique, of the poet. *How* does the poet achieve his or her effect? What specific techniques has he or she used in the making of this poem, and what is their effect?

To help you understand the major elements of crafsmanship, we provide the following outline.

STRUCTURE: How is this poem structured? Does it have a conventional structure such as a sonnet, or an ode? Does it have stanzas with a regular number of lines, or any other interesting features of structural 'design'?

LANGUAGE: How would you describe the poet's use of words – vivid, striking, effective or colourless and predictable? Is the language *appropriate* to subject and/or theme? What *effect* does the language have on the poem's achievement?

IMAGERY: Are there any striking examples of similes, metaphors, personifications or symbols in the poem? What is their effect?

MOVEMENT, or rhythm: Does the poem have a regular (slow or fast) rhythm? What is the effect of any rhythmic qualities?

SOUNDS: Does the poem have any significant *sound* features? Is it musical? Does the poet use onomatopoeia, alliteration, or assonance? Does the poem rhyme? What are the effects of these features of sound on the achievement of the poem?

Using the Guidelines

Let us now analyse a poem, using the guidelines suggested to see how they can usefully direct us to important aspects of a poem.

IT WAS LONG AGO

I'll tell you, shall I, something I remember?
Something that still means a great deal to me.
It was long ago.

A dusty road in summer I remember,
A mountain, and an old house, and a tree
That stood, you know

Behind the house. An old woman I remember
In a red shawl with a grey cat on her knee
Humming under a tree.

She seemed the oldest thing I can remember,
But then perhaps I was not more than three.
It was long ago.

I dragged on the dusty road, and I remember
How the old woman looked over the fence at me
And seemed to know

How it felt to be three, and called out, I remember
'Do you like bilberries and cream for tea?'
I went under the tree

And while she hummed, and the cat purred, I remember
How she filled a saucer with berries and cream for me
So long ago,

Such berries and such cream as I remember
I never had seen before, and never see
To-day, you know.

And that is almost all I can remember,
The house, the mountain, the grey cat on her knee,
Her red shawl, and the tree,

And the taste of the berries, the feel of the sun I remember,
And the smell of everything that used to be
So long ago,

Till the heat on the road outside again I remember,
And how the long dusty road seemed to have for me
No end, you know.

That is the farthest thing I can remember.
It won't mean much to you. It does to me.
Then I grew up, you see.

ELEANOR FARJEON

Appreciating 'It Was Long Ago'

SUBJECT-
MATTER

This simple poem, by Eleanor Farjeon, records the poet's earliest memory, an incident that occurred when she was around 3 years old. While she was walking along a dusty road, she saw an old lady sitting under a tree. The lady invited her over and gave her bilberries and cream to eat, a 'feast' that the poet recalls with pleasure.

PURPOSE
(Theme)

At first glance the poem may appear to have no serious purpose other than the recording of an early memory, but the last lines suggest some additional significance. The poet shows that this simple, pleasant memory means much to her because 'then I grew up, you see'. We are reminded that 'growing up' is not always so pleasant. Sadly, being an adult can sometimes dull us so that we no longer appreciate the simple pleasures of life.

EMOTION (Mood)	The poem is gentle and nostalgic. It seeks not only to re-create the scene for the reader, but to have him or her feel the child-world goodness of the incident. The poet begins by asking our permission: 'I shall tell you, shall I, something I remember?' In the manner of a small child, she regularly checks to see that we are attending, that we understand: 'You know'; 'You see'. Thus the poem has a confiding, warm feel to it.
CRAFTS-MANSHIP • Structure • Language • Imagery • Movement • Sounds	The poem has an interesting, simple structure built around three-line stanzas. Are we overdoing our analysis if we wonder whether the poet has deliberately settled on three-line stanzas as the most appropriate for a 3 year-old? At any rate the simple structure is certainly appropriate for the situation. Similarly the language and rhyming scheme are deliberately simple. Words are uncomplicated, tending to be single syllables, with considerable repetition of words. The first line in every stanza ends with the word 'remember', and there are only two other rhyme sounds – 'ee' and 'oh', used absolutely regularly throughout the poem. The rhythm is gentle and slow, appropriate to the subject-matter. Such structural economy and simplicity form a very appropriate vehicle with which to re-create a childhood memory.
	Throughout the re-creation the poet seeks to involve our senses. She introduces concrete objects ('a mountain, an old house, and a tree . . .'), and simple colours ('in a red shawl with a grey cat . . .'), to help us visualize the scene. She invites us to *hear* the memory ('and while she hummed, and the cat purred . . .'), to *taste* it ('. . . the taste of the berries . . .'), and *feel* it ('the feel of the sun I remember . . .') as she draws upon her own sense memories. Thus, the memory is evoked for us in a much clearer way.
SUMMARY	Because of the poet's skill in using appropriately simple words, structure and rhythm, to re-create her earliest memory, she successfully involves us in the poem. For all its simplicity, the poem has a gentle robustness to it. We share the uncluttered goodness of the incident and are left with some wistful longings for our own childhood.

Beyond the Guidelines

If every poem were slavishly analysed, using the pattern suggested by SPECS and SLIMS, the end product would certainly become boring very quickly. Once you are thoroughly familiar with the guidelines, it is important to examine different aspects of each poem with freedom. Some aspects of the guidelines will clearly be irrelevant to specific poems, and so will not need mention. Other aspects will be particularly important in certain poems, and so will need greater elaboration. While this freedom is the desired goal, however, we encourage you to use the guidelines until you are thoroughly familiar with them. Then, confident that you know how to begin 'seeing into' a poem, you can analyse and synthesize with greater freedom.

Below is an appreciation of the poem, 'Leopard skin'. You will note that the writer is clearly familiar with the guidelines, but has felt free to move beyond their suggested structure.

LEOPARD SKIN

Seven pairs of leopard skin underpants
Flying on the rotary clothes-line! Oh, look, look, virgins,
How with the shirts and pyjamas they whirl and dance.
And think no more, trembling in your own emergence
Like butterflies into the light, that tall soft boy
Who nightly over his radio crooned and capered
Alone in his room in weird adolescent joy
Is mother's boy, softy: has he not slain a leopard?

But more than that: does he not wear its skin,
Secretly, daily, superbly? Oh, girls, adore him,
For dreaming on velvet feet to slay and to sin
He prowls the suburb, the wild things flee before him.
He miaous at the leopardesses, and they stop:
He is a leopard – he bought himself in a shop.

DOUGLAS STEWART

Appreciating Leopard Skin

This poem represents an attempt to comment on a boy's emerging sexual maturity, using the image of leopard-skin underpants. The poet begins by expressing his surprise at the sight of seven pairs of leopard-skin underpants on a clothes-line. With a beautifully gentle simile he describes the emerging sexuality of young girls, '... trembling in your own emergence/Like butterflies into the light ...' and exhorts them to note these underpants and, especially, to note the change that they symbolize in the adolescent boy who wears them. Flying on the line, for all to see, they constitute a bold statement of the boy's developing sexuality, which contrasts with the timid emergence of the sexuality of the young girls. The poet asks the girls to revise their thinking about the owner of these underpants. He is no longer an immature childish boy, a 'mother's boy', pursuing his own interests in 'weird adolescent joy'. His self-absorbed world, previously not understood by the girls and therefore 'weird', has changed. He has become a man – the understandable, mate-seeking, sexually mature masculine member of the species. And his leopard-skin underpants declare it proudly to the world, as though he has heroically and mystically 'slain a leopard' to achieve this status.

In the second stanza the poet marvels at the dramatic changes that have come about in the boy because he has 'slain a leopard', and asks the girls to admire them too. Now he wears the leopard skin 'secretly, daily, superbly'. He exults in his masculinity, weaving his whole life around this wonderful change taking place in his body. 'Dreaming on velvet feet' is a strong image of the boy confident in his new-found sure-footed 'leopardness', daydreaming of conquests and of indulging his sexual drives. He 'prowls the suburb', imagining his power over girls, now that 'he *is* a leopard'.

It is at the very end that the poet most clearly reveals his attitude. He suddenly cuts the ground away from under this grand heroic presentation of emerging adolescence, and shows that the description has been tongue-in-cheek. He is really mocking. The irony of the last phrase is strong: 'he bought himself in a shop'! He is no real leopard, just a shop-bought imitation, and his true stature is revealed when instead of 'roaring' at leopardesses he, like a tame kitten, merely 'miaous'.

Now, Try the Guidelines for Yourself!

Read through the poem below, and then try your own hand at writing an appreciation of the poem, using the guidelines above to help you.

THE HUNCHBACK IN THE PARK

The hunchback in the park
A solitary mister
Propped between trees and water
From the opening of the garden lock
That lets the trees and water enter
Until the Sunday sombre bell at dark

Eating bread from a newspaper
Drinking water from the chained cup
That the children filled with gravel
In the fountain basin where I sailed my ship
Slept at night in a dog kennel
But nobody chained him up.

Like the park birds he came early
Like the water he sat down
And Mister they called Hey mister
The truant boys from the town
Running when he had heard them clearly
On out of sound

Past lake and rockery
Laughing when he shook his paper
Hunchbacked in mockery
Through the loud zoo of the willow groves
Dodging the park keeper
With his stick that picked up leaves.

And the old dog sleeper
Alone between nurses and swans
While the boys among willows
Made the tigers jump out of their eyes
To roar on the rockery stones
And the groves were blue with sailors

Made all day until bell time
A woman figure without fault
Straight as a young elm
Straight and tall from his crooked bones
That she might stand in the night
After the locks and the chains

All night in the unmade park
After the railings and shrubberies
The birds the grass the trees the lake
And the wild boys innocent as strawberries
Had followed the hunchback
To his kennel in the dark.

DYLAN THOMAS

2 All Creatures Great and Small

Birds

The homing instinct of birds provided the poet with the inspiration for this poem.

THE DEATH OF THE BIRD

For every bird there is this last migration;
Once more the cooling year kindles her heart;
With a warm passage to the summer station
Love pricks the course in lights across the chart.

Year after year a speck on the map, divided
By a whole hemisphere, summons her to come;
Season after season, sure and safely guided,
Going away she is also coming home.

And being home, memory becomes a passion
With which she feeds her brood and straws her nest.
Aware of ghosts that haunt the heart's possession
And exiled love mourning within the breast.

The sands are green with a mirage of valleys;
The palm-tree casts a shadow not its own;
Down the long architrave of temple or palace
Blows a cool air from moorland scarps of stone.

And day by day the whisper of love grows stronger;
That delicate voice, more urgent with despair,
Custom and fear constraining her no longer,
Drives her at last on the waste leagues of air.

A vanishing speck in those inane dominions,
Single and frail, uncertain of her place,
Alone in the bright host of her companions,
Lost in the blue unfriendliness of space.

She feels it close now, the appointed season:
The invisible thread is broken as she flies;
Suddenly, without warning, without reason,
The guiding spark of instinct winks and dies.

Try as she will, the trackless world delivers
No way, the wilderness of light no sign,
The immense and complex map of hills and rivers
Mocks her small wisdom with its vast design.

And darkness rises from the eastern valleys,
And the winds buffet her with their hungry breath,
And the great earth, with neither grief nor malice,
Receives the tiny burden of her death.

A. D. HOPE

The Poet Comments

The first idea came to me on reading an article in a science journal on the investigations into the problem of how migratory birds find their way to the same place each year. The poem itself, of course is not simply about this problem in natural science, but about divided loves and loyalties in human life, particularly those which have an equal and unavoidable claim on the individual. It may be of interest that the poem was written over a period of something like five years. I wrote about half of it and then could not see how to go on, left it for a long time and finished it at a single sitting. I have often wondered whether readers could detect a change in tone or intention.

A. D. Hope

Kookaburras provide a fascinating study for Douglas Stewart. He says: 'I wrote the poem very early one morning partly because I was up so early and I had to do something, partly because the kookaburras were then in full chorus, and partly because for a long time I had been outraged at the fact that so many writers unthinkingly say that the kookaburras "laugh", which they do not. The poem tries to analyse the meaning and purpose of their chorus more exactly.'

KOOKABURRAS

I see we have undervalued the kookaburras;
They think they are waking the world, and I think so, too.
They gobble the night in their throats like purple berries,
They plunge their beaks in the tide of darkness and dew
And fish up long rays of light; no wonder they howl
In such a triumph of trumpets, leaves fall from the trees,
Small birds fly backwards, snakes disappear in a hole.
And all day long they will rule the bush as they please.

Perched on high branches, cocking sharp eyes for the snake,
From treetop to treetop they watch the sun and follow it;
Far in the west they take it in that great beak
And bang it against a bluegum branch and swallow it;
Then nothing is left in the world but the kookaburras
Like waterfalls exulting down the gullies.

DOUGLAS STEWART

Contemplating Kookaburras

(1) 'I see we have undervalued the kookaburras'. What point is the poet making?
(2) Why is 'gobble' a better word than 'eat'?
(3) What is meant by 'the tide of darkness and dew'?
(4) How does the poet exaggerate when he says the kookaburras 'fish up long rays of light'? What other examples of exaggeration can you find in the poem?
(5) What is the meaning of 'they howl/In such a triumph of trumpets'?
(6) How does the poet prove that the kookaburras rule the bush and its life?
(7) What according to the poet do the kookaburras catch instead of a snake? What do they do after they have caught it?
(8) Explain the meaning of 'the kookaburras/Like waterfalls exulting down the gullies'.
(9) How does the poet prove that the kookaburras play a part in making day and night?
(10) What do you think are the poet's feelings towards the kookaburras?

Animals

William Hart-Smith presents us with a friendly and positive description of a rhinoceros.

RHINOCEROS

... and there he was –
the Rhinoceros! ...
his hide caked in sun-dried mud,
fresh from his daily wallow,
a very amiable and placid fellow,
smelling richly of straw and fermenting grass.

I am sorry, Rhinoceros,
you have been sadly misrepresented to us
as vicious, intractable and ponderous,
a blindly-charging
two-spiked battering-ram.
Rhinoceros,
you don't know how sorry I am.

Dürer saw you as if dressed
in riveted armour plate,
a medieval tank.
Your hide is flexible enough I think.

That's right – amble over
and rest your chin on the concrete.

Your little eye is bright
and surprisingly intelligent.

Your nostril hawse-holes are wet,
and I am surprised
how very sensitive your lips are.
Rhinoceros, you are far
more of a friend than I thought you were.

Here – you like them?
Have another cheese straw!

WILLIAM HART-SMITH

Some Questions about Rhinoceros

(1) What is the setting for this poem?
(2) What impression does the poet give you of the rhinoceros in the first stanza?
(3) 'Vicious, intractable and ponderous'. What impression of the rhinoceros do these words give you?

(4) Dürer was a German painter in the sixteenth century. How did he view the rhinoceros?
(5) 'Rest your chin on the concrete'. What judgements does the poet make about the rhinoceros when he studies it close at hand?
(6) What evidence can you find to show that the poet is sympathetic towards the rhinoceros?
(7) 'Have another cheese straw.' Do you think this was a good way of concluding the poem? Why or why not?
(8) Did you find the poet's approach to his subject unusual? Why or why not?
(9) What did you learn about the character of the poet himself from the poem?
(10) What do you think was the poet's purpose in writing 'Rhinoceros'?

Don Marquis shows us that the tom-cat at midnight in the alley is very different from the same tom-cat lying on the rug at home.

THE TOM-CAT

At midnight in the alley
   A tom-cat comes to wail,
And he chants the hate of a million years
   As he swings his snaky tail.

Malevolent, bony, brindled,
   Tiger and devil and bard,
His eyes are coals from the middle of Hell
   And his heart is black and hard.

He twists and crouches and capers
   And bares his curved sharp claws,
And he sings to the stars of the jungle nights,
   Ere cities were, or laws.

Beast from a world primeval,
   He and his leaping clan,
When the blotched red moon leers over the roofs,
   Give voice to their scorn of man.

He will lie on a rug to-morrow
   And lick his silky fur,
And veil the brute in his yellow eyes
   And play he's tame, and purr.

But at midnight in the alley
   He will crouch again and wail,
And beat the time for his demon's song
   With the swing of his demon's tail.

DON MARQUIS

THE GREY SQUIRREL

Like a small grey
coffee-pot,
sits the squirrel.
He is not

all he should be,
kills by dozens
trees, and eats
his red-brown cousins.

The keeper, on the
other hand,
who shot him, is
a Christian, and

loves his enemies,
which shows
the squirrel was not
one of those.

HUMBERT WOLFE

BATS

A bat is born
Naked and blind and pale.
His mother makes a pocket of her tail
And catches him. He clings to her long fur
By his thumbs and toes and teeth.
And then the mother dances through the night
Doubling and looping, soaring, somersaulting –
Her baby hangs on underneath.
All night, in happiness, she hunts and flies.
Her high sharp cries
Like shining needlepoints of sound
Go out into the night and, echoing back,
Tell her what they have touched.
She hears how far it is, how big it is,
Which way it's going:
She lives by hearing.

The mother eats the moths and gnats she catches
In full flight; in full flight
The mother drinks the water of the pond
She skims across. Her baby hangs on tight.
Her baby drinks the milk she makes him
In moonlight or starlight, in mid-air.
Their single shadow, printed on the moon
Or fluttering across the stars,
Whirls on all night; at daybreak
The tired mother flaps home to her rafter.
The others all are there.
They hang themselves up by their toes,
They wrap themselves in their brown wings.
Bunched upside-down, they sleep in air.
Their sharp ears, their sharp teeth, their quick sharp
    faces
Are dull and slow and mild.
All the bright day, as the mother sleeps,
She folds her wings about her sleeping child.

RANDALL JARRELL

John Foulcher sees the kangaroo as a creature that is full of latent power and beauty. It is intensely alive and yet there is a grave threat to its existence.

KANGAROOS NEAR HAY

Head like a horse, whip of backbone twisting the body
into a coil, a scythe,
legs smooth as the length of a shark, cowled
with claws black and tooth-strong,
the tail curling like a lip.
The whole animal is a single arch, its currents of sinew
traced under storm-grey skin,

spilling with tension,
its lope of bone and muscle tight as a fist.

Sometimes, they lunge past you,
battering silence from the uncut farm at evening,

but, mostly, morning lays them at the roadside,
wrenches them into angles,
legs snapped, brittle as branches stuck out from sand.
Or there's nothing
save for the crab-stain of blood beaten into gravel,
the body belched away in its last swathe of existence,
its eyes eaten with lies about light.

JOHN FOULCHER

Observing Kangaroos near Hay

(1) '... whip of background twisting the body
   into a coil, a scythe
   legs smooth as the length of a shark ...'
   How do these lines suggest that the kangaroo is an animal of suppressed strength and power?

(2) Explain the powerful comparison that is contained in the last two lines of the first stanza.

(3) How does the second stanza prepare the reader for the movement that is to follow in the next stanza?

(4) 'Sometimes, they lunge past you'. Why is the word 'lunge' a more expressive word to use than, say, 'run'?

(5) Explain what you think the poet means by 'battering silence'?

(6) What view of the kangaroo's life does the last stanza present to the reader?

(7) When the poet writes of the 'crab-stain of blood', is he emphasizing colour or shape? Explain your view point.

(8) 'Wrenches them into angles'. What has happened?

(9) How could the eyes of the dead kangaroo be 'eaten with lies about light'?

(10) To what extent is this poem in praise of kangaroos?

(11) What thoughtful issue does this poem explore?

Fish

Here, in his poem 'Pike', is one of Ted Hughes' prize catches.

PIKE

Pike, three inches long, perfect
Pike in all parts, green tigering the gold.
Killers from the egg: the malevolent aged grin.
They dance on the surface among the flies.

Or move, stunned by their own grandeur,
Over a bed of emerald, silhouette
Of submarine delicacy and horror.
A hundred feet long in their world.

In ponds, under the heat-struck lily pads –
Gloom of their stillness:
Logged on last year's black leaves, watching upwards.
Or hung in an amber cavern of weeds

The jaws' hooked clamp and fangs
Not to be changed at this date;
A life subdued to its instrument;
The gills kneading quietly, and the pectorals.

Three we kept behind glass,
Jungled in weed: three inches, four,
And four and a half: fed fry to them –
Suddenly there were two. Finally one

With a sag belly and the grin it was born with.
And indeed they spare nobody.
Two, six pounds each, over two feet long,
High and dry and dead in the willow-herb –

One jammed past its gills down the other's gullet:
The outside eye stared: as a vice locks –
The same iron in this eye
Though its film shrank in death.

A pond I fished, fifty yards across,
Whose lilies and muscular tench
Had outlasted every visible stone
Of the monastery that planted them –

Stilled legendary depth:
It was as deep as England. It held
Pike too immense to stir, so immense and old
That past nightfall I dared not cast

But silently cast and fished
With the hair frozen on my head
For what might move, for what eye might move.
The still splashes on the dark pond,

Owls hushing the floating woods
Frail on my ear against the dream
Darkness beneath night's darkness had freed,
That rose slowly towards me, watching.

TED HUGHES

The Poet Comments

I used to be a very keen angler for pike, as I still am when I get the chance, and I did most
of my early fishing in a quite small lake, really a large pond. This pond went down to a
great depth in one place. Sometimes, on hot days, we would see something like a railway
sleeper lying near the surface, and there certainly were huge pike in that pond. I suppose
they are even bigger by now. Recently I felt like doing some pike fishing, but in
circumstances where there was no chance of it, and over the days, as I remembered the
extreme pleasures of that sport, bits of the following poem began to arrive. As you will
see, by looking at the place in my memory very hard and very carefully and by using the
words that grew naturally out of the pictures and feelings, I captured not just a pike,
I captured the whole pond, including the monsters I never even hooked.

Ted Hughes

Insects

Karl Shapiro does not spare us a single disgusting detail of the sordid life and habits of the fly.

THE FLY

O hideous little bat, the size of snot,
With polyhedral eye and shabby clothes,
To populate the stinking cat you walk
The promontory of the dead man's nose,
Climb with the fine leg of a Duncan Phyfe
    The smoking mountains of my food
      And in a comic mood
In mid-air take to bed a wife.

Riding and riding with your filth of hair
On gluey foot or wing, forever coy,
Hot from the compost and green sweet decay,
Sounding your buzzer like an urchin toy –
You dot all whiteness with diminutive stool,
    In the tight belly of the dead
      Burrow with hungry head
And inlay maggots like a jewel.

At your approach the great horse stomps and paws
Bringing the hurricane of his heavy tail;
Shod in disease you dare to kiss my hand
Which sweeps against you like an angry flail;
Still you return, return, trusting your wing
    To draw you from the hunter's reach
      That learns to kill to teach
Disorder to the tinier thing.

My peace is your disaster. For your death
Children like spiders cup their pretty hands
And wives resort to chemistry of war.
In fens of sticky paper and quicksands
You glue yourself to death. Where you are stuck
    You struggle hideously and beg
      You amputate your leg
Imbedded in the amber muck.

But I, a man, must swat you with my hate,
Slap you across the air and crush your flight,
Must mangle with my shoe and smear your blood,
Expose your little guts pasty and white,
Knock your head sidewise like a drunkard's hat,
    Pin your wings under like a crow's,
      Tear off your flimsy clothes
And beat you as one beats a rat.

Then like Gargantua I stride among
The corpses strewn like raisins in the dust,
The broken bodies of the narrow dead
That catch the throat with fingers of disgust.
I sweep. One gyrates like a top and falls
   And stunned, stone blind, and deaf
      Buzzes its frightful F
   And dies between three cannibals.

KARL SHAPIRO

Line 5   Duncan Phyfe: *a brand of American furniture*

Thinking About the Poem

(1) How does the first line of the poem indicate that the poet is going to be critical of the fly?
(2) Explain how the poet's food appears to the fly.
(3) Why does the poet refer to 'decay' as sweet?
(4) Why is the tail of the horse described as a 'hurricane'?
(5) 'Shod in disease'. Which of the fly's habits does this phrase refer to?
(6) What is the fly really doing when it is daring to kiss the poet's hand? How does the poet react?
(7) Explain the meaning of 'My peace is your disaster'.
(8) Why do you think the poet compares children to spiders?
(9) Explain the meaning of 'And wives resort to chemistry of war'.
(10) What is the poet's attitude to the fly in the second last stanza of the poem?
(11) 'Then like Gargantua I stride ...' Gargantua was a giant. How is the idea of huge size continued in the second line of the last stanza?
(12) What habits of the fly did you find particularly repulsive?
(13) What was the poet's purpose in writing 'The Fly'?
(14) How did you react to this poem?

D. H. Lawrence has recorded his encounter with a mosquito.

MOSQUITO

When did you start your tricks,
Monsieur?

What do you stand on such high legs for?
Why this length of shredded shank,
You exaltation?

Is it so that you shall lift your centre of gravity upwards
And weigh no more than air as you alight upon me,
Stand upon me weightless, you phantom?

I heard a woman call you the Winged Victory
In sluggish Venice.
You turn your head towards your tail, and smile.

How can you put so much devilry
Into that translucent phantom shred
Of a frail corpus?

Queer, with your thin wings and your streaming legs,
How you sail like a heron, or a dull clot of air,
A nothingness.

Yet what an aura surrounds you;
Your evil little aura, prowling, and casting numbness on
  my mind.
That is your trick, your bit of filthy magic:
Invisibility, and the anaesthetic power
To deaden my attention in your direction.

But I know your game now, streaky sorcerer.
Queer, how you stalk and prowl the air
In circles and evasions, enveloping me,
Ghoul on wings,
Winged Victory.

Settle, and stand on long thin shanks
Eyeing me sideways, and cunningly conscious that I am
  aware,
You speck.

I hate the way you lurch off sideways into the air
Having read my thoughts against you.
Come then, let us play at unawares,
And see who wins in this sly game of bluff.
Man or mosquito.

You don't know that I exist, and I don't know that you
  exist.
Now then!

It is your trump,
It is your hateful little trump,
You pointed fiend,
Which shakes my sudden blood to hatred of you:
It is your small, high, hateful bugle in my ear.

Why do you do it?
Surely it is bad policy.
They say you can't help it.

If that is so, then I believe a little in Providence protecting
  the innocent.
But it sounds so amazingly like a slogan,
A yell of triumph as you snatch my scalp.

Blood, red blood
Super-magical
Forbidden liquor.

I behold you stand
For a second enspasmed in oblivion,
Obscenely ecstasied
Sucking live blood,
My blood.

Such silence, such suspended transport,
Such gorging,
Such obscenity of trespass.

You stagger
As well as you may.
Only your accursed hairy frailty,
Your own imponderable weightlessness
Saves you, wafts you away on the very draught my anger
   makes in its snatching.

Away with a paean of derision,
You winged blood-drop.

Can I not overtake you?
Are you one too many for me,
Winged Victory?
Am I not mosquito enough to out-mosquito you?

Queer what a big stain my sucked blood makes
Beside the infinitesimal faint smear of you!
Queer, what a dim dark smudge you have disappeared
   into!

D. H. LAWRENCE

3 The Sounds of Poetry

One of the identifiable skills of successful poetry-writing is the ability to put words together in such a way that the *sounds* have a specific effect upon the reader/hearer. Since poetry is, ideally, written for people to *hear*, the skilful poet achieves his or her impact, not only through the meaning of the words, but also through their sounds.

The following passage, not strictly poetry, contains examples of the most important 'sound techniques'. Read through the passage, allowing yourself to experience the effect of the writer's rich sound combinations.

SOUNDS

FIRST VOICE: There's the clip clop of horses on the sunhoneyed cobbles of the humming streets, hammering of horse-shoes, gobble quack and cackle, tomtit twitter from the bird-ounced boughs, braying on Donkey Down. Bread is baking, pigs are grunting, chop goes the butcher, milk-churns bell, tills ring, sheep cough, dogs shout, saws sing. Oh the Spring whinny and morning moo from the clog dancing farms, the gulls' gab and rabble on the boat-bobbing river and sea and the cockles bubbling in the sand, scamper of sanderlings, curlew cry, crow caw, pigeon coo, clock strike, bull bellow, and the ragged gabble of the beargarden school as the women scratch and babble in Mrs Organ Morgan's general shop where everything is sold: custard, buckets, henna, rat-traps, shrimp-nets, sugar, stamps, confetti, paraffin, hatchets, whistles.

from *Under Milk Wood* by DYLAN THOMAS

Notice that there is a noisy liveliness to the scene thus described; action and energy abound. The passage achieves its effect predominantly through the skilful combination of specific sounds. The three major techniques used are Alliteration, Assonance and Onomatopoeia. Let us look at each one separately.

Alliteration

Alliteration is a device which involves the repetition of initial consonant sounds to produce a rhythmical, usually-musical, effect. Notice in the Dylan Thomas passage above, examples such as: '*b*read is *b*aking'; '*m*orning *m*oo'.

Or, look carefully at the example below, taken from Coleridge's 'The Rime of the Ancient Mariner'.

The fair breeze blew, the white foam flew,
The furrow followed free ...

The repetition of the 'f' sound, in particular, gives a rhythmical, musical effect to these lines, somehow creating a feeling of freedom as we imagine the ship sailing across the ocean.

Assonance

Assonance is the repetition of vowel sounds, without regard for the following sounds. (Note that when a vowel sound is repeated *and* the following sound is identical, we have not assonance, but rhyme.) Thus, for example, 'reed' and 'wheel' is an example of assonance; 'reed' and 'weed' is an example or rhyme.

Look at the following line from the Dylan Thomas extract at the start of this chapter. You will notice that it contains several examples of assonance.

EXAMPLE: '... gobble quack and cackle, tomtit twitter from the bird-ounced boughs ...'

Notice the repetition of the short 'a' sound in 'gobble quack and cackle', the repetition of the short 'i' sound in 'tomtit twitter', and the repetition of the 'ow' sound in 'bird-ounced boughs'. The effect of these vowel sound repetitions, along with the other sound devices, gives the language a liveliness that helps to create the atmosphere of bubbling life which fits the scene being described.

Onomatopoeia

Onomatopoeia is the formation of words which echo the sounds that they describe. Once again, look at the Dylan Thomas extract at the start of this chapter, and note the following examples:

EXAMPLES: 1. '... gobble quack and cackle ...'
2. '... crow caw, pigeon coo...bull bellow ...'

Notice that these words echo the sound they describe. For example, the cry of a crow sounds like 'caw'; the call of a pigeon sounds like 'coo'; the sound of a bull calling is akin to 'bellow'.

The effect of these onomatopoeic words is enhanced by the fact that, at times, they concurrently occur in examples of alliteration or assonance. For example, we have already noticed that 'gobble quack and cackle' is an example of assonance, as well as onomatopoeia. The line 'Oh the Spring whinny and morning moo ...' is an example of the co-occurrence of both assonance and onomatopoeia, and the co-occurrence of alliteration and onomatopoeia. Can you identify both of these?

This co-occurrence of the major devices of sound is a frequent feature of Dylan Thomas' writing and gives it a particularly musical effect, important for the creation of atmosphere. In this specific example we can see how the combined use of these techniques creates a sense of lively energy, of life bursting forth as the Spring morning gets under way.

Coleridge makes good use of alliteration and assonance in his famous poem, 'Kubla Khan'.
Read through the poem and consider the issues raised below.

KUBLA KHAN

In Xanadu did Kubla Khan
A stately pleasure-dome decree:
Where Alph, the sacred river, ran
Through caverns measureless to man
   Down to a sunless sea.
So twice five miles of fertile ground
With walls and towers were girdled round:
And there were gardens bright with sinuous rills,
Where blossomed many an incense-bearing tree;
And here were forests ancient as the hills,
Enfolding sunny spots of greenery.

But oh! that deep romantic chasm which slanted
Down the green hill athwart a cedarn cover!
A savage place! as holy and enchanted
As e'er beneath a waning moon was haunted
By woman wailing for her demon-lover!
And from this chasm with ceaseless turmoil seething,
As if this earth in fast thick pants were breathing,
A mighty fountain momently was forced:
Amid whose swift half-intermitted burst
Huge fragments vaulted like rebounding hail,
Or chaffy grain beneath the thresher's flail:
And 'mid these dancing rocks at once and ever
It flung up momentarily the sacred river.
Five miles meandering with a mazy motion
Through wood and dale the sacred river ran,
Then reached the caverns measureless to man,
And sank in tumult to a lifeless ocean:
And 'mid this tumult Kubla heard from far
Ancestral voices prophesying war!
   The shadow of the dome of pleasure
   Floated midway on the waves;
   Where was heard the mingled measure
   From the fountain and the caves.
It was a miracle of rare device,
A sunny pleasure-dome with caves of ice!

   A damsel with a dulcimer
   In a vision once I saw:
   It was an Abyssinian maid,
   And on her dulcimer she played,
   Singing of Mount Abora.
   Could I revive within me
   Her symphony and song,

To such a deep delight 'twould win me,
That with music loud and long,
I would build that dome in air,
That sunny dome! those caves of ice!
And all who heard should see them there,
And all should cry, 'Beware! Beware!
His flashing eyes, his floating hair!
Weave a circle round him thrice,
And close your eyes with holy dread,
For he on honey-dew hath fed,
And drunk the milk of Paradise.'

SAMUEL TAYLOR COLERIDGE

Sound Devices in Kubla Khan

(1) 'So twice five miles of fertile ground . . .' Identify the major device of sound used in this line. What effect does it create for you, in the context of the poem?
(2) Listen to the line: 'Five miles meandering with a mazy motion . . .' Identify any devices of sound and comment on their effect.
(3) Identify three examples of alliteration from the poem. Underline the repeated consonant sounds.
(4) Identify three examples of assonance from the poem. Underline the repeated vowel sounds.
(5) Is 'cedarn cover' an example of alliteration? Explain your answer.
(6) How would you describe the achievement of this poem?
(7) How important to the overall achievement of the poem are these devices of sound?
(8) Do you think Coleridge over-uses alliteration or assonance in the poem? Comment.

Two Short Poems

SAILING

Consider the Viking keel
Cutting keen,
Slicing over the green deep.

Hear the hiss of the salt foam
Curling off at the bow.
And the wake closing quietly
In bubbles behind.

Listen to the sound of the thumping drum,
See the helmets shine in the sun.
Feel, with your finger,
The full sail drawn tight
As they drive home before the wind.

DAVID ENGLISH

The Sounds of Sailing

(1) Read through the poem above, 'feeling' the sounds, allowing them to affect your senses. Notice the assonance in the first verse. What vowel sound is repeated? Does this have an identifiable effect?
(2) Look at the alliteration in the second stanza. Does it have an identifiable effect on mood, or atmosphere, or the more-vivid creation of a 'picture'? Is 'closing quietly' an example of alliteration?
(3) Where is the assonance in the first line of the third stanza? What senses are we invited to use in the third stanza, to experience this 'sailing'?
(4) Look at the structure of the poem. What do you notice about it? Is this relevant to the poem's achievement?

SUMMER REMEMBERED

Sounds sum and summon the remembering of
summers.
The humming of the sun
The mumbling in the honeysuckle vine
The whirring in the clovered grass
The pizzicato plinkle of ice in an auburn
uncle's amber glass.
The whing of father's racquet and the whack
of brother's bat on cousin's ball
and calling voices calling
voices spilling voices . . .

ISABELLA GARDNER

Summer Sounds

(1) In your own words, what does the first line mean?
(2) Identify the assonance in the first three lines. Comment on the effect of this repeated sound.
(3) 'The humming of the sun ...' Surely the sun doesn't hum. What can the poet mean?
(4) Identify an example of alliteration in the poem and comment upon its effect.
(5) What is 'plinkle' an example of?
(6) Comment on the use of 'whing' and 'whack'.
(7) What is the overall effect of these devices of sound in this poem?

'The Windhover'

One of Gerard Manley Hopkins' most brilliant sonnets, this poem is full of arresting word-sounds which are used to build a poem with powerful impact.

THE WINDHOVER

To Christ Our Lord

I caught this morning morning's minion, kingdom of daylight's dauphin,
    dapple-dawn-drawn Falcon, in his riding
Of the rolling level underneath him steady air, and striding
High there, how he rung upon the rein of a wimpling wing
In his ecstasy! then off, off forth on swing,
    As a skate's heel sweeps smooth on a bow-bend: the hurl and gliding
    Rebuffed the big wind. My heart in hiding
Stirred for a bird, – the achieve of, the mastery of the thing!

Brute beauty and valour and act, oh, air, pride, plume here
Buckle! AND the fire that breaks from thee then, a billion
Times told lovelier, more dangerous, O my chevalier!

    No wonder of it: sheér plód makes plough down sillion
Shine, and blue-bleak embers, ah my dear,
    Fall, gall themselves, and gash gold-vermilion.

GERARD MANLEY HOPKINS

Appreciating The Windhover

At first reading the poem's meaning is somewhat obscure, partly because of the use of archaic words, and partly because of Hopkins' tendency to compress words. The first four lines describe how Hopkins observed a bird, the windhover, hovering perfectly still, balanced against the currents of air. (A 'minion' is a favourite child; 'dauphin', the heir-apparent to the French throne.) Hopkins then observes the bird suddenly break from hovering and swoop off in a beautiful, gliding dive, 'As a skate's heel sweeps smooth on a bow-bend'. His heart is exultant ('My heart . . . stirred for a bird'), deeply moved by the beauty of this incident. Notice the use of 'achieve' as a shortened form of achievement.

The last six lines are Hopkins' reflection on the incident. First, he is struck by the beauty of the hovering, but even more so by the greater beauty which breaks forth when the bird destroys the 'still' picture by suddenly swooping. The new picture is 'a billion/Times told lovelier'. (A 'chevalier' is a knight of honour.) Notice the several meanings of 'buckle'. It can carry a sense of preparing for action as in 'to buckle down to a task'. It can also mean to bring together, to clasp. Further, it may mean to give way under pressure. This richness in a single word is characteristic of Hopkins' poetry.

But Hopkins reflects further. It is not surprising ('No wonder of it') that when something that is already beautiful 'buckles', a greater beauty shines forth. It happens when the earth is torn by ploughing so that the furrows ('sillion') shine. And a beautiful coal-fire, when it breaks apart ('gall' means injure), shines with deeper beauty as its gold-vermilion colour is revealed.

All of this is the theme of a poem sub-titled 'To Christ our Lord'. It is possible that this is simply the poem's dedication. But it is also possible that Hopkins wants us to make a more significant connection. The 'still picture' of the life of Christ is beautiful. But when that life was broken, through death on a cross, the deeper beauty of God's love for men was revealed.

Noting . . .

(1) Note the elaborate use of the 'aw' sound in the assonance in the first two lines: caught, morning, dawn-dawn. How would Hopkins have intended us to pronounce the word 'Falcon'?
(2) Select an example of alliteration from the poem. What is its effect?
(3) How important do you think devices of sound are to the message of this poem? What contribution do they make to its achievement?

In 'Poem in October', Dylan Thomas reflects on his hometown of Laugharne, a Welsh seaside village, during a walk in an autumn shower. The present moment recalls mornings from his past and these mingle in the poem. Thomas relies on creating a series of images to leave us with an impression. Like Hopkins, he loves to play with the sounds of words, as part of the creation of images. At times he almost appears intoxicated with the sounds of words, so richly does he combine them. How much do you like the poem? How well do you feel you understand what he is saying? How important to its achievement is the poet's use of alliteration and assonance?

POEM IN OCTOBER

It was my thirtieth year to heaven
Woke to my hearing from harbour and neighbour wood
   And the mussel pooled and the heron
      Priested shore
     The morning beckon
With water praying and call of seagull and rook
And the knock of sailing boats on the net webbed wall
    Myself to set foot
     That second
In the still sleeping town and set forth.

My birthday began with the water –
Birds and the birds of the winged trees flying my name
   Above the farms and the white horses
      And I rose
     In rainy autumn
And walked abroad in a shower of all my days.
High tide and the heron dived when I took the road
    Over the border
     And the gates
Of the town closed as the town awoke.

A springful of larks in a rolling
Cloud and the roadside bushes brimming with whistling
   Blackbirds and the sun of October
      Summery
     On the hill's shoulder,
Here were fond climates and sweet singers suddenly
Come in the morning where I wandered and listened
    To the rain wringing
     Wind blow cold
In the wood faraway under me.

Pale rain over the dwindling harbour
And over the sea wet church the size of a snail
   With its horns through mist and the castle
      Brown as owls
    But all the gardens
Of spring and summer were blooming in the tall tales
Beyond the border and under the lark full cloud.
   There could I marvel
    My birthday
  Away but the weather turned around.

  It turned away from the blithe country
And down the other air and the blue altered sky
   Streamed again a wonder of summer
     With apples
    Pears and red currants
And I saw in the turning so clearly a child's
Forgotten mornings when he walked with his mother
   Through the parables
    Of sunlight
And the legends of the green chapels

  And the twice told fields of infancy
That his tears burned my cheeks and his heart moved in
    mine.
   These were the woods the river and sea
     Where a boy
    In the listening
Summertime of the dead whispered the truth of his joy
To the trees and the stones and the fish in the tide.
   And the mystery
    Sang alive
Still in the water and singingbirds.

  And there could I marvel my birthday
Away but the weather turned around. And the true
   Joy of the long dead child sang burning
     In the sun.
   It was my thirtieth
Year to heaven stood there then in the summer noon
Though the town below lay leaved with October blood.
   O may my heart's truth
    Still be sung
On this high hill in a year's turning.

               DYLAN THOMAS

4 A Sunburnt Country

A. D. Hope was born in 1907 at Cooma in New South Wales. Educated at Sydney University and later at Oxford, he became a teacher, then a lecturer and finally Professor of English at Canberra.

In 'Australia' the poet is critical of the anti-intellectual atmosphere in his homeland and yet he is still drawn to the cultural wasteland of Australia in the hope that inspiration and endeavour will one day emerge.

AUSTRALIA

A Nation of trees, drab green and desolate grey
In the field uniform of modern wars,
Darkens her hills, those endless, outstretched paws
Of Sphinx demolished or stone lion worn away.

They call her a young country, but they lie:
She is the last of lands, the emptiest,
A woman beyond her change of life, a breast
Still tender but within the womb is dry.

Without songs, architecture, history:
The emotions and superstitions of younger lands,
Her rivers of water drown among inland sands,
The river of her immense stupidity

Floods her monotonous tribes from Cairns to Perth.
In them at last the ultimate men arrive
Whose boast is not: 'we live' but 'we survive',
A type who will inhabit the dying earth.

And her five cities, like five teeming sores,
Each drains her: a vast parasite robber-state
Where second-hand Europeans pullulate
Timidly on the edge of alien shores.

Yet there are some like me turn gladly home
From the lush jungle of modern thought, to find
The Arabian desert of the human mind,
Hoping, if still from the deserts the prophets come,

Such savage and scarlet as no green hills dare
Springs in that waste, some spirit which escapes
The learned doubt, the chatter of cultured apes
Which is called civilization over there.

A. D. HOPE

Thinking About the Poem's Meaning

(1) How does the poet convey a sense of the sameness of the Australian landscape?
(2) To what does he liken her hills?
(3) How does the poet suggest the tremendous age and antiquity of Australia?
(4) According to the poet, why is it a lie to call Australia a young country?

(5) What comparison does the poet use to contradict the idea of Australia's youthfulness?

(6) The first and second stanzas of the poem are concerned with the Australian landscape. What shift of emphasis occurs in the third stanza?

(7) 'The river of her immense stupidity'. Explain what you think the poet is referring to in this line.

(8) According to the poet, what characteristic do the people who inhabit Australia from Cairns to Perth share?

(9) 'The ultimate men arrive'. Explain the significance of the word 'ultimate'.

(10) Explain the difference between 'live' and 'survive' in the line 'Whose boast is not: "we live" but "we survive"'.

(11) Why do you think the poet compares the five cities of Australia to 'five teeming sores'?

(12) What is the poet's attitude to the white population of Australia?

(13) What change of mood occurs in the second last stanza of the poem?

(14) Explain the comparison that is contained in the phrase, 'the lush jungle of modern thought'.

(15) In the second last stanza, what words are used by the poet to depict the intellectual wasteland of Australia?

(16) How does the poet express his optimism for the eventual emergence of intellectual inspiration in Australia?

(17) Do you agree with the sentiments expressed in this poem? Why? Why not?

Kath Walker, the aboriginal poet, sees with great clarity the dilemma of the dispossessed. An aboriginal bora ring has been desecrated and the remnant of the tribe that once conducted its ceremonies on the tribal ground feel powerless to act or even express their thoughts. Once they were the keepers of the sacred ground now they are just like ghosts, silent and hardly seen by the white people of the town who now possess, but do not respect, the legendary land.

WE ARE GOING
for Grannie Coolwell

They came in to the little town
A semi-naked band subdued and silent,
All that remained of their tribe.
They came here to the place of their old bora ground
Where now the many white men hurry about like ants.
Notice of estate agent reads: 'Rubbish May Be Tipped Here.'
Now it half covers the traces of the old bora ring.
They sit and are confused, they cannot say their thoughts:
'We are as strangers here now, but the white tribe are the
    strangers.
We belong here, we are of the old ways.
We are the corroboree and the bora ground,
We are the old sacred ceremonies, the laws of the elders.
We are the wonder tales of Dream Time, the tribal legends
    told.
We are the past, the hunts and the laughing games, the
    wandering camp fires.
We are the lightning-bolt over Gaphembah Hill
Quick and terrible,

And the Thunderer after him, that loud fellow.
We are the quiet daybreak paling the dark lagoon.
We are the shadow-ghosts creeping back as the camp fires
    burn low.
We are nature and the past, all the old ways
Gone now and scattered.
The scrubs are gone, the hunting and the laughter.
The eagle is gone, the emu and the kangaroo are gone from
    this place.
The bora ring is gone.
The corroboree is gone.
And we are going.'

KATH WALKER

Understanding the Poem's Significance

(1) Why do you think the aboriginals were 'subdued and silent'?
(2) Why is the comparison between the white people and ants a suitable one?
(3) What made the estate agent's notice hurtful for the aborigines?
(4) Explain the meaning of 'We are as strangers here now, but the white tribe are the strangers'.
(5) The tribal people identify themselves with aspects of their legendary past. Which one of these do you find the most appealing?
(6) Explain the shift of mood that occurs in the second part of the poem.
(7) What contrast is there between the present and the past?
(8) What does the poet achieve by her repetition of the word 'gone'?
(9) How does the last line of the poem sum up all the ideas that have gone before?
(10) Why do you think the aboriginal poet, Kath Walker, has written this poem?

The poet, Len Fox, draws our attention to one of our national heroes, whose achievements most of us have never acknowledged. The poem was written in the 1950s.

NATIONAL HERO

(An Asian girl, shown a postage stamp with the head of an
Australian Aborigine, asked: 'Is he a national hero?')

Postage stamps
Often show national heroes,
But this chap didn't make the grade.
Was never top of his class at school,
Didn't finish his University degree
And couldn't tell one end of a machine-gun
From the other.
All he could do was kill a kangaroo
With a spear at two hundred yards,
And how could Sir Anthony
have captured the Canal
If his army had been able
Only to throw spears?

He had talent, mind you,
Could have made a singer, painter,
Might even have won the right
To own a house or buy a beer
Like a white man,
But he seemed to lack initiative,
Just roamed round the desert
Getting in the way of
Guided missiles
And probably ended up
Dying of consumption –
These fellows go round half naked
You know.

But we treat them very well,
Missions and schools
And that sort of thing,
And we give them jobs and sometimes
Pay them good wages,
And it'll be a pity if they die out
Because they're awfully decorative
For Christmas cards
And souvenirs
And postage stamps.

LEN FOX

TOM FARLEY

Tom Farley, up to his knees in sheep
By the drafting yard, moves in a red fog
Of summer dust; moves, bent, in a rhythm deep
As the seasons, his hard-soft hands
Holding gentle conversation with his dog.

Tom Farley on his Mid-North run
Has a face as fresh and kindly as his sheep;
Wears an old felt hat with its brim full of sun,
Sees the waves of wool move as soothingly as sleep.

Tom Farley lives a life of moving sheep:
Sheep flowing down the slopes
In broad falls
Or unwinding slowly like slack ropes
From knots at dams;
Cataracts of sheep in flood down ledges
Leaping and bucking in angles and edges,
Tossing up like flotsam the horns of rams;
Sheep held in the hollows and valleys
In friendly lakes rippling gently in the sun
On Farley's run.

And Tom, sometimes caught in the rucking tide
Of backs, feels them break against him,
Carry him forward in their jostle and surge
Till, fingers crooked deep in wool, he wades wide
To the fence and at last stands free
Like a tired surfer plodding from the sea.

But Tom finds himself most deeply once a year
When the sheep-dog trials come to test his dog ...

Then, by riddled stump or fallen log
He sucks his pipe and – eyes alight,
Though ringed by the crows'-feet treading round their hollows –
Sums up the sheep and the brain of the dog that follows;

But when Tom and his noiseless shadow slip
On to the oval green where the renegade ewes
Fidget and shift, people pity the others' chances,
For these two are always surer, a little faster,
Fluid with the knowing talk of nods and glances –
A spiritual union of the dog and master.

Tom Farley and his dog, they say, will wipe
The field – so much at one in paddocks, yards and races
That folk would hardly be surprised
Some day to see them interchange their places,
See the dog stand up to fill his brier pipe,
And old Tom, dropping to the turf behind the flock,
Creep stealthily with feints and cunning graces,
And, nose to the ground, sink his teeth in a lagging hock.

COLIN THIELE

THE MUSHROOMER

Over the brow of the hill the mushroomer, walking,
Felt the wind playing with arrows of hidden frost,
Felt the air in his face like a steep cold river,
Felt the crying of lost

Lambs in his ears, and the airy ripple of wings.
Small wonder that he quite forgot his art
And, leaving his bucket empty, sat collecting these things
Instead, in his heart.

Down in the gully where the autumn creek
Was yarning to the reeds about last week's rain
He flung away his bucket, his wife, and ten years' lamplight,
And clutched at himself again.

The reeds trembled with pleasure, and all things too,
At the sight of it: a magpie broke song on the steep
Downward air, a cricket itched, and the long slope of sheep
Cried out anew.

Even a young gum in the warmth of the hollow there,
Where the sun was golden pollen on its leaves,
Echoed his joy, lifted its head in the air,
And sang with bees.

COLIN THIELE

Henry Lawson, who has been called the Father of Australian Poetry, knew all about carrying a swag Out Back while looking for work. He also valued highly the idea and ideal of 'mateship'. Mateship meant that a man relied on his mates to share his joys and his troubles and, in return, he shared theirs. Lawson knew that a man without mates was a man who was courting disaster in the Out Back. This is a poem about a man without mates.

OUT BACK

The old year went, and the new returned, in the withering weeks of drought;
The cheque was spent that the shearer earned, and the sheds were all cut out;
The publican's words were short and few, and the publican's looks were black –
And the time had come, as the shearer knew, to carry his swag Out Back.

For time means tucker, and tramp you must, where the scrubs and plains are wide,
With seldom a track that a man can trust, or a mountain peak to guide;
All day long in the dust and heat – when summer is on the track –
With stinted stomachs and blistered feet, they carry their swags Out Back.

He tramped away from the shanty there, when the days were long and hot,
With never a soul to know or care if he died on the track or not.
The poor of the city have friends in woe, no matter how much they lack,
But only God and the swagmen know how a poor man fares Out Back.

He begged his way on the parched Paroo and the Warrego tracks once more,
And lived like a dog, as the swagmen do, till the Western stations shore;
But men were many, and the sheds were full, for work in the town was slack –
The traveller never got hands in wool, though he tramped for a year Out Back.

In stifling noons when his back was wrung by its load, and the air seemed dead,
And the water swarmed in the bag that hung to his aching arm like lead.
Or in times of flood, when plains were seas and the scrubs were cold and black.
He ploughed in mud to his trembling knees, and paid for his sins Out Back.

36

And dirty and careless and old he wore, as his lamp of hope grew dim;
He tramped for years, till the swag he bore seemed part of himself to him.
As a bullock drags in the sandy ruts, he followed the dreary track,
Within never a thought but to reach the huts when the sun went down Out Back.

It chanced one day when the north wind blew in his face like a furnace-breath,
He left the track for a tank he knew – 'twas a shorter cut to death;
For the bed of the tank was hard and dry, and crossed with many a crack,
And, oh! it's a terrible thing to die of thirst in the scrub Out Back.

A drover came, but the fringe of law was eastward many a mile;
He never reported the thing he saw, for it was not worth his while.
The tanks are full, and the grass is high in the mulga off the track,
Where the bleaching bones of a white man lie by his mouldering swag Out Back.

For time means tucker, and tramp they must, where the plains and scrubs are wide,
With seldom a track that a man can trust, or a mountain peak to guide;
All day long in the flies and heat the men of the outside track,
With stinted stomachs and blistered feet, must carry their swags Out Back.

HENRY LAWSON

Quite often Henry Lawson would depict in his poetry characters he had met when he worked and wandered in the country. There is no doubt that Henry Lawson would have seen many a young man who worked as a rouseabout – an odd job man on a sheep or cattle property – and some, like Andy below, might well have hidden their true character behind a loutish-looking face.

MIDDLETON'S ROUSEABOUT

Tall and freckled and sandy,
    Face of a country lout;
This was the picture of Andy,
    Middleton's Rouseabout.

Type of a coming nation
    In the land of cattle and sheep;
Worked on Middleton's station,
    Pound a week and his keep;

On Middleton's wide dominions
    Plied the stockwhip and shears;
Hadn't any opinions,
    Hadn't any 'idears'.

Swiftly the years went over,
    Liquor and drought prevailed;
Middleton went as a drover
    After his station had failed.

Type of a careless nation,
    Men who are soon played out,
Middleton was: – and his station
    Was bought by the Rouseabout.

Flourishing beard and sandy,
    Tall and solid and stout,
This is the picture of Andy,
    Middleton's Rouseabout.

Now on his own dominions
    Works with his overseers;
Hasn't any opinions,
    Hasn't any idears.

HENRY LAWSON

A sheep-dog knows the ways of human beings and when it becomes a sheep-killer it becomes adept at deceiving its master. It has to appear innocent while all the time harbouring the urge to slaughter the very sheep it has to look after. This poem analyses the mind of a sheep-dog transformed by the killer instinct.

SHEEP-KILLER

I should have known, when I undid his chain,
That darkness had been busy at his brain
As at an anvil, sharpening a fang.
I should have known it by the glint that sprang
Into his eyes when the chain fell and he
Stood stiffly there, as though to let me see
That he had all the time in the world to spare,
If I so felt, to match me stare for stare,
His heart being innocent.
              I watched him go
Out through the gate with just the slightest show
Of hurry in his trot, as though he kept
His body back from where his thoughts leapt
Ahead to the red kill; that holding back
A dog will never show unless the track
He follows is a secret he would keep
From men whose fingers smell of lambs and sheep.

I should have known, had I but had the eye,
That strain in hip and curving flank and thigh
For what must happen in a hawk's neck when
He spots the quail way down there, but with men
Too near in yard or paddock to make safe
The whistling lunge; the tension of that chafe
That is when lust has the red tongue on fire
But cunning is the muzzle on desire.

So he went slowly till I lost him quite
In the thick fog that made another night
Over the paddocks where beneath the trees
The lambs would be hard at it on their knees
Draining the heavy udders. In that fog
A lamb would learn the coming of a dog
Too late even to get upon its feet.
Or in one wild and lost and desperate bleat
To say that death was hard and life was sweet.

He got his fifty in a mile that day,
Crunched through the shoulders in the killer's way,
Ribs broken in to crush the leaping heart.
Though great my loss, I recognized the art
With which the thing was done. What speed, what power,
He must have known for that one breathless hour,
When long restraint was straw before the urge
Of instinct, the red longing, the hot surge
That leapt and thundered and would not be still
Till fifty lambs lay dead about the hill!

He always liked to work the sheep close in,
Sniffing the blood, no doubt, beneath the skin
He dared not tear because of watching eyes.
Why did I trust that shifty compromise!
Why must sheep stand, by fear together drifted,
Helpless as flowers when the scythe is lifted!
Who was at fault, the dog, or I, or the sheep?

But since a farmer needs must have his sleep,
That night I put a bullet in his head,
Gave the world back to God, and went to bed.

ERNEST G. MOLL

Gaining a Deeper Understanding of Sheep-Killer

(1) What do you think the poet means by 'That darkness had been busy at his brain'?
(2) How does the poet create in our minds a stark image of the darkness at work on the animal's brain?
(3) The poet reproaches himself for missing the one sign of guilt made by the dog. What was that sign?
(4) How does the dog pretend innocence?
(5) What thought does the dog restrain himself from acting on as he trots away?
(6) What comparison does the poet make between the dog and the hawk in the third stanza?
(7) What image do you see in your mind's eye when you read of 'the whistling lunge' made by the hawk?
(8) Explain the meaning of 'lust has the red tongue on fire'.
(9) Why would the lambs be defenceless and taken by surprise when the sheep-killer made its appearance?
(10) What method did the dog use to kill each lamb?
(11) Despite the loss that it caused him as a farmer, the poet still admires the work of the sheep-killer. Why does he do this?

(12) Explain the meaning of 'When long restraint was straw before the urge/Of instinct'.
(13) Why did the dog always like 'to work the sheep close in'?
(14) Why does the poet describe the way the sheep come together as 'drifted'?
(15) Why do you think the last, short stanza is so matter-of-fact and devoid of feeling?
(16) After he had put a bullet in the dog's head, the poet says he 'gave back the world to God'. What do you think he means by this?

'Merinos' is concerned with the incredible stubbornness and perversity of the creatures called sheep!

MERINOS

Sheep! You can keep them! What cynic godhead made them?
Or did they think themselves through the sheep-pad paths
Of evolution? A little wool to warm savages,
And nibbling at tuber peelings around the hearths.

Sheep! Move a mob one way, it elects the other;
Cross a creek, sheep stamp the pebbles and ring around,
And when they do start leaping, follow the current
Downstream to a cliff-face. Half a dozen drowned!

Sheep! They're not dumb, they know every trick in the book:
Bale up, go down, dig in, at the cry of 'Sheep!'
Ask the penner-up. Ask Paterson: merinos,
He wrote, made our men sardonic or they would weep!

DAVID CAMPBELL

This poem provides us with a sad picture of what life can become in a small Australian town.

SMALL TOWN

Down here the starlings sit
on our television aerials (tall
for city reception) and yesterday a woman drank Dettol.

Next door the forty-year-old
child is a collector of junk:
bits of old motorbikes, picture
frames, toilet seats, Singer

stands and old chairs. His father
died last week and the son
lives now in a Home. Their old
house sinks further into

itself each day. There are three
policemen, three hotels
and two schools. The woman who
drank Dettol died, and

Councillor P. might run
for Mayor again this
year and they're finally
building conveniences, for tourists.

Oh, and I forgot to put
the rubbish out last night.
Another visit to the Tip. I
always bring back something.

B. A. BREEN

5 Similes and Metaphors

Similes

A poet works with words, putting them together so skilfully that they call up pictures in our minds. Such picture-giving word-patterns are called *figures of speech*.

One of the most important figures of speech is the *simile*. A simile asks us to picture one thing as being similar to another, and uses the word 'like', 'as' or 'than' to create the linkage in our minds.

All the following sayings are similes:
- as warm as toast
- as proud as a peacock
- as sober as a judge
- as sick as a dog
- as light as a feather
- like a cat on a hot tin roof
- like a bull in a china shop

In our everyday language, we often use common similes such as: 'She's as fit as a fiddle' or 'He's as strong as an ox'. We hope to give a clearer picture about one thing by comparing it with another. However, very often these comparisons become stale from too much repetition. A good poet who wishes to hold our attention will not use everyday similes for fear of losing our interest.

Similes from Famous Poets

Below are a number of similes chosen from the poetry of famous poets. Write down four of the similes that you have found vivid or unusual. Then give reasons for your choice.

(1) 'Her lips were red, her looks were free,
Her locks were yellow as gold:
Her skin was as white as leprosy,'
Samuel Taylor Coleridge

(2) 'Let us go then, you and I,
When the evening is spread out against the sky
Like a patient etherised upon a table;'
T. S. Eliot

(3) 'Youth like summer morn
Age like winter weather.'
William Shakespeare

(4) 'The wild tulip, at the end of its tube, blows out its great red bell
Like a thin clear bubble of blood.'
Robert Browning

(5) 'There is sweet music here that softer falls
Than petals from blown roses on the grass.'
Alfred Lord Tennyson

(6) 'I wandered lonely as a cloud,
    That floats on high o'er vales and hills.'
                                    William Wordsworth

(7) 'It is a beauteous evening, calm and free,
    The holy time is quiet as a Nun
    Breathless with adoration.'
                                    William Wordsworth

(8) 'They're tearing down, tearing up
    this city, block by block.
    Rooms, cut in half,
    hang like flayed carcasses,'
                                    Adrienne Rich

(9) 'Her lips are like two budded roses.'
                                    Thomas Lodge

(10) 'Think of the storm roaming the sky uneasily
     like a dog looking for a place to sleep in,
     listen to it growling.'
                                    Elizabeth Bishop

Similes from the *Canterbury Tales*

Geoffrey Chaucer was one of the first English poets to use similes. Before his time, during the Old English period, the simile was not frequently used. Chaucer's similes in his famous *Canterbury Tales* are short, simple ones. Here in a modern translation by Nevill Coghill is a description of a rooster called Chanticleer, which featured in 'The Nun's Priest's Tale'.

CHANTICLEER

She had a yard that was enclosed about
By a stockade and a dry ditch without,
In which she kept a cock called Chanticleer.
In all the land for crowing he'd no peer;
His voice was jollier than the organ blowing
In church on Sundays, he was great at crowing.
His comb was redder than fine coral, tall
And battlemented like a castle wall,
His bill was black and shone as bright as jet,
Like azure were his legs and they were set
On azure toes with nails of lily white,
Like burnished gold his feathers, flaming bright.

from *The Canterbury Tales* by GEOFFREY CHAUCER
(translated by Nevill Coghill)

Chanticleer Similes

(1) Which simile suggests that Chanticleer's crowing was pleasant to hear?
(2) Make a list of the similes Chaucer uses to describe Chanticleer's colouring.
(3) What was the shape of Chanticleer's comb like?
(4) What do you learn about Chanticleer's character from this description?
(5) What comments would you make about Chaucer's use of similes? Are they successful or not?

The following portrait of an attractive young lady comes from Chaucer's 'The Miller's Tale'.

ALISON

And she had plucked her eyebrows into bows,
Slenderly arched they were, and black as sloes.
And a more truly blissful sight to see
She was than blossom on a cherry-tree,
And softer than the wool upon a wether.
And by her girdle hung a purse of leather,
Tasselled in silk, with metal droplets, pearled.
If you went seeking up and down the world
The wisest man you met would have to wrench
His fancy to imagine such a wench.
She had a shining colour, gaily tinted,
And brighter than a florin newly minted,
And when she sang it was as loud and quick
As any swallow perched above a rick.
And she would skip or play some game or other
Like any kid or calf behind its mother.
Her mouth was sweet as mead or honey – say
A hoard of apples lying in the hay.
Skittish she was and jolly as a colt,
Tall as a mast and upright as a bolt
Out of a bow. Her collaret revealed
A brooch as big as boss upon a shield.
High shoes she wore, and laced them to the top.
She was a daisy, O a lollypop.

from *The Canterbury Tales* by GEOFFREY CHAUCER
(translated by Nevill Coghill)

Alison Similes

(1) 'Sloes' are small blue-black wild plums. Why has Chaucer compared Alison's eyebrows to sloes?
(2) What simile used by the poet emphasizes that Alison is very appealing to the eye?
(3) What simile reveals Alison's softness?
(4) In England in the fourteenth century a florin was a golden coin. Why does Chaucer compare Alison to 'a florin newly minted'?
(5) What is Alison's singing similar to?
(6) What simile reveals Alison's playfulness?
(7) How does Chaucer emphasize the sweetness of Alison's mouth?
(8) What similes show that Alison is tall and straight?
(9) What simile tells you that Alison was wearing a very large brooch?
(10) What overall impression has Chaucer given you of Alison?

Simile Poems

THE WARM AND THE COLD

Freezing dusk is closing
　　Like a slow trap of steel
On trees and roads and hills and all
　　That can no longer feel.
　　　　But the carp is in its depth
　　　　　　Like a planet in its heaven.
　　　　And the badger in its bedding
　　　　　　Like a loaf in the oven.
　　　　And the butterfly in its mummy
　　　　　　Like a viol in its case.
　　　　And the owl in its feathers
　　　　　　Like a doll in its lace.

Freezing dusk has tightened
　　Like a nut screwed tight
On the starry aeroplane
　　Of the soaring night.
　　　　But the trout is in its hole
　　　　　　Like a chuckle in a sleeper.
　　　　The hare strays down the highway
　　　　　　Like a root going deeper.
　　　　The snail is dry in the outhouse
　　　　　　Like a seed in a sunflower.
　　　　The owl is pale on the gatepost
　　　　　　Like a clock on its tower.

Moonlight freezes the shaggy world
　　Like a mammoth of ice –
The past and the future
　　Are the jaws of a steel vice.
　　　　But the cod is in the tide-rip
　　　　　　Like a key in a purse.
　　　　The deer are on the bare-blown hill
　　　　　　Like smiles on a nurse.
　　　　The flies are behind the plaster
　　　　　　Like the lost score of a jig.
　　　　Sparrows are in the ivy-clump
　　　　　　Like money in a pig.

Such a frost
　　The flimsy moon
　　　　Has lost her wits.

　　　A star falls.

The sweating farmers
　　Turn in their sleep
　　　　Like oxen on spits.

TED HUGHES

Simile Questions

(1) What does the simile 'Like a slow trap of steel' suggest about the closing of the freezing dusk?

(2) What simile suggests that the carp will not be affected by the cold?

(3) What simile suggests that the badger is warm and cosy?

(4) What does the simile 'Like a chuckle in the sleeper' suggest about the trout in its hole?

(5) What simile emphasizes that the snail is dry?

(6) What does the simile 'Like a key in a purse' suggest about the cod in the tide-rip?

(7) What does the simile 'Like smiles on a nurse' suggest about the deer on the bare-blown hill?

(8) Why does the poet compare the farmers to 'oxen on spits'?

(9) What comments would you make about Ted Hughes' similes? Did you find them successful or not?

(10) Why do you think Ted Hughes called his poem, 'The Warm and the Cold'?

It's always easy to identify similes because they begin with 'like', 'as' or 'than'. 'The Picture' is a poem full of similes. Read through the poem, identify three or four of the similes and explain why they are effective. After you have done this, see whether you can understand why the poem was called 'The Picture'. The last line of the poem provides the answer.

THE PICTURE

The sun bears down on to a grassy hill
like a cake in a cook's oven.
The flower tosses and turns in the wind
like a boat in an ocean gale.
The leaves come streaming down
like a group of sky-divers from a plane.
The noise from a tractor interrupts the peace
like a goal scored at Wembley.
The river carries a broken branch
like the shopping crowds carry a lost little boy.
Picnickers arrive in a car, squashing life in their tracks
like a Government suppressing the people.
The birds come down from their nests to collect crumbs
like a Salvation Army collector at your door,
and darkness descends on that grassy hill
like a slowly shutting pair of curtains.
The woods become silent
like a road after a curfew in El Salvador.

The next picture is our holiday in Germany in '79.

DEAN OSBORNE

Metaphors

The metaphor takes us one step further than the simile. Instead of asking us to picture one thing as *being like* another, we are asked to picture one thing as *being* another.

- Her nerves were like steel. (*simile*)
- She had nerves of steel. (*metaphor*)

The poet Wes Magee by his use of metaphors stimulates our imagination so that we see the sun with a new vision.

WHAT IS ... THE SUN?

The sun is an orange dinghy
    sailing across a calm sea.

It is a gold coin
    dropped down a drain in heaven.

It is a yellow beach ball
    kicked high into the summer sky.

It is a red thumb-print
    on a sheet of pale blue paper.

It is the gold top from a milk bottle
    floating on a puddle.

WES MAGEE

In 'The Thought-Fox' even though the fox is vividly present the poem is not about a fox at all. The poem is purely metaphorical. It's about how a poet's inspiration comes to him as he writes a poem.

Here is an excellent opportunity to allow the poet, Ted Hughes himself, to introduce his own poem. 'An animal I never succeeded in keeping alive is the fox. I was always frustrated: twice by a farmer, who killed cubs I had caught before I could get to them, and once by a poultry keeper who freed my cub while his dog waited. Years after those events I was sitting up late one snowy night in dreary lodgings in London. I had written nothing for a year or so but that night I got the idea I might write something and I wrote in a few minutes the following poem: the first 'animal' poem I ever wrote. Here it is – "The Thought-Fox".'

THE THOUGHT-FOX

I imagine this midnight moment's forest:
Something else is alive
Beside the clock's loneliness
And this blank page where my fingers move.

Through the window I see no star:
Something more near
Though deeper within darkness
Is entering the loneliness:

Cold, delicately as the dark snow
A fox's nose touches twig, leaf;
Two eyes serve a movement, that now
And again now, and now, and now

Sets neat prints into the snow
Between trees, and warily a lame
Shadow lags by stump and in hollow
Of a body that is bold to come

Across clearings, an eye,
A widening deepening greenness,
Brilliantly, concentratedly,
Coming about its own business

Till, with a sudden sharp hot stink of fox
It enters the dark hole of the head.
The window is starless still; the clock ticks,
The page is printed.

TED HUGHES

The Poet Comments

This poem does not have anything you could easily call a meaning. It is about a fox, obviously enough, but a fox that is both a fox and not a fox. What sort of a fox is it that can step right into my head where presumably it still sits...smiling to itself when the dogs bark. It is both a fox and a spirit. It is a real fox; as I read the poem I see it move, I see it setting its prints, I see its shadow going over the irregular surface of the snow. The words show me all this, bringing it nearer and nearer. It is very real to me. The words have made a body for it and given it somewhere to walk.

If, at the time of writing this poem, I had found livelier words, words that could give me much more vividly its movements, the twitch and craning of its ears, the slight tremor of its hanging tongue and its breath making little clouds, its teeth bared in the cold, the snow-crumbs dropping from its pads as it lifts each one in turn, if I could have got the words for all this, the fox would probably be even more real and alive to me now, than it is as I read the poem. Still, it is there as it is. If I had not caught the real fox there in the words I would never have saved the poem. I would have thrown it into the waste-paper basket as I have thrown so many other hunts that did not get what I was after. As it is, every time I read the poem the fox comes up again out of the darkness and steps into my head. And I suppose that long after I am gone, as long as a copy of the poem exists, every time anyone reads it the fox will get up somewhere out in the darkness and come walking towards them.

So, you see, in some ways my fox is better than an ordinary fox. It will live for ever, it will never suffer from hunger or hounds. I have it with me wherever I go. And I made it. And all through imagining it clearly enough and finding the living words.

Ted Hughes

Metaphor Poems

Each of the following poems has a metaphor that extends through them. When this happens the metaphor is called an extended metaphor.

The American Indians used to refer to the locomotive thundering across the plains as 'the iron horse'. Emily Dickinson expands on this metaphor in her poem 'The Railway Train'.

THE RAILWAY TRAIN

I like to see it lap the miles,
And lick the valleys up,
And stop to feed itself at tanks;
And then, prodigious step

Around a pile of mountains,
And, supercilious, peer
In shanties by the sides of roads;
And then a quarry pare

To fit its sides, and crawl between,
Complaining all the while
In horrid, hooting stanza:
Then chase itself downhill

And neigh like Boanerges;
Then, punctual as a star,
Stop – docile and omnipotent –
At its own stable door.

EMILY DICKINSON

Metaphor Questions

(1) What words in the first stanza suggest that the railway train is a living creature?
(2) What words of the poet create the impression that the train rapidly covers great distances?
(3) *Supercilious* means 'contemptuous'. What reasons would the train have for being contemptuous?
(4) Boanerges was a loud preacher who lived in biblical times. What is the meaning of 'And neigh like Boanerges'?
(5) What is the meaning of 'punctual as a star'?
(6) 'Docile and omnipotent'. What do these words suggest about the train?
(7) What is the extended metaphor used in the poem?
(8) What impression of the train did the poet create for you?

In the next poem, C. Day Lewis' plane becomes a 'winged bull'.

FLIGHT TO ITALY –
THE PLANE TAKES OFF

The winged bull trundles to the wired perimeter.
Cumbrously turns. Shivers, brakes clamped,
Bellowing four times, each engine tested
With routine ritual. Advances to the runway.
Halts again as if gathering heart
Or warily snuffling for picador cross-winds.
Then, then, a roar open-throated
Affronts the arena. Then fast, faster
Drawn by the magnet of his *idée fixe*,
Head down, tail up, he's charging the horizon.
And the grass of the airfield grows smooth as a fur.
The runway's elastic and we the projectile;
Installations control-tower mechanics parked aeroplanes –
Units all woven to a ribbon unreeling,
Concrete melts and condenses to an abstract
Blur and our blood thickens to think of
Rending, burning, as suburban terraces
Make for us, wave after wave.

C. DAY LEWIS

Winged Bull Questions

(1) When the poet compares the plane to a 'winged bull', what characteristics of the plane is he trying to make the reader aware of?
(2) 'Bellowing four times'. What is happening to the plane?
(3) 'Halts again as if gathering heart'. What is happening?
(4) Why do you think the poet refers to the cross-winds as 'picador'?
(5) What is the plane's *idée fixe*?
(6) 'He's charging the horizon'. What is happening?
(7) What is the meaning of 'we the projectile'?
(8) 'Concrete melts and condenses to an abstract/Blur'. What is happening?
(9) What does the poet think of as the plane passes over suburban terraces?
(10) Do you think C. Day Lewis' extended metaphor is effective? Why or why not?

In 'Night Ride' the road at night takes on the appearance of a black leather strap and in the daylight it becomes a white ribbon.

NIGHT RIDE

Along the black
leather strap
of the night
deserted road

swiftly rolls
the freighted bus.
Huddled together
two lovers doze

their hands linkt
across their laps
their bodies loosely
interlockt

their heads resting
two heavy fruits
on the plaited
basket of their limbs.

Slowly the bus
slides into the light.
Here are hills
detach'd from dark

the road, uncoils
a white ribbon
the lovers with
the hills unfold

wake cold
to face the fate
of those who love
despite the world.

HERBERT READ

Thinking About the Metaphors

(1) Do you think the poet's comparison of the road at night to a black leather strap is a good one? Why or why not?
(2) 'Two heavy fruits'. Explain the metaphor.
(3) 'The plaited basket of their limbs'. Explain the metaphor.
(4) Why does the road for the poet change to 'a white ribbon'?
(5) Why is the shape of the poem appropriate for the subject matter?

Read below to see how Charles Cook's fire becomes a crimson serpent.

THE CRIMSON SERPENT

Fire; a serpent, hissing and crackling
Now pacified, now demanding
Climbing and swirling through countless
    grotesque forms –
Hungrily eying the next morsel of food
    in its path to self-destruction.
Fire – now secluded, now rampant through
    the charred ruins of its meal
Now friendly and warm, the next moment
    fierce and hot
Desperately trying to escape an inescapable fate –
A crimson serpent with an insatiable appetite,
Doomed to death through its own greediness.

CHARLES COOK

6 People

At the lunch counter the young girl mocks the blind boy while others are listening and watching. But she wants them to go away so that she can show her true kindness.

AT THE LUNCH COUNTER

A girl, fifteen perhaps,
licking her finger-tips,
smoothing splotches
of butter and salt
off her blue pants,
cheek muscles rippling.

Nathan who is blind
sidles to the stool beside her.

They talk, he pompously,
she making faces
he can't see,
telling the boys she isn't serious.

I'm Barbara, she says,
blowing her cheeks out,
wrinkling her forehead,
Fred Ward's Barbara.
I have red hair!

She giggles
since her hair is brown
with aluminum
fishes at the temples.

But he can't see.

Then,
she stiffens and frowns
wanting us to go away
so she can be kind.

ALDEN NOWLAN

Seeing Human Nature

(1) In the first stanza how does the poet create the impression that the young girl is full of life?
(2) Why is 'sidles' a better word than 'moves'?
(3) Why do you think the blind boy would talk 'pompously'?
(4) How does the girl deceive Nathan?
(5) Why does the poet repeat the words, 'he can't see'?
(6) How does the last stanza present us with a surprise?
(7) What do you learn about human nature from this poem?
(8) Why do you think the poet wrote 'At the Lunch Counter'?

Even though the gardener is *not quite all there*, he enjoys life to the full.

THE GARDENER

He was not able to read or write,
He did odd jobs on gentlemen's places
Cutting the hedge or hoeing the drive
With the smile of a saint,
With the pride of a feudal chief,
For he was not quite all there.

Crippled by rheumatism
By the time his hair was white,
He would reach the garden by twelve,
His legs in soiled puttees,
A clay pipe in his teeth,
A tiny flag in his cap,
A white cat behind him,
And his eyes a cornflower blue.

And between the clack of his shears
Or the honing of the scythe
Or the rattle of the rake on the gravel
He would talk to amuse the children,
He would talk to amuse himself or the cat
Or the robin waiting for worms
Perched on the handle of the spade;
Would remember snatches of verse
From the elementary school
About a bee and a wasp
Or the cat by the barndoor spinning;
And would talk about himself for ever –
You would never find his like –
Always in the third person;

And he would level his stick like a gun
(With a glint in his eye)
Saying 'Now I'm a Frenchman' –
He was not quite right in the head.

LOUIS MACNEICE

Appreciating the Gardener as a Person

(1) What attitude does the gardener have to his work?
(2) Why do you think the last line of the first stanza is placed in italics?
(3) The second stanza gives us a description of the gardener's appearance. Even though he is crippled by rheumatism, what do you find appealing about the gardener in this description?

(4) Why are the poet's words 'clack', 'honing' and 'rattle' so expressive of the work the gardener is doing?

(5) How do you know that the gardener enjoyed the company of various living creatures?

(6) What evidence in the poem indicates that the gardener enjoyed his childhood?

(7) 'You would never find his like'. What is unusual about the gardener?

(8) What does the last stanza reveal about the gardener?

(9) Do you think the poet wrote this poem from personal experience? Why?

(10) What do you think are the poet's feelings towards the gardener?

(11) What are your feelings towards the gardener?

The Nile landscape is bountiful both in fish and beauty. Yet the natural rhythm of an environment into which the Nile fishermen easily harmonize is shattered by the appearance of the police boat and the officials.

NILE FISHERMEN

Naked men, fishing in Nile without a licence,
kneedeep in it, pulling gaunt at stretched ropes.
Round the next bend is the police-boat and the officials
ready to make an arrest on the yellow sand.

The splendid bodies are stark to the swimming sand,
taut to the ruffled water, the flickering palms,
yet swelling and quivering as they tug at the trembling ropes.
Their faces are bent along the arms and still.

Sun is torn in coloured petals on the water,
the water shivering in the heat and the north wind;
and near and far billow out white swollen crescents,
the clipping wings of feluccas, seagull sails.

A plunge in the turbid water, a quick joke stirs
a flashing of teeth, an invocation of God.
Here is food to be fetched and living from labour.
The tight ropes strain and the glittering backs for the haul.

Round the bend comes the police-boat. The men scatter.
The officials blow their whistles on the golden sand.
They overtake and arrest strong bodies of men
who follow with sullen faces, and leave their nets behind.

REX WARNER

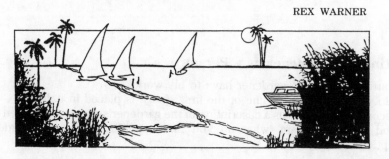

Through the eyes of the drover's sweetheart we look for the return of the drover and we feel
the anguish of her separation but then all is well: 'Jack's dog . . . he's coming – up – the track'.

THE DROVER'S SWEETHEART

An hour before the sun goes down
Behind the ragged boughs,
I go across the little run
To bring the dusty cows;
And once I used to sit and rest
Beneath the fading dome,
For there was one that I loved best
Who'd bring the cattle home.

Our yard is fixed with double bails;
Round one the grass is green,
The bush is growing through the rails,
The spike is rusted in;
It was from there his freckled face
Would turn and smile at me;
For he'd milk seven in the race
While I was milking three.

He kissed me twice and once again
And rode across the hill;
The pint-pots and the hobble-chain
I hear them jingling still . . .
About the hut the sunlight fails,
The fire shines through the cracks –
I climb the broken stockyard rails
And watch the bridle-tracks.

And he is coming back again –
He wrote from Evatt's Rock;
A flood was in the Darling then
And foot-rot in the flock.
The sheep were falling thick and fast
A hundred miles from town,
And when he reached the line at last
He trucked the remnant down.

And so he'll have to stand the cost;
His luck was always bad,
Instead of making more, he lost
The money that he had;
And how he'll manage, Heaven knows
(My eyes are getting dim)
He says – he says – he don't – suppose
I'll want – to – marry him.

As if I wouldn't take his hand
Without a golden glove –
Oh! Jack, you men won't understand
How much a girl can love.
I long to see his face once more –
Jack's dog! thank God, it's Jack! –
(I never thought I'd faint before)
He's coming – up – the track.

HENRY LAWSON

The machine gives Cynddylan a new kind of freedom from the soil to which he was 'yoked'.

CYNDDYLAN ON A TRACTOR

Ah, you should see Cynddylan on a tractor.
Gone the old look that yoked him to the soil;
He's a new man now, part of the machine,
His nerves of metal and his blood oil.
The clutch curses, but the gears obey
His least bidding, and lo, he's away
Out of the farmyard, scattering hens.
Riding to work now as a great man should,
He is the knight at arms breaking the fields'
Mirror of silence, emptying the wood
Of foxes and squirrels and bright jays.
The sun comes over the tall trees
Kindling all the hedges, but not for him
Who runs his engine on a different fuel.
And all the birds are singing, bills wide in vain,
As Cynddylan passes proudly up the lane.

R. S. THOMAS

Observing Cynddylan on a Tractor

(1) What are the poet's feelings towards Cynddylan on a tractor?
(2) Why was Cynddylan 'yoked' to the soil before he got his tractor?
(3) What words of the poet suggest that Cynddylan has become part of his machine?
(4) Explain how the poet uses personification to show how the machine responds to Cynddylan's driving?
(5) Why is Cynddylan now a 'great man'?
(6) What kind of romantic figure does Cynddylan become as he rides to work on his tractor?
(7) Why would Cynddylan be 'emptying the wood of foxes and squirrels and bright jays'?
(8) 'The sun comes over the tall trees/Kindling all the hedges'. What is happening?
(9) Why are all the birds singing with their 'bills wide in vain'?
(10) What are Cynddylan's feelings as he drives his tractor?

As you read through 'Follower' you'll come to understand how important the title is for your understanding of the poem.

FOLLOWER

My father worked with a horse-plough,
His shoulders globed like a full sail strung
Between the shafts and the furrow.
The horses strained at his clicking tongue.

An expert. He would set the wing
And fit the bright steel-pointed sock.
The sod rolled over without breaking.
At the headrig, with a single pluck

Of reins, the sweating team turned round
And back into the land. His eye
Narrowed and angled at the ground,
Mapping the furrow exactly.

I stumbled in his hob-nailed wake,
Fell sometimes on the polished sod;
Sometimes he rode me on his back
Dipping and rising to his plod.

I wanted to grow up and plough,
To close one eye, stiffen my arm.
All I ever did was follow
In his broad shadow round the farm.

I was a nuisance, tripping, falling,
Yapping always. But today
It is my father who keeps stumbling
Behind me, and will not go away.

SEAMUS HEANEY

In London, the bowler hat is worn by white collar workers commuting to the City. It helps to confer on them the kind of anonymity which the poet, A. S. J. Tessimond examines in his poem, 'The Man in the Bowler Hat'.

THE MAN IN THE BOWLER HAT

I am the unnoticed, the unnoticeable man:
The man who sat on your right in the morning train:
The man you looked through like a windowpane:
The man who was the colour of the carriage, the
    colour of the mounting
Morning pipe smoke.

I am the man too busy with a living to live,
Too hurried and worried to see and smell and touch:
The man who is patient too long and obeys too much
And wishes too softly and seldom.

I am the man they call the nation's backbone,
Who am boneless – playable catgut, pliable clay:
The Man they label Little lest one day
I dare to grow.

I am the rails on which the moment passes,
The megaphone for many words and voices:
I am graph, diagram,
Composite face.

I am the led, the easily-fed,
The tool, the not-quite-fool,
The would-be-safe-and-sound,
The uncomplaining, bound,
The dust fine-ground,
Stone-for-a-statue waveworn pebble-round.

A. S. J. TESSIMOND

Appraising the Man in the Bowler Hat

(1) What is the man in the bowler hat emphasizing about himself when he says: 'I am the unnoticed, the unnoticeable man'?
(2) What does the man in the bowler hat suggest about himself when he says: 'The man who was the colour of the carriage'?
(3) What is the meaning of 'I am the man too busy with a living to live'?
(4) What judgement would you make about a person 'who is patient too long and obeys too much'?
(5) Why does the man in the bowler hat refer to himself as 'pliable clay'?
(6) What is the meaning of 'I am the man they call the nation's backbone'?
(7) 'The would-be-safe-and-sound'. What is the man in the bowler hat telling us about himself?
(8) What does the poet gain from having the man in the bowler hat personally describing his existence?
(9) What are your feelings towards the man in the bowler hat?
(10) What is the poet's message to the reader?

A young man is saved from a life of hardship. However there is a price he must pay for comfort and security.

WARREN PRYOR

When every pencil meant a sacrifice
his parents boarded him at school in town,
slaving to free him from the stony fields,
the meager acreage that bore them down.

They blushed with pride when, at his graduation,
they watched him picking up the slender scroll,
his passport from the years of brutal toil
and lonely patience in a barren hole.

When he went in the Bank their cups ran over.
They marveled how he wore a milk-white shirt
work days and jeans on Sundays. He was saved
from their thistle-strewn farm and its red dirt.

And he said nothing. Hard and serious
like a young bear inside his teller's cage,
his axe-hewn hands upon the paper bills
aching with empty strength and throttled rage.

ALDEN NOWLAN

7 Personification

Personification is a special kind of metaphor in which human characteristics are given to non-human things. Look carefully at these examples.

- Slowly, silently, now the moon
  Walks the night in her silver shoon.

- But look, the dawn, in russet mantle clad,
  Walks o'er the dew of yon high eastern hill.

You can clearly see that both the moon and the dawn have taken on human qualities. Here are some more examples of personification. Explain how each of the things in heavy type has been given human qualities.

- Jocund **day** stands tiptoe on the misty mountain tops.
- And **Time** took up his solar swag.
- The dusky **night** rides down the sky.
- Ol' man **River**, he jes' keeps rolling along.
- **September** the maid, with her swift silver feet.
- The **Fir Tree** sobbed through all its robes of darkness.
- The **stars** watched over the sleeping child.
- The **trees** waved their arms in distress.
- The **ravine** yawned at my feet.
- The **wind** kicked the withered leaves about.

62

Personification Poems

You'll readily understand what personification is as you look closely at these two brief poems. In the first, the fog has become a hunch-shouldered, blind man groping his way up through the streets from the harbour. In the second, a cicada is transformed into a violinist.

THE FOG

Slowly, the fog,
Hunch-shouldered with a grey face,
Arms wide, advances,
Finger tips touching the way
Past the dark houses
And dark gardens of roses.
Up the short street from the harbour,
Slowly the fog,
Seeking, seeking;
Arms wide, shoulders hunched,
Searching, searching.
Out through the streets to the fields,
Slowly, the fog –
A blind man hunting the moon.

F. R. MCCREARY

HAIKU

Listlessly on a bare bough
a cicada scrapes
with his bow a few dry notes.

ALISTAIR CAMPBELL

Nature Personified

As you read the next poem, you will observe how Osbert Sitwell has personified Winter as a huntsman.

WINTER THE HUNTSMAN

Through his iron glades
Rides Winter the Huntsman.
All colour fades
As his horn is heard sighing.

Far through the forest
His wild hooves crash and thunder
Till many a mighty branch
Is torn asunder.

And the red reynard creeps
To his hole near the river,
The copper leaves fall
And the bare trees shiver,

As night creeps from the ground,
Hides each tree from its brother,
And each dying sound
Reveals yet another.

Is it Winter the Huntsman
Who gallops through his iron glades,
Cracking his cruel whip
To the gathering shades?

OSBERT SITWELL

Witnessing Winter's Coming

(1) Why do you think the poet has called Winter 'a huntsman'?
(2) Why does the poet describe the glades as 'iron'?
(3) 'All colour fades'. Explain what is happening?
(4) What effect does Winter have on the forest?
(5) Why does the red fox creep to his hole?
(6) 'And the bare trees shiver'. Explain how the poet has personified the trees?
(7) 'Cracking his cruel whip'. What is happening?
(8) What are some of the onomatopoeic words used by the poet?

The short poems that follow depend on the poet's use of personification for their success.
Read them through and answer the questions.

LAST WEEK IN OCTOBER

The trees are undressing, and fling in many places
On the gray road, the roof, the window-sill –
Their radiant robes and ribbons and yellow laces;
A leaf each second so is flung at will,
Here, there, another and another, still and still.

A spider's web has caught one while downcoming,
That stays there dangling when the rest pass on;
Like a suspended criminal hangs he, mumming,
In golden garb, while one yet green, high yon,
Trembles, as fearing such a fate for himself anon.

THOMAS HARDY

A Sight to Behold

(1) Explain the poet's use of personification in 'The trees are undressing'.
(2) 'Their radiant robes and ribbons and yellow laces'. What are these?
(3) How does the poet convey the impression that many leaves are falling?
(4) Why has the poet likened one of the leaves to 'a suspended criminal'?
(5) Explain the poet's use of personification in: '. . . while one yet green, high yon,/Trembles, as fearing such a fate for himself anon.'
(6) Did you enjoy the poet's description of autumn in 'Last Week in October'? Why or why not?

The dread King Drought has become master of the great West Land in Will Ogilvie's poem.

DROUGHT

My road is fenced with the bleached, white bones
    And strewn with the blind, white sand,
Beside me a suffering, dumb world moans
    On the breast of a lonely land.

On the rim of the world the lightnings play,
    The heat-waves quiver and dance,
And the breath of the wind is a sword to slay
    And the sunbeams each a lance.

I have withered the grass where my hot hoofs tread.
    I have whitened the sapless trees,
I have driven the faint-heart rains ahead
    To hide in their soft green seas.

I have bound the plains with an iron band,
    I have stricken the slow streams dumb!
To the charge of my vanguards who shall stand?
    Who stay when my cohorts come?

The dust-storms follow and wrap me round,
    The hot winds ride as a guard;
Before me the fret of the swamps is bound
    And the way of the wild-fowl barred.

I drop the whips on the loose-flanked steers;
    I burn their necks with the bow;
And the green-hide rips and the iron sears
    Where the staggering, lean beasts go.

I lure the swagman out of the road
    To the gleam of a phantom lake;
I have laid him down. I have taken his load,
    And he sleeps till the dead men wake.

My hurrying hoofs in the night go by,
 And the great flocks bleat their fear
And follow the curve of the creeks burnt dry
 And the plains scorched brown and sere.

The worn men start from their sleepless rest
 With faces haggard and drawn;
They cursed the red Sun into the west
 And they curse him out of the dawn.

They have carried their outposts far, far out,
 But – blade of my sword for a sign! –
I am the Master, the dread King Drought,
 And the great West Land is mine!

WILL H. OGILVIE

Observing the Mastery of the Dread King Drought

(1) How does the poet make the dread King Drought appear to be human?
(2) What powers does the dread King Drought possess?
(3) Explain the meaning of 'a suffering, dumb world moans'.
(4) What is the meaning of 'And the breath of the wind is a sword to slay'?
(5) What do you learn about the character of King Drought from the words: 'I have bound the plains with an iron band'?
(6) Why does the poet speak of the streams as *dumb*?
(7) What do you learn about the character of King Drought from the following words?
  'I lure the swagman out of the road
   To the gleam of a phantom lake;'
(8) 'And the great West Land is mine!' Why does the dread King Drought believe this?
(9) What words in the poem suggest that King Drought is a warrior engaged in battle?
(10) Do you think the poet wrote this poem from personal experience or not? Give reasons for your viewpoint.

Appreciating Personification

In the following poem, the metho drinker's methylated spirits becomes his 'woman of fire' who must eventually destroy him.

METHO DRINKER

Under the death of winter's leaves he lies
who cried to Nothing and the terrible night
to be his home and bread. 'O take from me
the weight and waterfall of ceaseless Time
that batters down my weakness; the knives of light
whose thrust I cannot turn; the cruelty
of human eyes that dare not touch nor pity.'
Under the worn leaves of the winter city
safe in the house of Nothing now he lies.

His white and burning girl, his woman of fire,
creeps to his heart and sets a candle there
to melt away the flesh that hides the bone,
to eat the nerve that tethers him in Time.
He will lie warm until the bone is bare
and on a dead dark moon he wakes alone.
It was for Death he took her; death is but this;
and yet he is uneasy under her kiss
and winces from that acid of her desire.

JUDITH WRIGHT

Appreciating a Poem

In the first stanza of 'Metho Drinker', Judith Wright reveals her compassion and concern for a metho drinker she has observed in everyday life. She uses the imagery she knows best, imagery which in the main she draws from natural phenomena, to describe his situation.

In life, the metho drinker's proximity to death is seen in his having to seek refuge 'in the death of winter's leaves'. The poet uses imagery from nature to show that the metho drinker finds it impossible to face life. Her metaphor of the waterfall emphasizes the pressure and battering that reality imposes upon the metho drinker.

Judith Wright evokes pity for the metho drinker and also reveals some of the forces that motivate his actions. He seeks 'the terrible night' as a hiding place and refuge from human problems. His aim is to find refuge in oblivion. When he is 'safe in the house of Nothing', he defeats Time and forgets about 'the cruelty of human eyes'.

For Judith Wright, the metho drinker is a human being who deserves to be understood rather than be condemned. The metho drinker's inability to overcome his problem is vividly evoked in her metaphor 'the knives of light whose thrust I cannot turn'. She then suggests that some of the blame for the metho drinker's plight lies with us. We, with our lack of compassion, have not the moral strength to touch or pity the drunkard.

In the second stanza, the poet describes the intensity of the metho drinker's passion for methylated spirits. She takes the comparison of a man enthralled by his desire for his mistress and applies it with all its implications to the metho drinker and his addiction. The methylated spirits is personified as his 'White and burning girl'. One becomes acutely aware of the destructive and consuming qualities of the metho drinker's mistress. His love for methylated spirits is consummated through the physical experience of drinking it. As the lover in sexual union with his mistress forgets all else, so now the metho drinker united with his mistress, loses awareness of the physical world and Time itself. However, the metho drinker's union with methylated spirits is not satisfying. Once his intoxication with her wears off, he is alone. The pathos of the situation is brought out in the words: 'It was for Death he took her'. The words 'he took her' convey his blind passion and complete infatuation with his mistress. But once more, the poet emphasizes the sadness and deterioration that this relationship brings the metho drinker. He is virtually embracing death – 'death is but this'.

The concluding lines of the poem present us with a sorrowful picture of the metho drinker's dominance by his mistress. His passion does not bring him peace. The repetition of the 's' sounds in words such as 'desire', 'acid', 'winces' and 'uneasy' suggest both the sensuous and vitiating qualities of this union. We, the readers, know full well that the metho drinker's continued submission to his passion will ultimately destroy him.

Personifying Death

John Donne (1572–1631) is thought of today as the 'father' of the Metaphysical Poets. His poetry is marked by vigour and freshness, and his lyrics are frequently quite dramatic. Much of his poetry is religious. In 'Death Be Not Proud', Donne questions, confronts and challenges the power of death over man.

DEATH BE NOT PROUD

Death be not proud, though some have called thee
Mighty and dreadful, for, thou art not so,
For, those whom thou think'st thou dost overthrow
Die not, poor death, nor yet canst thou kill me.
From rest and sleep, which but thy pictures be,
Much pleasure, then from thee much more must flow,
And soonest our best men with thee do go,
Rest of their bones, and soul's delivery.
Thou art slave to fate, chance, kings, and desperate men,
And dost with poison, war, and sickness dwell,
And poppy, or charms can make us sleep as well,
And better than thy stroke; why swell'st thou then?
One short sleep past, we wake eternally,
And death shall be no more; death, thou shalt die.

JOHN DONNE

Challenging Death

(1) What is Donne's first command to death?
(2) How does Donne create the impression throughout the poem that death is a person?
(3) Why does the poet refer to death as *'poor* death'?
(4) What does the poet mean when he says that those death thinks it overthrows, do not die?
(5) In what way are rest and sleep 'pictures' of death?
(6) How do we gain pleasure from rest and sleep?
(7) Explain the poet's argument when he says that we must gain 'much pleasure' from death.
(8) In what way is death 'slave to fate, chance, kings and desperate men'?
(9) Death dwells with 'poison, war and sickness'. How does this cause us to view death?
(10) What other things can make us sleep as well, or better, than death?
(11) 'Why swell'st thou then?' What does the poet mean?
(12) What 'short sleep' is the poet referring to in the second last line?
(13) Why does the poet say 'death, thou shalt die'?
(14) Is the tone of this poem light hearted or serious? Explain your viewpoint.

Fun with Personification

In 'The Fight of the Year', Spring and Winter are boxers fighting it out, until finally, Spring is the winner.

'THE FIGHT OF THE YEAR'

And there goes the bell for the third month
and Winter comes out of its corner looking groggy
Spring leads with a left to the head
followed by a sharp right to the body
    daffodils
    primroses
    crocuses
    snowdrops
    lilacs
    violets
    pussywillow
Winter can't take much more punishment
and Spring shows no signs of tiring
    tadpoles
    squirrels
    baalambs
    badgers
    bunny rabbits
    mad march hares
    horses and hounds
Spring is merciless
Winter won't go the full twelve rounds
    bobtail clouds
    scallywaggy winds
    the sun
    a pavement artist
    in every town
A left to the chin
and Winter's down!
    tomatoes
    radish
    cucumber
    onions
    beetroot
    celery
    and any
    amount
    of lettuce
    for dinner
'Winter's out for the count
Spring is the winner!'

R. MCGOUGH

8 Appealing to the Senses

Poetry, more than any other form of literature, appeals to the reader's senses. The five senses are sight, sound, touch, smell and taste.

Let us look at brief examples of the appeal to the senses in poetry.

The Sense of Sight:

He strikes a match – and instantly
The lovely flower of light

from 'The Match' by W. W. Gibson

Notice what a colourful, shapely vision this calls up in the imagination.

The Sense of Sound:

And nearer, nearer, rolls the sound,
Louder the throb and roar of wheels

from 'The Bridge' by John Redwood Anderson

Here the sound of the approaching train beats on the ear.

The Sense of Touch:

In a cool curving world he lies
And ripples with dark ecstasies

from 'The Fish' by Rupert Brooke

Touch and feeling impinge on the fish and on the reader in these lines.

The Sense of Smell:

The old strange fragrance filled the air,
A fragrance like the garden pink,
But tinged with vague medicinal stink
Of camphor, soap, new sponges, blent
With chloroform and violet scent.

from 'Miss Thompson Goes Shopping'
by Martin Armstrong

Miss Thompson shops in a pharmacy, and her nose identifies a variety of odours pleasant and strange. These are evoked in the reader's imagination.

The Sense of Taste:

Sandalwood, cedarwood, and sweet white wine

from 'Cargoes' by John Masefield

Notice how the word 'sweet' appeals directly to the reader's sense of taste.

The Five Senses

In 'The Great Lover', Rupert Brooke titillates the reader's five senses – sight, sound, taste, touch and smell.

THE GREAT LOVER

These I have loved:
    White plates and cups, clean-gleaming,
Ringed with blue lines; and feathery, fairy dust;
Wet roofs, beneath the lamp-light; the strong crusts
Of friendly bread; and many-tasting food;
Rainbows; and the blue bitter smoke of wood;
And radiant raindrops couching in cool flowers;
And flowers themselves, that sway through sunny hours,
Dreaming of moths that drink them under the moon;
Then, the cool kindliness of sheets, that soon
Smooth away trouble; and the rough male kiss
Of blankets; grainy wood; live hair that is
Shining and free; blue massing clouds; the keen
Unpassioned beauty of a great machine;
The benison of hot water, furs to touch;
The good smell of old clothes; and others such –
The comfortable smell of friendly fingers,
Hair's fragrance, and the musty reek that lingers
About dead leaves and the last years ferns . . .
                              Dear names,
And thousand others throng to me! Royal flames;
Sweet water's dimpling laugh from tap or spring;
Holes in the ground; and voices that do sing;
Voices in laughter, too; and body's pain,
Soon turned to peace; and deep panting train;
Firm sands; the little dulling edge of foam
That browns and dwindles as the wave goes home;
And washen stones, gay for an hour; the cold
Graveness of iron; moist black earth mould;
Sleep; and high places; footprints in the dew;
And oaks; and brown horse-chestnuts, glossy-new;
And new peeled sticks; and shining pools on grass; –
All these have been my loves.

                              RUPERT BROOKE

Appealing to the Senses

(1) Why has the poet called this poem, 'The Great Lover'?
(2) Why do you think the poet refers to the bread as 'friendly'?
(3) What picture do you see in the words 'radiant raindrops couching in cool flowers'?
(4) What does the poet mean by 'the cool kindliness of sheets?' Which one of your senses is the poet appealing to?

(5) What does the poet mean by 'The benison of hot water'?

(6) What are some of the smells the poet describes?

(7) What does the poet mean by 'Sweet water's dimpling laugh from tap or spring;'?

(8) What are the human sounds the poet has loved?

(9) What does the poet mean by 'the cold/Graveness of iron'? Which one of your senses is the poet appealing to?

(10) Which one of Rupert Brooke's loves is one of your favourites? Why? Which one of his loves doesn't appeal to you?

Your Turn to Write

In 'The Great Lover' Rupert Brooke has described the things in his life that he has loved. See whether you can write a poem of your own using a similar approach to Rupert Brooke's. First of all jot down a list of things – experiences, places, people or whatever else you enjoy or have enjoyed in your own life. Then try to make your list as alluring as possible. You may like to call your poem 'Some of my Favourite Things' or 'These Have I Loved'.

Here is another poem that appeals to every one of the senses and makes use of comparisons, contrasts and imagery to present the reader with grape harvest time in all its rich diversity capturing the sounds, shapes, colours, tastes and scents of the ripe vineyards.

GRAPE HARVEST

There was a great heat on the land,
But crackle-dry as wing of a dragon fly;
Breast-high over the baked brown earth
Stretched dappled green lines of dark flat leaves,
And, in the ponderous mass of light and shade,
The pulsing shapes of grapes. Cool from the white canal
Where I had swum beneath a cloudless sky,
Over a burning acre I came at a run
To the shaded tables on trestles, to the purple-white bunches
Each with a short brown curving stalk,
To the snip of wine-stained scissors, the dextrous fingers
Of women and men, the hot pulpy scent, to the bees
Clinging and humming, sipping sweet nectar,
And I thrilled as if I had come upon Heaven.

Down the long rows, thin in perspective,
Came the pickers with heavy full baskets
Out from the glare into awninged sharp shade,
The packers down bending to set the white paper,
With coarse-sensitive fingers layering the fruit,
Bunch on bunch of white-purple grapes; then hammer
And nails, a brand, and away to the horse-drawn carts;
And I said to myself, 'O man, what a world thou hast here
In thy two hands,' for I knew full well
The labour of man and maiden, the sweat of the labourer's brow,
Was keystone of all the heavens; and I said again,
Watching the flash of limbs in the wide canal,
Dappled with light as the sun retreated –
'What harvest as this have the cities?'

BRIAN VREPONT

Marvelling at the Grape Harvest

(1) 'Crackle-dry' effectively combines two words to give us a feeling of the heat that was upon the land. Which of the senses are appealed to in this unusual word?
(2) What visual image does the word 'dappled' call up in your mind's eye?
(3) 'And, in the ponderous mass of light and shade,/The pulsing shapes of grapes'. Within these lines the poet uses alliteration and rhyme to suggest the richness of the vines and the full growth of the grapes. Comment on the poet's use of alliteration and the rhyme that contribute to these images.
(4) At the moment when the poet approaches the trestle tables of the grape pickers the sense of sight is uppermost. How does the poet emphasize colour and shape in the sight that confronts him?
(5) Why is 'snip' a more expressive word to use than 'cut' when referring to the action of the scissors on the stems of bunches of grapes?
(6) 'The hot pulpy scent'. Explain how a scent could be both 'hot' and 'pulpy'.
(7) Explain how the senses of touch, taste, sound and smell are appealed to in this description of the bees: 'Clinging and humming, sipping sweet nectar'.
(8) How did the poet feel after he had arrived at the place where the grapes lay?
(9) Explain the meaning of 'Down the long rows, thin in perspective'.
(10) How is the reader's sense of sight appealed to in the line, 'Out from the glare into awninged sharp shade'?
(11) The pickers' fingers are both coarse and sensitive. How could they be both at the same time?
(12) What, according to the poet, made the vineyard a heaven on earth?
(13) What contrast is the poet making in the final line of the poem?
(14) How would you describe the mood that pervades the poem?
(15) What message is carried in this poem?
(16) How does the appeal to the senses throughout the poem help to enrich the poem's theme?

In the following poem the senses and feelings of the reader are engaged as the poet unfolds in symbolism the plight of city dwellers alienated from one another by the indifference and insularity of urban existence.

ACQUAINTED WITH THE NIGHT

I have been one acquainted with the night.
I have walked out in rain – and back in rain.
I have outwalked the furthest city light.

I have looked down the saddest city lane.
I have passed by the watchman on his beat
And dropped my eyes unwilling to explain.

I have stood still and stopped the sound of feet
When far away an interrupted cry
Came over houses from another street,

But not to call me back or say goodbye;
And further still at an unearthly height,
One luminary clock against the sky
Proclaimed the time was neither wrong nor right.
I have been one acquainted with the night.

ROBERT FROST

Appreciating Acquainted with the Night

Robert Frost, who lived in the New England district of the United States from 1874 to 1963 and whose poetry is mainly derived from nature, was deeply concerned at the alienation suffered by the city dweller both from nature and from society. 'Acquainted with the Night' is one of his poems which depicts the dark, unforgiving side of the urban existence. Many of Frost's poems begin with a familiar situation then work, stanza by stanza, to unfold some deep and unsuspected core of truth.

In 'Acquainted with the Night', the first stanza presents us with the ordinary, recognizable situation of walking through the city in the rain. However, even in this stanza, we begin to suspect that the night is a symbol for some feeling or quality inherent in the wanderer. The poem proceeds to reveal that night is symbolic of the insularity and isolation of the city dweller.

In the second line of the first stanza, the pendulum-like swing of 'out in rain – and back in rain' seems to indicate the aimlessness of city life in which it is possible to search for, but not to find, a stable social relationship with the other dwellers amidst the indifference of the city. The rain falling – rain has often been used as a poetic symbol for sadness – leads us to the second stanza, where the sadness and the lack of communication become explicit. The feeling of sadness cannot be explained and, in any case, there is no one to accept responsibility for its cause.

Just as the first and second stanzas appeal to the reader's sense of sight, so the third stanza appeals to the sense of hearing: 'the sound of feet', 'an interrupted cry'. However, the interrupted cry is not for the poet. He hears, just as many others hear, but in the city there is no necessary connection between what is seen or heard and any reaction such as going to the help of another human being in trouble. Streets and houses intervene and each person's fate must remain his or her own concern.

In the poem's last stanza there comes the welcome vision of a light in the darkness: 'One luminary clock against the sky'. However, its message is ambiguous – 'neither wrong nor right'. The poem ends on this pendulum-like swing which recalls that of the first stanza and emphasizes the irrelevance of even right or wrong to those who dwell without meaningful contact with each other, as each gropes and treads an individual path amidst the night imposed by the impersonal city.

Sydney's William Street runs from Hyde Park, dips into a kind of valley and rises again in King Cross. At night, the length of the street is lit by many neon signs. The lights, the pawnshops, food shops and cafes all contribute to the street's character.

WILLIAM STREET

THE red globes of light, the liquor-green,
The pulsing arrows and the running fire
Spilt on the stones, go deeper than a stream;
You find this ugly, I find it lovely.

Ghosts' trousers, like the dangle of hung men,
In pawnshop-windows, bumping knee by knee,
But none inside to suffer or condemn;
You find this ugly, I find it lovely.

Smells rich and rasping, smoke and fat and fish
And puffs of paraffin that crimp the nose,
Or grease that blesses onions with a hiss;
You find it ugly, I find it lovely.

The dips and molls, with flip and shiny gaze
(Death at their elbows, hunger at their heels)
Ranging the pavements of their pasturage;
You find it ugly, I find it lovely.

KENNETH SLESSOR

How the Poet Appeals to the Senses

(1) What visual aspect of the city life is the poet describing in the opening lines of the poem?
(2) What words and phrases in the first stanza show that the movement of the lights in William Street seems to resemble water?
(3) Why do you think the poet says at the end of each stanza: 'You find it ugly, I find it lovely'?
(4) What scene is the poet describing in the second stanza?
(5) Why does the poet think of the trousers hanging in the pawnshop windows as belonging to ghosts?
(6) Which two of the reader's senses does the third stanza appeal to?
(7) What do you think the poet intends you to experience as you read, 'puffs of paraffin that crimp the nose'?
(8) Why is 'hiss' an effective word?
(9) Explain the meaning of 'Death at their elbows, hunger at their heels'.
(10) It is not necessary to live in Sydney to enjoy and appreciate this poem. Explain why this is so.

Here is a poem which treats a skyscraper as being alive and tormented by men and yet, at the same time, as being worshipped by them.

CRUCIFIXION OF THE SKYSCRAPER

Men took the skyscraper
And nailed it to the rock. Each nerve and vein
Were searched by iron hammers. Hour on hour,
The bolts were riveted tighter. Steel and stone
Did what they could to quench the fiery core
That blazed within. Till when the work was done,
Solid as a sepulchre, square-rooted to the rock,
The skyscraper, a well-polished tomb of hope,
Guarded by busy throngs of acolytes,
Shouldered aside the sun. Within its walls
Men laid a little gold.
                              But yet not dead
However long battered by furious life,
However buried under tons of frozen weight
That structure was. At night when crowds no more
Jostled its angles, but the weary streets
Of a worn planet stared out at the stars;
Its towering strength grown ghostly, pure, remote,
Lone on the velvet night in flights of gold
The tower rose. The skyscraper dripped light.

                    J. GOULD FLETCHER

In 'Winter Stock Route' the poet stirs us to visualize the same setting in different seasons and different eras, as a vehicle for his message.

WINTER STOCK ROUTE

Here where red dust rose
To raddle sheep and men
And the kelpie tongued at noon,
Silence has come again.
The great-boled gumtrees bow
Beneath their load of snow.

The drover and his dray
Have gone; and on this hill
I find myself alone
And Time standing still.
Printless the white road lies
Before my quiet skis.

But where my skis trace
Their transient snow furrow,
For generations both
Man and beast will follow.
Now in this winter passage
I cross the deserted stage.

DAVID CAMPBELL

Thinking about the Poet's Intention

(1) Explain the meaning of 'the kelpie tongued at noon'.
(2) 'Silence has come again.' What is the reason for the advent of silence?
(3) Notice the marvellous use the poet makes of the rounded sound of the vowel 'o' in the last two lines of the first stanza. How does the poet's use of this sound help us to form an image of the changed scene?
(4) What contrast of feeling is there between the first and second parts of stanza one?
(5) Why do you think the poet uses a capital 'T' for Time in the second stanza?
(6) Why does the poet feel that Time is standing still?
(7) Explain the meaning of 'Printless the white road lies'.
(8) What movement does the poet begin to make in the last stanza?
(9) How do we know that the poet thinks of himself as only a temporary visitor?
(10) How do we learn that the poet is thinking of the future in the last stanza?

GIVE ME NATURE

Give me the splendid silent sun with all his beams full – dazzling,
Give me juicy autumnal fruit ripe and red from the orchard,
Give me a field where the unmown grass grows,
Give me an arbour, give me the trellised grape,
Give me fresh corn and wheat, give me serene-moving animals teaching content,
Give me nights perfectly quiet as on a high plateau west of the Mississippi, and I looking
   up at the stars,
Give me odorous at sunrise a garden of beautiful flowers where I can walk undisturbed,
Give me for marriage a sweet-breath'd woman of whom I should never tire,
Give me a perfect child, give me away from the noise of the world a rural domestic life,
Give me to warble spontaneous songs recluse by myself, for my own ears only,
Give me solitude, give me Nature, give me again, O Nature, your primal sanities!

WALT WHITMAN

Appreciating Give Me Nature

Walt Whitman (1819–92) is well known as an American nature poet and 'Give Me Nature' is a good example of his work. It is really a hymn of praise to nature and, at the same time, a plea that nature will satisfy his deepest needs and feelings – those of his soul.

The poem begins with the sun, the source of all growth and life on earth. Then in the orchard, the field, the arbour and wherever else the poet experiences nature, he pleads for the most fruitful and bountiful conditions to prevail. He wants fruit to be as juicy and as ripe and red as possible, the grass in the field to be unmown and therefore as lush as possible. He desires the full and complete gratification of all his senses. To emphasize the fullness of his desires, the poet makes use of alliteration in the first three lines of the poem: 'the splendid silent sun', 'fruit ripe and red', 'unmown grass grows'.

In the fifth line of the poem the long, slow moving word picture – 'serene-moving animals teaching content' – aptly conjures up in the imagination a browsing herd of cattle. In this line too, the words 'content' and 'serene' seem to sum up the kind of experience the poet seeks from life. Notice, too, the gentleness of the appeals to both sight and smell – as the poet looks up at the stars and smells the odour of a garden of beautiful flowers at sunrise.

There is a shift of emphasis from natural to human affairs in the line beginning 'Give me for marriage . . .' and here the poet prays that the harmony in nature, as he sees it, will extend to his own family world.

In the last two lines of the poem the poet addresses nature just as a priest would address a deity. Here the poet seems to suggest that he seeks no personal fame for his poetry: 'Give me to warble spontaneous songs recluse by myself, for my own ears only'. A sufficient reward for him would be the 'primal sanities' of nature, the appreciation and enjoyment of the simple, everyday gifts of natural life.

Here is a poem that appeals primarily to the reader's sense of sound. The memories of sounds heard in childhood by the poet are disturbing, startling, terrifying, weird, lonely, and even alien, so that we are left with the impression that childhood was a wild and irrational time for the poet. The poem is a catalogue of sounds arising on all sides like the trees in a wood, aimless and menacing. Even the sound of his mother singing was a lonely, self-indulgent sound.

I REMEMBER

I remember, when I was a boy,
I heard the scream of a frog, which was caught with his foot
   in the mouth of an up-starting snake;
I remember when I first heard bull-frogs break into sound in
   the spring;
I remember hearing a wild goose out of the throat of night
Cry loudly, beyond the lake of waters;
I remember the first time, out of a bush in the darkness, a
   nightingale's piercing cries and gurgles startled the depths
   of my soul;
I remember the scream of a rabbit as I went through a wood at
   midnight;
I remember the heifer in her heat, blorting and blorting
   through the hours, persistent and irrepressible;
I remember my first terror hearing the howl of weird, amorous
   cats;
I remember the scream of a terrified, injured horse, the
   sheet-lightning,
And running away from the sound of a woman in labour,
   something like an owl whooing,
And listening inwardly to the first bleat of a lamb,
The first wail of an infant,
And my mother singing to herself,
And the first tenor singing of the passionate throat of a young
   collier, who has long since drunk himself to death,
The first elements of foreign speech
On wild dark lips.

D. H. LAWRENCE

79

The boy fishing is at one with the strange, cold environment of the fish he patiently seeks . . .

BOY FISHING

I am cold and alone,
On my tree-root sitting as still as stone.
The fish come to my net. I scorned the sun,
The voices on the road, and they have gone.
My eyes are buried in the cold pond, under
The cold, spread leaves; my thoughts are silver-wet.
I have ten stickleback, a half-day's plunder,
Safe in my jar. I shall have ten more yet.

E. J. SCOVELL

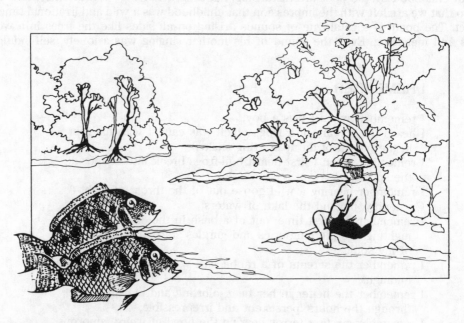

Appreciating the Boy's Feelings

(1) How is the boy feeling as the poem opens?
(2) What comparison does the poet use to indicate that the boy is concerned not to make any movement?
(3) What words in the poem show that the boy successfully closes his mind to his surroundings and concentrates on his fishing?
(4) 'My eyes are buried in the cold pond, under/The cold, spread leaves; my thoughts are silver-wet.' What do these words tell you about the involvement of the boy in his fishing?
(5) Explain the meaning of 'my thoughts are silver-wet'.
(6) Why is the word 'plunder' used instead of, say, 'catch'?
(7) Explain how this poem describes more than just the action of fishing.
(8) What are your feelings towards the boy?

In the following poem, the poet has some fun with his nose. For a number of reasons that you will discover he is not entirely satisfied with his organ of smell because it betrays him. It soon becomes apparent that he is ashamed of his nose and blames it for some of his misfortunes.

SMELL!

Oh strong-ridged and deeply hollowed
nose of mine! what will you not be smelling?
What tactless asses we are, you and I boney nose
always indiscriminate, always unashamed,
and now it is the souring flowers of the bedraggled
poplars: a festering pulp on the wet earth
beneath them. With what deep thirst
we quicken our desires
to that rank odor of a passing springtime!
Can you not be decent? Can you not reserve your ardors
for something less unlovely? What girl will care
for us, do you think, if we continue in these ways?
Must you taste everything? Must you know everything?
Must you have a part in everything?

WILLIAM CARLOS WILLIAMS

9 Rhyme and Rhythm

Two of the most important structural elements of poetry are *rhyme* and *rhythm*.

1. Rhyme

Rhyme is usually accepted as the repetition of an accented vowel sound (usually, although not always, followed by an identical consonant sound), and *preceded* by a letter or letters which are unlike in sound.

Thus, true rhyme has the following features:

(a) *unlike* sounds preceding a rhymed vowel sound;
(b) *identical* vowel sounds;
(c) when consonant sounds follow the rhymed vowel sound, these also must be identical.

EXAMPLES OF TRUE RHYME:
fight/night; cat/mat; slow/toe; eat/feet.

EXAMPLES WHICH ARE NOT TRUE RHYME:
fight/hide; cat/can; threw/through.

2. Rhyme Pattern Variations

(a) End Rhyme

The most common rhyme pattern used by poets is that called *end rhyme*. This simply means that the end words of lines rhyme. Two consecutive lines may rhyme, or alternate lines may rhyme, or even more distant lines. Many variations are possible within a single poem. The consistent feature is that the rhyme occurs only at the end of lines. In the following examples each new rhyme is given a new letter of the alphabet, following the end of the line.

EXAMPLE 1: He clasps the crag with crooked hands;   a
Close to the sun in lonely lands,   a
Ringed with the azure world, he stands.   a

from 'The Eagle' by Alfred, Lord Tennyson

2: Sunset and evening star,   a
And one clear call for me!   b
And may there be no moaning of the bar,   a
When I put out to sea   b

from 'Crossing the Bar' by Alfred, Lord Tennyson

(b) Internal Rhyme

When the rhyme pattern involves rhyming a word half-way through a single line of poetry with the end word of the same line, it is called *internal rhyme*. It is used fairly frequently in ballads, and occasionally in other kinds of poetry.

EXAMPLE: And I had done a hellish thing
And it would work 'em woe:
For all *averred*, I had killed the *bird*
That made the breeze to blow.
Ah wretch! said *they*, the bird to *slay*,
That made the breeze to blow.

from 'The Rime of the Ancient Mariner' by S. T. Coleridge

(c) Half Rhyme

Half rhyme involves the use of words which suggest rhyme but, for some reason, fail to satisfy the criteria of true rhyme. Sometimes the final consonant varies, so that the half rhyme is really assonance. More commonly, the final consonant is identical, but the vowel sound varies slightly (e.g. hall / hell). The effect of half rhyme is to create a sense of rhyme, with a slightly discordant feel. Two examples are provided. The first is from 'Sir Patrick Spens' and is, in fact, assonance. The second is a poem by the British poet, Wilfred Owen who, perhaps more than most poets, refined the art of deliberately using half rhyme.

EXAMPLE 1: The anchor broke, the topmast split,
'Twas such a deadly storm
The waves came over the broken ship
Till all her sides were torn.

from 'Sir Patrick Spens' (anonymous)

EXAMPLE 2:

MINERS

There was a whispering in my hearth,
A sigh of the coal,
Grown wistful of a former earth
It might recall.

I listened for a tale of leaves
And smothered ferns;
Frond-forests; and the low, sly lives
Before the fawns.

My fire might show steam-phantoms simmer
From Time's old cauldron,
Before the birds made nests in summer,
Or men had children.

But the coals were murmuring of their mine,
    And moans down there
Of boys that slept wry sleep, and men
    Writhing for air.

And I saw white bones in the cinder-shard.
    Bones without number;
For many hearts with coal are charred
    And few remember.

I thought of some who worked dark pits
    Of war, and died
Digging the rock where Death reputes
    Peace lies indeed.

Comforted years will sit soft-chaired
    In rooms of amber;
The years will stretch their hands, well-cheered
    By our lives' ember.

The centuries will burn rich loads
    With which we groaned,
Whose warmth shall lull their dreaming lids
    While songs are crooned.
But they will not dream of us poor lads
    Lost in the ground.

WILFRED OWEN

Notes on Miners

In 'Miners', Owen is pensive before his coal fire. He expects his imagination to re-create tales of the prehistoric plant life that gave birth to this coal, but instead finds himself thinking only of those whose toil beneath the earth has mined this coal. Look back over the rhyme pattern carefully and you will be intrigued at Owen's craftsmanship. He systematically alters the vowel sound slightly in each rhyming pair to make half rhymes (e.g. hearth/earth; coal/recall). What do you feel is the overall effect of this in the poem?

3 Blank Verse

The distinctive quality of *blank verse* is that it is unrhymed. It is important to note that it still has clear rhythmic qualities and so qualifies as verse, rather than prose. Most of Shakespeare's dramas are written in blank verse. Here is an example from John Milton's *Paradise Lost*.

EXAMPLE:
                             ... His pride
    Had cast him out from Heaven with all his host
    Of rebel Angels, by whose aid, aspiring
    To set himself in glory above his peers,
    He trusted to have equalled the Most High ...

Rhythm

Rhythm refers to the beat, or the pattern of stresses, which occur in poetry. It is a vital part of a poet's craft, for rhythm can be used to give great variety of effect in poetry. It can evoke the rhythm of a train or a bulldozer, the lazy motion of a river or the urgent rush of a sprinter. Usually, we can feel the rhythm best when we read aloud. We can mark the beats, or stresses and, thus, see the pattern built in by the poet. Usually, we mark the stresses in a line of poetry with a small sloping dash above the accented syllable.

Read through the poem below and consider the effect of the pattern of accents which provides the rhythm.

BREAK, BREAK, BREAK

Break, break, break,
   On thy cold grey stones, O Sea!
And I would that my tongue could utter
   The thoughts that arise in me.

O well for the fisherman's boy,
   That he shouts with his sister at play!
O well for the sailor lad,
   That he sings in his boat on the bay!

And the stately ships go on
   To their haven under the hill;
But O for the touch of a vanish'd hand,
   And the sound of a voice that is still!

Break, break, break,
   At the foot of thy crags, O Sea!
But the tender grace of a day that is dead
   Will never come back to me.

ALFRED, LORD TENNYSON

Looking at Rhyme and Rhythm

(1) There are six beats or accents which occur in the first two lines. Rewrite the lines and mark the accents over the respective syllables.
(2) What effect does the pattern of accents in the first line have upon the pace, or speed, at which the line should be read?
(3) Try to formulate a general rule from the effect of the grouping of strong accents in the first line upon the pace of the line.
(4) What effect does the pattern of accents, and the pace of the poem, have upon the *mood* of the poem?
(5) Comment upon the effect of the phrase 'cold grey stones' in evoking the mood of this poem.
(6) What is the overall mood of the poem?
(7) How appropriate is this mood to the subject matter of the poem?

(8) The rhythm of the poem is intended to evoke another rhythm for us. What is this other rhythm?

(9) How effective is the poem's rhythm pattern?

(10) Using letters of the alphabet, identify the rhyme scheme of the poem.

Henry Kendall, the Australian poet after whom the New South Wales country town of Kendall was named, uses rhythm to excellent effect in this poem.

SONG OF THE CATTLE HUNTERS

While the morning light beams on the fern-matted streams,
And the waterfalls flash in its glow,
Down the ridges we fly, with a loud ringing cry –
Down the ridges and gullies we go!
And the cattle we hunt, they are racing in front,
With a roar like the thunder of waves,
And the beat and the beat of our swift horses' feet
Start the echoes away from their caves –
As the beat and the beat
Of our swift horses' feet
Start the echoes away from their caves.

Like the wintry shore that the waters ride o'er
All the lowlands are filling with sound:
For swiftly we gain where the herds on the plain
Like a tempest are tearing the ground!
But we follow them hard to the rails of the yard,
Over gulches and mountain-tops grey,
Where the beat and the beat of our swift horses' feet
Will die with the echoes away –
Where the beat and the beat of our swift horses' feet
Will die with the echoes away.

HENRY KENDALL

Hunting

(1) Identify the type of rhyme used in the poem's opening line.

(2) Use letters of the alphabet to identify the rhyme scheme of the first stanza.

(3) Write out the lines: 'And the beat and the beat /Of our swift horses' feet /Start the echoes away from their caves.' Mark in the accents over the syllables where they occur.

(4) What other rhythm does the poet intend to evoke for us via the rhythm of the poem?

(5) How successfully does the poet evoke this other rhythm?

(6) Comment on the pace at which this poem should be read, as compared with 'Break, Break, Break'.

(7) Try to identify a general rule about the pace of a poem's movement based upon the closeness of the strong accents to each other.

(8) Why is the repetition of 'the beat and the beat of our swift horses' feet' appropriate in each verse?

(9) Consider the repetition of 'the beat and the beat of our swift horses' feet' in the first stanza. If you were reading the poem aloud, how should you vary the expression in the repeat line? Why?

(10) What do you see as the most important techniques in this poem?

(11) How successful would you rate this poem? Why?

The following extract from Shakespeare's *Macbeth* is another excellent example of regular rhythm used to create an atmosphere, a 'feeling' for the event being described.

DOUBLE, DOUBLE TOIL AND TROUBLE

Round about the cauldron go:
In the poisoned entrails throw.
Toad, that under cold stone
Days and nights has thirty-one
Sweltered venom sleeping got
Boil thou first i' th' charmed pot!

Double, double toil and trouble;
Fire burn and cauldron bubble.
Fillet of a fenny snake,
In the cauldron boil and bake:
Eye of newt and toe of frog,
Wool of bat and tongue of dog,
Adder's fork and blind-worm's sting,
Lizard's leg and howlet's wing,
For a charm of powerful trouble,
Like a hell-broth boil and bubble.

Double, double toil and trouble;
Fire burn and cauldron bubble.
Cool it with a baboon's blood,
Then the charm is firm and good.

from *Macbeth*, Act IV, Scene 1
WILLIAM SHAKESPEARE

Looking into the Cauldron

(1) What scene is the poet attempting to re-create for us?

(2) Rewrite the first six lines, marking in where the accents fall.

(3) What effect is the writer wanting to create through the rhythm?

(4) How successfully is rhythm used to achieve this?

(5) What pace does the rhythm tend to call forth from the reader?

(6) How appropriate is this pace to the scene being described? Explain your answer.

(7) Much of the vitality of this extract also derives from the use of alliteration. Identify three examples.

(8) The extract is, in fact, a kind of song. What are the features which tend to give it the character of a song.

(9) What is the effect upon the reader of listing all the unlikely ingredients in the brew?

(10) How would you rate the poet's achievement? Justify your answer.

Contrast

Finally, to help you appreciate the tremendous variations in rhythm available to a poet, consider the following two poems. Notice how, in each case, the rhythm is used to give a sense of pace or speed, and also to set an atmosphere. In 'The Burial of Sir John Moore at Corunna' the rhythm is slow and dignified, perhaps recalling the rhythm of the funeral drum even though none is heard at the funeral. In 'Two Chronometers' the rhythm re-creates the ticking of clocks, one lively and urgent and the other slower.

THE BURIAL OF SIR JOHN MOORE AT CORUNNA

Not a drum was heard, not a funeral note,
   As his corse to the rampart we hurried;
Not a soldier discharged his farewell shot
   O'er the grave where our hero we buried.

We buried him darkly at dead of night,
   The sods with our bayonets turning;
By the struggling moonbeam's misty light
   And the lantern dimly burning.

No useless coffin enclosed his breast,
   Not in sheet or in shroud we wound him;
But he lay like a warrior taking his rest,
   With his martial cloak around him.

Few and short were the prayers we said,
   And we spoke not a word of sorrow;
But we steadfastly gazed on the face that was dead,
   And we bitterly thought of the morrow.

We thought, as we hollow'd his narrow bed
   And smoothed down his lonely pillow,
That the foe and the stranger would tread o'er his head
   And we far away on the billow!

Lightly they'll talk of the spirit that's gone
   And o'er his cold ashes upbraid him, –
But little he'll reck, if they let him sleep on
   In the grave where a Briton has laid him.

But half of our heavy task was done
   When the clock struck the hour for retiring,
And we heard the distant and random gun
   That the foe was sullenly firing.

Slowly and sadly we laid him down,
   From the field of his fame fresh and gory;
We carved not a line, and we raised not a stone,
   But we left him alone with his glory.

CHARLES WOLFE

TWO CHRONOMETERS

Two chronometers the captain had,
One by Arnold that ran like mad,
One by Kendal in a walnut case,
Poor devoted creature with a hangdog face.

Arnold always hurried with a crazed click-click
Dancing over Greenwich like a lunatic,
Kendal panted faithfully his watch-dog beat,
Climbing out of Yesterday with sticky little feet.

Arnold choked with appetite to wolf up time,
Madly round the numerals his hands would climb,
His cogs rushed over and his wheels ran miles,
Dragging Captain Cook to the Sandwich Isles.

But Kendal dawdled in the tombstoned past,
With a sentimental prejudice to going fast,
And he thought very often of a haberdasher's door
And a yellow-haired boy who would knock no more.

All through the night-time, clock talked to clock,
In the captain's cabin tock-tock-tock,
One ticked fast and one ticked slow,
And Time went over them a hundred years ago.

KENNETH SLESSOR

10 Modern Living

PRELUDES

I

The winter evening settles down
With smell of steaks in passageways.
Six o'clock.
The burnt-out ends of smoky days.
And now a gusty shower wraps
The grimy scraps
Of withered leaves about your feet
And newspapers from vacant lots;
The showers beat
On broken blinds and chimney-pots,
And at the corner of the street
A lonely cab-horse steams and stamps.

And then the lighting of the lamps.

II

The morning comes to consciousness
Of faint stale smells of beer
From the sawdust-trampled street
With all its muddy feet that press
To early coffee-stands.

With the other masquerades
That time resumes,
One thinks of all the hands
That are raising dingy shades
In a thousand furnished rooms.

III

You tossed a blanket from the bed,
You lay upon your back, and waited;
You dozed, and watched the night revealing
The thousand sordid images
Of which your soul was constituted;
They flickered against the ceiling.
And when all the world came back
And the light crept up between the shutters
And you heard the sparrows in the gutters,
You had such a vision of the street
As the street hardly understands;
Sitting along the bed's edge, where
You curled the papers from your hair,
Or clasped the yellow soles of feet
In the palms of both soiled hands.

IV

His soul stretched tight across the skies
That fade behind a city block,
Or trampled by insistent feet
At four and five and six o'clock;
And short square fingers stuffing pipes,
And evening newspapers, and eyes
Assured of certain certainties,
The conscience of a blackened street
Impatient to assume the world.

I am moved by fancies that are curled
Around these images, and cling:
The notion of some infinitely gentle
Infinitely suffering thing.

Wipe your hand across your mouth, and laugh;
The worlds revolve like ancient women
Gathering fuel in vacant lots.

T. S. ELIOT

Appreciating Preludes

Each section of this poem is called a 'prelude', or a beginning, a title that contrasts with the mood of futility and hopelessness which permeates the description. Rather than beginnings, these brief verses all seem, in some way, to describe 'burnt-out ends'.

Prelude I confronts the reader with the atmosphere of the passageways which lead out onto the sordid streets of an urban slum. Upon these streets the evening has settled down. All the images used to picture the winter evening are vivid, but depressing. On the streets the wind blows 'The grimy scraps/Of withered leaves' and 'newspapers from vacant lots' around. It is raining and the blinds on windows are 'broken'. The only sign of life at all is a cab-horse, which is described as 'lonely'. The poet leaves us with a picture, a sense-impression, of hopeless desolation, a landscape not conducive to human life at all. Notice how the sameness of this prevailing mood is enhanced by the repetition of the 'st' and 'l' sounds in the alliteration of the last two lines: 'A lonely cab-horse steams and stamps/And then the lighting of the lamps.'

Prelude II complements Prelude I and begins at the other end of the day, morning. The technique of personification is used to help us picture the arrival of morning. In this sordid setting morning does not awaken. Instead, like a boxer who has taken a beating, it 'comes to consciousness', vague and uncertain of itself. The first signs of this stirring of consciousness are the 'faint stale smells of beer', but as morning's bleary vision improves it encompasses the meanness of the streets and the inhabitants and then, dimly, the occupants of 'a thousand furnished rooms'. As in the first prelude, the use of descriptive words such as 'stale', 'muddy' and 'dingy' help to create the mood of emptiness and quiet despair. Notice, also, how the repetition of 'all' and the use of 'a thousand' emphasize the pervasive nature of the morning's depressing revelations.

Prelude III moves us into one of the 'thousand furnished rooms' where a woman, who is addressed as 'you', has waited and dozed and 'watched the night revealing /The thousand sordid images' of her soul. In the previous prelude morning came to consciousness; here, a woman comes to consciousness. So the woman and the street are linked by the images they share and she is one of the thousand other inhabitants of the 'thousand furnished rooms' who continually adopt the evening masquerade, only to have it prised away from her with the beginning of each day.

Notice the climax that occurs in the words: 'You had such a vision of the street /As the street hardly understands.' The fourth prelude will show us just how limited is the vision possessed by the street. But the question remains: What is the woman's vision of the street, of the world beyond her room? Is her 'vision' the awareness that the street's appalling meanness is all that there is, that there is no other reality? This third prelude ends with an image of the woman clasping the soles of her feet in the palms of her hands, tucked in a position that suggests she does not want to be open to the reality of the morning or the world outside.

Prelude IV is divided into three parts. In the first part the street is personified: 'His soul stretched tight against the skies.' The reality of the drabness and routine intrude quickly with the image of the street being 'trampled by insistent feet /At four and five and six o'clock'. This last line serves as a good example of the poet's use of rhythm to heighten poetic effect. We 'hear' the trampling feet in the rhythm of 'at four and five and six o'clock'. The fingers 'stuffing pipes' are 'short' and 'square', and these descriptive words somehow epitomize the limited horizons of the 'world' we are looking at, this street. Yet in the words 'impatient to assume the world' there is a suggestion that perhaps civilization is so infected with meanness and poverty of spirit that this will some day turn the whole world into literal and spiritual slums.

In the second section of this prelude, beginning with the words 'I am moved . . .', the poet reveals something of his own feelings. The emptiness of these situations and people move him deeply, though perhaps not in the way we might expect. He is not moved to despair or anger. Instead, akin to a god looking in on these prelude scenes, he marvels at the gentle suffering he sees, and we are left with the faintest impression that something profound beyond our understanding is being worked out here.

In the last three lines there occurs a reversal of feeling. The poet seems to scorn sentiment. He advises co-viewers of these scenes: 'Wipe your hand across your mouth, and laugh.' His final comparison seems to deny any purpose at all to such human suffering. The actions of the world, it seems, are meaningless, futile and empty.

A Modern Daniel

Daniel is a modern man and the world news waits for him at his breakfast table. He doesn't like what he reads but it doesn't spoil his breakfast either. His own serious cares are really trivial and ultimately he inflates their importance until they become the world for him.

DANIEL AT BREAKFAST

His paper propped against the electric toaster
   (Nicely adjusted to his morning use),
Daniel at breakfast studies world disaster
   And sips his orange juice.

The words dismay him. Headlines shrilly chatter
   Of famine, storm, death, pestilence, decay.
Daniel is gloomy, reaching for the butter.
   He shudders at the way

War stalks the planet still, and men know hunger,
    Go shelterless, betrayed, may perish soon.
The coffee's weak again. In sudden anger
    Daniel throws down his spoon

And broods a moment on the kitchen faucet
    The plumber mended, but has mended ill;
Recalls tomorrow means a dental visit,
    Laments the grocery bill.

Then, having shifted from his human shoulder
    The universal woe, he drains his cup,
Rebukes the weather (surely turning colder),
    Crumples his napkin up
And, kissing his wife abruptly at the door,
Stamps fiercely off to catch the 8:04.

PHYLLIS MCGINLEY

Judging Daniel

(1) What words in the first stanza suggest that Daniel's life is governed by a pleasant routine?
(2) What contrast does the poet present you with in the first stanza?
(3) What feelings are experienced by Daniel as he reads the paper?
(4) 'Headlines shrilly chatter'. In what way could headlines ever be said to 'shrilly chatter'?
(5) How does Daniel physically react to the bad news he reads?
(6) 'And broods a moment on the kitchen faucet'. Why do you think 'broods' is a more expressive word to use than, say, 'thinks'?
(7) What comments would you make about Daniel's way of life?
(8) What does the poet mean by saying that Daniel 'rebukes the weather'?
(9) In the last line Daniel 'stamps fiercely off to catch the 8:04'; but why 'fiercely'?
(10) What is the poet's message to the reader?

Here is a poem which entertains because of the way it focuses on the many items of chaos that lurk in a household where a marriage has lost its magic. As you begin to read the poem you'll notice that Pam Ayres leads us towards the house as if we were visitors looking around. First we move through the strangled garden into the yard and the dilapidation that has taken place. Words such as 'chucked', 'smashed', 'sagging', 'bodged' aptly illustrate the indifference that has caused the chaos that is described.

Next we enter the living room and we follow the poet's gaze to 'fag ends in saucers', 'peelings in the sink' and to other areas of neglect. With the fifth stanza comes a change of emphasis as the husband remembers the romance of courtship only to be faced with the reality of his wife now looking slovenly and acting in a disgusting way.

In the poem's last stanza the husband points out that a long marriage is not necessarily one that can be praised. After twenty years of marriage, he and his wife have ceased to communicate with each other.

THE HUSBAND'S LAMENT

or Well, You Certainly Proved Them Wrong

The flowers round our garden gate
Are strangled now with nettles,
The caterpillars got the leaves,
The road dust got the petals,
There's cracks across the asphalt path,
And the dusty wind do blow,
I know they say 'domestic bliss',
But I dunno . . . .

There's trikes chucked on the garden
And there's writing on the wall,
The kids have smashed the wash house
With their little rubber ball.
The paint's peeled off the woodwork,
And the gutter's sagging fast,
I bodged it up last autumn,
But . . . it didn't last.

And in our shattered living room,
The telly's on the blink,
There's fag ends in the saucers,
And peelings in the sink,
There's holes burned in the carpet,
Where it smouldered half the night.
'A Woman's Work is Never Done'
And you certainly proved that right.

There's barnacles in the goldfish bowl
And curlers on the floor,
The budgie's out the window
And the woodworm's in the door.
The leaves fell off the rubber plant,
The leg fell off the bed,
The smiles fell off our faces
And the back fell off the shed.

And *you*, who I adored,
One look and I knew I was falling,
You stole away my heart,
Beneath the moon and that tarpaulin,
It *can't* be you beside me,
With your tights so full of holes,
Chewing through your supper,
All them picalilli rolls.

We've been together twenty years today,
And there's a moral,
Since we have no conversation,
We have never had a quarrel,
We hardly see each other,
So we never have a fight,
For 'Silence it is Golden'
And we've certainly proved that right.

PAM AYRES

A car driver thinks of his wife and the quarrel he's had with her but because he's driving a car he uses that as a weapon. The result is predictable.

MEDITATION ON THE A30

A man on his own in a car
  Is revenging himself on his wife;
He opens the throttle and bubbles with dottle
  And puffs at his pitiful life.

'She's losing her looks very fast,
  She loses her temper all day;
That lorry won't let me get past,
  This Mini is blocking my way.

'Why can't you step on it and shift her!
  I can't go on crawling like this!
At breakfast she said she wished I was dead –
  Thank heavens we don't have to kiss.

'I'd like a nice blonde on my knee
  And one who won't argue or nag.
Who dares to come hooting at me?
  I only give way to a Jag.

'You're barmy or plastered, I'll pass you, you bastard –
  I *will* overtake you. I *will*!'
As he clenches his pipe, his moment is ripe
  And the corner's accepting its kill.

JOHN BETJEMAN

Meditating on the A30

(1) Do you think the title 'Meditation on the A30' is suitable for the poem? Why?
(2) What do we know about the feelings of the car driver?
(3) How is the fact that the man is smoking a pipe linked by the poet with the way he is driving his car and the way he is thinking?
(4) In the second stanza, what complaints does the driver make about his wife?

(5) How is his frustration with his wife expressed in the way he feels about the traffic around him?
(6) What is happening to the traffic in the third stanza?
(7) What fantasy does the driver have?
(8) What rudely dispels this fantasy?
(9) What is the meaning of 'the corner's accepting its kill'?
(10) Throughout the poem, what technique does the poet use to indicate that the domestic problems of the driver are worrying him while he is driving?
(11) To what extent does this poem explore a genuine aspect of modern living?

As you will soon discover as you read the poem, the title 'The Improvers' is ironic. The poet sees those who work on unimproved land as desecrating 'the whole miraculous earth' with their huge earth-moving machines.

THE IMPROVERS

I see they are at it again with their bloody bulldozers,
tournapulls, mastertorques, and God knows what other
inventions directed by Big Brother –
damnable tamed dinosaurs and mechanical mastodons
munching the red earth, spilling it, dripping,
half-masticated from the corners of their mouths.

All breeds and offspring grind and acerbate,
charge like bulls, toss up the dust, plough
insensately among their clods and furrows.
Some like nightmare beetles butt about,
strike attitudes, throw feelers up, and shout
their day-long platitudes in holes and burrows,
One fat old waddler fills its apron up –
tons it with earth and stone – and, gorged grotesquely,
lumbers off like an old crone
with a bag of melons stuffed inside her jumper.

'Unimproved land' is the keeper's meat they feed on,
so, slaver and yammer, they must need go improve it.
The iron mandibles twitch, jaws champ,
pipe of each nostril snorts, rectum huffs,
at the heave and strain that brutes against their shoulders –
And trees come down, cliffs crack, the green
gift of grass lies mouthed and mutilated;
till, creeks filled in and hills made flat, the whole
miraculous earth lies lathed for traffic snooker.

Now the highway builders rub their stomachs' fat,
for coloured cars can hurtle to nowhere and back,
and good-time Charlie can outdo lame-brain Jack.

Strangely how the language keeps us sane –
ironic old elephant that can't forget –
for where the roadmen carve and desecrate
the green waywardness of each old byway, then
unwittingly they fly their proper flag:
'State Highwaymen!'

COLIN THIELE

Evaluating the Improvers

(1) At the very beginning of the poem, what are the poet's feelings towards the developers?
(2) Who do you think is Big Brother?
(3) What does the reference to Big Brother suggest about the world in which the poet finds himself?
(4) Why do you think the poet likens the machinery to prehistoric monsters?
(5) 'Mechanical mastodons munching' is an example of alliteration in the first stanza, and there are several other examples as well. What is the poet's purpose in employing such alliteration?
(6) Why is 'munching' in 'munching the red earth' a more expressive word to use than, say, 'eating'?
(7) What comparison is the poet making in the first three lines of the second stanza?
(8) What image does the description, 'gorged grotesquely' call up in your imagination?
(9) Explain the striking comparison made by the poet in the last four lines of the second stanza.
(10) What confronts us in the second half of the third stanza?
(11) What picture do you think was in the poet's mind when he wrote of 'traffic snooker'?
(12) What purposeless reasons for the desecration of the land are given in the fourth stanza?
(13) Explain the meaning of, 'the green waywardness of each old byway'.
(14) 'State Highwaymen!' What condemnation is the poet making of the roadmen and the developers?

The houses in this poem reflect and demonstrate the kinds of fears possessed by the idiosyncratic creatures called people.

HOUSES

People who are afraid of themselves
multiply themselves into families
and so divide themselves
and so become less afraid.

People who might have to go out
into clanging strangers' laughter,
crowd under roofs, make compacts
to no more than smile at each other.

People who might meet their own faces
or surprise their own faces in doorways
build themselves rooms without mirrors
and live between walls without echoes.

People who might meet other faces
and unknown voices round corners
build themselves rooms all mirrors
and live between walls all echoes.

People who are afraid to go naked
clothe themselves in families, houses,
but are still afraid of death
because death one day will undress them.

A. S. J. TESSIMOND

In 'Office Block' the reader is given a glimpse of the future but it is a future in which human beings are strangely misplaced.

OFFICE BLOCK

The main construction is in flexibrick,
Pre-stressed, fatigue-proof, never used before.
It's only fifteen millimetres thick
But carries eighteen thousand tons and more.

The lifts are – damn it, this one seems to stick –
The lifts are atom-driven – mind the door! –
With cybernetic halts. They're pretty slick.
Now up we go again. Excelsior!

The helicopter-park is just behind
With robots in attendance. But it's queer;
You'd never dream how hard it's been to find
The class of tenant we expected here.

There have been applicants; but now and then
I've had suspicions they were only men.

JOHN MANIFOLD

Here is a poem that examines the way humans have been inhuman to each other at critical times in history.

FIVE WAYS TO KILL A MAN

There are many cumbersome ways to kill a man:
you can make him carry a plank of wood
to the top of a hill and nail him to it. To do this
properly you require a crowd of people
wearing sandals, a cock that crows, a cloak
to dissect, a sponge, some vinegar and one
man to hammer the nails home.

Or you can take a length of steel,
shaped and chased in a traditional way,
and attempt to pierce the metal cage he wears.
But for this you need white horses,
English trees, men with bows and arrows,
at least two flags, a prince and a
castle to hold your banquet in.

Dispensing with nobility, you may, if the wind
allows, blow gas at him. But then you need
a mile of mud sliced through with ditches,
not to mention black boots, bomb craters,
more mud, a plague of rats, a dozen songs
and some round hats made of steel.

In an age of aeroplanes, you may fly
miles above your victim and dispose of him by
pressing one small switch. All you then
require is an ocean to separate you, two
systems of government, a nation's scientists,
several factories, a psychopath and
land that no one needs for several years.

These are, as I began, cumbersome ways
to kill a man. Simpler, direct, and much more neat
is to see that he is living somewhere in the middle
of the twentieth century, and leave him there.

EDWIN BROCK

11 Sonnets

Classical or Petrarchan Sonnets

The sonnet is a form of lyric poem which always follows a set structure of fourteen lines. As a poetic form it appeared first in Italy in the late 13th century and was given its classical form by the Italian poet, Petrarch. His sonnets were consistently divided into an *octave* (a stanza of eight lines), and a *sestet* (a concluding stanza of six lines), marked by a pause between them in the movement of the poem. His sonnets also limited rhyme variations to a total of five, with the octave rhyming as ABBA ABBA and the sestet as CDECDE. The common theme running through Petrarch's sonnets was unrequited love. Each poem was a love poem to an idealized woman who failed to return his love.

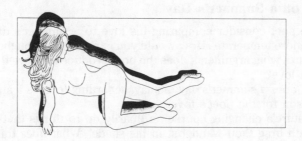

English Sonnets

Brought into English by the Earl of Surrey and Sir Thomas Wyatt, the sonnet was most brilliantly developed by Shakespeare.

(a) *Structure*: Shakespeare's sonnets were written as three quatrains (stanzas of four lines each) with a concluding couplet. Other English sonnet writers, such as Donne and Hopkins, followed the more classical division of an octave and a sestet.

(b) *Theme*: Shakespeare's themes centre on aspects of love, though other English poets such as Milton, Wordsworth, Byron, Keats and Hopkins extend the sonnet to cover descriptions of nature, inner struggles of the soul, hymns of praise, and other diverse subjects.

(c) *Rhythm*: Classical, and Shakespearean, sonnets follow a predominantly *iambic* rhythm. Iambic rhythms have two syllables, with the accent always on the second syllable as, for example, in the word 'compare'. Other English sonneteers have adopted much greater rhythmic freedom in their poems.

Shakespearean Sonnets

Each of the following sonnets by Shakespeare, deals with some aspect of love, or the effects of time on physical beauty.

SHALL I COMPARE THEE TO A SUMMER'S DAY?

Shall I compare thee to a summer's day?
Thou art more lovely and more temperate:
Rough winds do shake the darling buds of May,
And summer's lease hath all too short a date:
Sometime too hot the eye of heaven shines,
And often is his gold complexion dimmed;
And every fair from fair sometime declines,
By chance or nature's changing course untrimmed.
But thy eternal summer shall not fade,
Nor lose possession of that fair thou ow'st;
Nor shall death brag thou wander'st in his shade,
When in eternal lines to time thou grow'st:
    So long as men can breathe, or eyes can see,
    So long lives this, and this gives life to thee.

WILLIAM SHAKESPEARE

Shedding Light on a Summer's Day

(1) Why does the poet consider comparing his love to a summer's day?
(2) 'Thou . . . art more temperate'. How would you express this thought in your own words?
(3) In the first stanza what arguments does the poet produce to prove that a summer's day is inferior to his love?
(4) What 'deficits' does a summer's day display, according to lines 5 and 6, which make it a poor comparison for the poet's love?
(5) What does 'nature's changing course' ordinarily do to things that are 'fair'?
(6) 'Nor shall death brag thou wander'st in his shade'. What does this line mean?
(7) What are the 'eternal lines to time' which enable his love to continue to grow?
(8) 'So long lives this . . .' What does 'this' refer to?
(9) 'So long as . . . eyes can see'. Why is this relevant to the poem's argument?
(10) What is the theme of this poem?

THAT TIME OF YEAR

That time of year thou may'st in me behold
When yellow leaves, or none, or few, do hang
Upon those boughs which shake against the cold –
Bare ruined choirs, where late the sweet birds sang.
In me thou seest the twilight of such day
As after sunset fadeth in the west,
Which by-and-by black night doth take away,
Death's second self, that seals up all in rest:
In me thou seest the glowing of such fire
That on the ashes of his youth doth lie,
As the death-bed whereon it must expire,
Consumed with that which it was nourished by.
    This thou perceiv'st, which makes thy love more strong,
    To love that well which thou must leave ere long.

WILLIAM SHAKESPEARE

Thinking About That Time of Year

(1) 'That time of year ...' What time of year is the poet referring to?
(2) 'Bare ruined choirs ...' Explain the appropriateness of this image.
(3) In the second quatrain (stanze of four lines), the poet changes the comparison of his stage of life with a time of year. What new comparison does he make?
(4) To what time of day does he compare his stage of life?
(5) Explain how this comparison is appropriate.
(6) In what way is night 'Death's second self'?
(7) In the third quatrain the image changes to a fire. What stage of a fire's life does the poet see his life as fitting?
(8) How is a fire 'consumed with that which it was nourished by'? How is this an appropriate comparison for the poet's life?
(9) How does the final perception make 'thy love more strong'?
(10) What is the poet's theme or message?
(11) How would you describe the mood of this poem?

MY MISTRESS' EYES ARE NOTHING LIKE THE SUN

My mistress' eyes are nothing like the sun;
Coral is far more red than her lips' red:
If snow be white, why then her breasts are dun;
If hairs be wires, black wires grow on her head.
I have seen roses damasked, red and white,
But no such roses see I in her cheeks;
And in some perfumes is there more delight
Than in the breath that from my mistress reeks.
I love to hear her speak, yet well I know
That music hath a far more pleasing sound:
I grant I never saw a goddess go,
My mistress, when she walks, treads on the ground:
    And yet, by heaven, I think my love as rare
    As any she belied with false compare.

WILLIAM SHAKESPEARE

Looking into my Mistress' Eyes

(1) Why is the opening line a startling one?
(2) What is there in common about most of the items the poet contrasts with his mistress?
(3) Comment on the impact of the word 'reeks'. How would you explain its apparent harshness in the poem?
(4) What does the poem imply about the way a goddess walks?
(5) What meaning does 'rare' have in this poem?
(6) What quality, then, does the poet seem to prize in his mistress?
(7) Would this poet approve of flattery? Support your answer from the poem.
(8) How would you state the poet's theme or message?
(9) Is the poem intended to be humorous or serious? Explain.
(10) How would you describe the technique being used throughout this poem?
(11) What is the effect of this technique on the poem's achievement?
(12) Summarize the achievement of the poem.

Other Classical English Sonnets

'Batter My Heart' is a sonnet, written at the beginning of the seventeenth century, in which the poet, John Donne, dramatically expresses his desire for a better relationship with God. At the violent beginning of this sonnet, God is a blacksmith and Donne himself is the object being reshaped. Donne next compares himself to 'an usurpt towne' which the devil has taken control of. Then, finally, in the sestet, Donne, betrothed to the devil, entreats God to ravish him spiritually.

BATTER MY HEART . . .

Batter my heart, three person'd God; for, you
As yet but knocke, breathe, shine, and seeke to mend;
That I may rise, and stand, o'erthrow mee,' and bend
Your force, to breake, blowe, burn and make me new.
I, like an usurpt towne, to' another due,
Labour to'admit you, but Oh, to no end,
Reason your viceroy in mee, mee should defend,
But is captiv'd, and proves weake or untrue.
Yet dearely' I love you,' and would be loved faine,
But am betroth'd unto your enemie:
Divorce mee,' untie, or breake that knot againe,
Take mee to you, imprison mee, for I
Except you'enthrall mee, never shall be free,
Nor ever chast, except you ravish mee.

JOHN DONNE

Meditating on a Holy Sonnet

 (1) What words in the first four lines indicate that God is a blacksmith?
 (2) What does Donne mean by: 'That I may rise, and stand, o'erthrow mee'?
 (3) What does the poet achieve by the repetition of the 'b' sounds in 'breake, blowe, burn'?
 (4) How do you know that Donne is very conscious of his past sins?
 (5) What do you learn about Donne's feelings towards God from your reading of this poem?
 (6) Explain the meaning of: 'But am betroth'd unto your enemie'.
 (7) 'Take mee to you, imprison mee.' Why does Donne want God to imprison him?
 (8) What have you learned about the personality of the poet from this sonnet?
 (9) What evidence can you find to show that this sonnet was written some centuries ago?
(10) What are some of the things you have found unusual about this religious sonnet?

John Milton (1608–74) is recognized as one of the great English poets. This sonnet records part of his struggle at the time of life when he became aware that he was going blind. The poet's sight progressively deteriorated from 1644 onwards, and he was completely blind by 1651. Because he was predominantly a religious poet, Milton draws on Scriptural images in his writing. He laments his blindness because he fears it will deprive him of the use of the 'one talent' which his Maker has entrusted him with – the ability to compose poetry. He is recalling the Parable of the Talents, told by Jesus about a servant who is condemned by his Master because he refused to use the talent given to him. Milton's soul, because of the tragedy, is 'more bent' to serve God, yet he still feels the pain of his situation. In his time of doubt he seems to hear a word of wisdom, reminding him of the importance of submission to his omnipotent God. In fact, Milton's greatest poems, including *Paradise Lost* and *Paradise Regained* were written after he had completely lost his sight.

ON HIS BLINDNESS

When I consider how my light is spent,
   Ere half my days in this dark world and wide,
   And that one talent which is death to hide
   Lodged with me useless, though my soul more bent
To serve therewith my Maker, and present
   My true account, lest He returning chide;
   'Doth God exact day-labour, light denied?'
   I fondly ask: but Patience, to prevent
That murmur, soon replies, 'God doth not need
   Either man's work or his own gifts. Who best
   Bear his mild yoke, they serve him best: his state
Is kingly: thousands at his bidding speed,
   And post o'er land and ocean without rest;
   They also serve who only stand and wait.'

JOHN MILTON

Percy Bysshe Shelley (1792–1822), a contemporary of Keats, wrote this well-known sonnet on the achievements of King Ozymandias, thought to be Rameses II of Egypt.

OZYMANDIAS

I met a traveller from an antique land
Who said: Two vast and trunkless legs of stone
Stand in the desert ... Near them on the sand,
Half sunk, a shatter'd visage lies, whose frown
And wrinkled lip and sneer of cold command
Tell that its sculptor well those passions read
Which yet survive, stamped on these lifeless things,
The hand that mocked them and the heart that fed:
And on the pedestal these words appear:
'My name is Ozymandias, king of kings:
Look on my works, ye Mighty, and despair!'
Nothing beside remains. Round the decay
Of that colossal wreck, boundless and bare
The lone and level sands stretch far away.

PERCY BYSSHE SHELLEY

Ozymandias – Probing the Ruins

(1) If you did not know that the country referred to in the poem was Egypt, identify two clues that might suggest it as a possibility.
(2) How do we know that the original monument was large?
(3) What was the complete original monument to Ozymandias?
(4) What is the 'shatter'd visage' referred to in the poem?
(5) What evidence is there that the sculptor was skilled?
(6) What are the 'lifeless things' referred to in the poem?
(7) What is the message that Ozymandias intended to convey to other kings?
(8) The inscription on the pedestal contrasts with the way things have turned out. Explain how this is so.
(9) What sort of person do you imagine Ozymandias to have been?
(10) 'Nothing beside remains.' What is the effect of this short sentence?
(11) What linguistic device does the poet make use of in the last two lines?
(12) How would you state the theme of this poem?
(13) Comment on the achievement of this poem.

Modern Sonnets

Gerard Manley Hopkins (1844–89), although technically not a modern poet, is usually considered to be so because his poetry was not published until well into the twentieth century. Since publication his poetry has been recognized as being amongst the most original in modern times. A Jesuit priest, Hopkins naturally tended to write about the revelation of God which he found in nature and in the events of the world around him.

In 'Spring', many of the novel features of Hopkins' poetry are evident. There is his skill in compressing language, his ability to create euphonious sounds with creative use of alliteration and assonance, and his tendency to invert word order to achieve rhyme at times. Because Hopkins is such a unique poet, he tends to be quite complicated and, at times, difficult to understand. Nevertheless, his poetry is so rich that it amply repays those who persevere.

SPRING

Nothing is so beautiful as spring –
　　When weeds, in wheels, shoot long and lovely and lush;
　　Thrush's eggs look little low heavens, and thrush
Through the echoing timber does so rinse and wring
The ear, it strikes like lightnings to hear him sing;
　　The glassy peartree leaves and blooms, they brush
　　The descending blue; that blue is all in a rush
With richness; the racing lambs too have fair their fling.

What is all this juice and all this joy?
　　A strain of the earth's sweet being in the beginning
In Eden garden. – Have, get, before it cloy,
　　Before it cloud, Christ, lord, and sour with sinning,
Innocent mind and Mayday in girl and boy,
　　Most, O maid's child, thy choice and worthy the winning.

GERARD MANLEY HOPKINS

Spring – Explaining Meaning and Achievement

(1) Identify the alliteration in the second line.
(2) What is unusual about the poet focusing on weeds? Why do you think he does this?
(3) 'Look little low heavens ...' What word has the poet omitted in this example of compressed language? What is the effect of this?
(4) What words suggest that the thrush's song is heard with something of a shock?
(5) What kind of a picture of the peartree leaves does the word 'glassy' create?
(6) What is meant by 'all in a rush'?
(7) How would you describe the poet's feelings as expressed in the octave?
(8) In the opening lines of the sestet the poet identifies the significance of Spring. What does this season represent?
(9) The poet finishes with a prayer to Christ. In your own words what is the prayer?
(10) Write a brief reaction to the sonnet, identifying aspects that impressed you.

A Pair of Sonnets

Both these sonnets are descriptions of people whose lives appear to be fairly trivial, yet in each case, the poet sees some evidence of greatness beyond the superficial appearance. Read through both poems and see which one you prefer. What are the qualities that appeal to you? What are the merits of each poem?

THE SERF

His naked skin clothed in the torrid mist
That puffs in smoke around the patient hooves,
The ploughman drives, a slow somnambulist,
And through the green his crimson furrow grooves.
His heart, more deeply than he wounds the plain,
Long by the rasping share of insult torn,
Red clod, to which the war-cry once was rain
And tribal spears the fatal sheaves of corn,
Lies fallow now. But as the turf divides
I see in the slow progress of his strides
Over the toppled clods and falling flowers,
The timeless, surly patience of the serf
That moves the nearest to the naked earth
And ploughs down palaces, and thrones, and towers.

ROY CAMPBELL

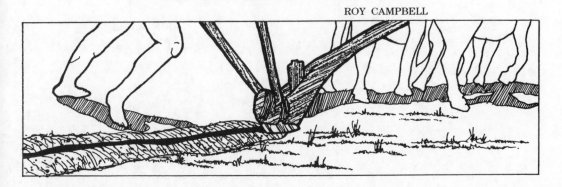

SUBURBAN SONNET

She practises a fugue, though it can matter
to no one now if she plays well or not.
Beside her on the floor two children chatter,
then scream and fight. She hushes them. A pot
boils over. As she rushes to the stove
too late, a wave of nausea overpowers
subject and counter-subject. Zest and love
drain out with soapy water as she scours
the crusted milk. Her veins ache. Once she played
for Rubinstein, who yawned. The children caper
round a sprung mousetrap where a mouse lies dead.
When the soft corpse won't move they seem afraid.
She comforts them; and wraps it in a paper
featuring: *Tasty dishes from stale bread.*

GWEN HARWOOD

In this sonnet, John Magee, a 19-year-old American fighter pilot describes some of his feelings about flying. This poem was written on the back of a letter to his parents. Not long after this he was killed in active service.

HIGH FLIGHT

Oh, I have slipped the surly bonds of earth
    And danced the skies on laughter-silvered wings;
Sunward I've climbed and joined the tumbling mirth
    Of sun-split clouds – and done a hundred things
You have not dreamed of – wheeled and soared and swung
    High in the sunlit silence. Hov'ring there
I've chased the shouting wind along and flung
    My eager craft through footless halls of air.
Up, up the long delirious burning blue
    I've topped the windswept heights with easy grace
Where never lark, or even eagle flew.
    And, while with silent, lifting mind I've trod
The high untrespassed sanctity of space,
    Put out my hand, and touched the face of God.

JOHN MAGEE

12 Sport

The following selection of poems seeks to offer some insight into the world of athletes of various kinds and some of the distinctive experiences they go through. Here you will encounter the world of the professional athlete, the amateur, and the spectator. You will have the opportunity to reflect on the glory of competitive sport, the ephemeral nature of fame, and some of the harsher realities behind all the 'glitter'.

FOOTBALL HERO

Bewdy! Kickut! Gees – ah – have a go, ya mug!
What are youse – women?
Gaud, I'd do a better job meself
With half a crutch ...

Yet, watching, sitting, waiting till the
siren blew, and
crowds sighed with relief and went to get their
pies and grog and hot dogs for the kids,
he turned and shuffled gamely towards
the rooms – a flier with a crippled wing,
a ruckman with no power to jump and weave
and duck and kick; a leg cast
weighed him down.

Gidday, Kenny!
Good ter see yer, mate!
How's that bloody leg of yours? Gees, looks
like that bump has put ya out ten weeks ...
Ah, Kenny, mate, sit down here
out of the way, eh. Comfy? Good! ... Now fellas ...

Ken's leg throbbed and now and then the
smell of sweat and gum and mouthguards
wafted in and out –
The stink of eucalyptus oil surrounded him
and bare bums smiled like kids as
shorts were changed and boots were checked.

Yes, he was part of all this once,
but now it seemed like ages since he ran out
free and tall and proud,
a member of the team.

Smoke wreathed and grinned its way around
the rooms, whilst oaths and earnest
conversation popped and buzzed about –
important words like
'When he gets the ball, just go in ...' or
'Haul his flamin' shorts off but just
slow him up ...'

They'd built a wall up round themselves and
Ken was not inside it.
Grim faced and tired, he hauled his useless
leg up to its foot and
trip-tapped out the door
and left –
no longer tall, or proud or free,
no longer then
a member of that team.

KEITH LAING

Feeling for a Football Hero

(1) What scene is recreated for us by the language and 'flavour' of the opening stanza? Who is responsible for all these shouts?

(2) In the second stanza we meet the football hero for the first time. As yet he remains unnamed, being referred to only as 'he'. What descriptive information are we given about him in this stanza?

(3) Identify the sport which is the focus of this poem. What evidence is there for your conclusion?

(4) Comment on the effect achieved by starting the third stanza with 'Gidday Kenny!' and finishing it with 'Now, fellas ...' How does the poet picture Kenny's situation?

(5) What evidence is there in the poem to suggest that the scene occurs during the quarter, half-time or three-quarter break?

(6) The sights, sounds and smells in the dressing room all bring back memories to Kenny. Identify some of these sights, sounds and smells.

(7) What memories do these trigger in Kenny?

(8) Comment on 'Smoke wreathed and grinned its way around'.

(9) Why does Kenny leave the dressing room?

(10) How does Kenny feel at the end of the poem?

(11) In your own words briefly state the theme of this poem.

'Rythm' communicates some of the inner thoughts and feelings of a soccer hero.

RYTHM

They dunno how it is. I smack a ball
right through the goals. But they dunno how the words
get muddled in my head, get tired somehow.
I look through the window, see. And there's a wall
I'd kick the ball against, just smack and smack.
Old Jerry he can't play, he don't know how,
not now at any rate. He's too flicking small.
See him in shorts, out in the crazy black.
Rythm, he says, and ryme. See him at back.
He don't know nuthing about Law. He'd fall
flat on his face, just like a big sack,
when you're going down the wing, the wind behind you
and crossing into the goalmouth and they're roaring
the whole great crowd. They're up on their feet cheering.
The ball's at your feet and there it goes, just crack.
Old Jerry dives – the wrong way. And they're jearing
and I run to the centre and old Bash
jumps up and down, and I feel great, and wearing
my gold and purpel strip, fresh from the wash.

IAIN CRICHTON SMITH

Kick-off on Rythm

(1) 'They dunno how it is.' Who do you think 'they' refers to?
(2) What is it that 'they' don't really know or understand?
(3) The poem unfolds the inner thoughts of the soccer player in short, apparently-unconnected phrases and sentences. Why has the poet written this way?
(4) '. . . there's a wall /I'd kick the ball against, just smack and smack.' What aspect of the soccer player's life do these lines describe?
(5) What is the intended effect of the spelling mistakes in the poem? Why is the poem's title spelled incorrectly?
(6) Old Jerry is the one who says 'rythm . . . and ryme'. What information and hints about Old Jerry does the poem give us?
(7) How does the soccer player feel about Old Jerry?
(8) What technique does the poet use to create a sense of the soccer player's excitement as he scores a goal?
(9) How does the soccer player feel after scoring?
(10) Some great athletes, beyond all the practice, seem to rely largely on intuition and natural ability. Others are brilliant because of their ability to think and plan on the field. In which category would you place this player? What evidence is there for your viewpoint?

In 'Ex-Basketball Player', John Updike provides a portrait of Flick Webb, former high school basketball star, who now 'sells gas' (petrol) and, perhaps, dreams of former glories.

EX-BASKETBALL PLAYER

Pearl Avenue runs past the high school lot,
Bends with the trolley tracks, and stops, cut off
Before it has a chance to go two blocks,
At Colonel McComsky Plaza. Berth's Garage
Is on the corner facing west, and there,
Most days, you'll find Flick Webb, who helps Berth out.

Flick stands tall among the idiot pumps –
Five on a side, the old bubble-head style,
Their rubber elbows hanging loose and low,
One's nostrils are two S's, and his eyes
An E and O. And one is squat, without
A head at all – more of a football type.

Once, Flick played for the high-school team, the Wizards.
He was good – in fact, the best. In '46,
He bucketed three hundred ninety points,
A county record still. The ball loved Flick.
I saw him rack up thirty-eight of forty
In one home game. His hands were like wild birds.

He never learned a trade; he just sells gas,
Checks oil, and changes flats. Once in a while
As a gag, he dribbles an inner tube.
But most of us remember anyway.
His hands are fine and nervous on the lug wrench.
It makes no difference to the lug wrench, though.

Off work, he hangs around Mae's Luncheonette.
Grease-grey and kind of coiled, he plays pinball,
Sips lemon cokes, and smokes those thin cigars;
Flick seldom speaks to Mae, just sits and nods
Beyond her face towards bright applauding tiers
Of Necco Wafers, Nibs, and Juju Beads.

JOHN UPDIKE

Looking Back on a Basketballer's Life

(1) 'Pearl Avenue ... stops, cut off ...' In what way might Pearl Avenue serve as a metaphor for Flick Webb's life?
(2) 'Flick stands tall among the idiot pumps ...' Explain the two possible meanings of 'stands tall'.
(3) What brand of petrol does the garage sell? (The second stanza provides enough clues for you to work this out!)
(4) Find a slang expression for scoring a goal in basketball, used in the poem.
(5) What made it appear to the poet that 'the ball loved Flick'?

(6) What does the poet mean by 'his hands were like wild birds'?

(7) Explain why dribbling an inner tube is a 'gag'.

(8) Comment on the effect of the word 'anyway' in the line: 'But most of us remember anyway'.

(9) In the fourth stanza the poet's feelings towards Flick's situation begin to emerge. What feelings are these? Find evidence to support your claim.

(10) Why is Flick described as 'grease-grey'?

(11) What feelings about Flick does this poem arouse in you? Do you see this as fitting in with the poet's purpose?

Sport can be a metaphor for life. There is the thrill of the contest, the discipline of the athlete, the determination of the competitor, and the triumph of winning. All of these aspects remind this poet of the race of life.

TO JAMÈS

Do you remember
How you won
That last race?
How you flung your body
At the start ...
How your spikes
Ripped the cinders
In the stretch ...
How you catapulted
Through the tape ...
Do you remember?
Don't you think
I lurched with you
Out of those starting holes?
Don't you think
My sinews tightened
At those first
Few strides ...
And when you flew into the stretch
Was not all my thrill
Of a thousand races
In your blood?
At your final drive
Through the finish line
Did not my shout
Tell of the
Triumphant ecstasy
Of victory?
Live
As I have taught you
To run, Boy –
It's a short dash
Dig your starting holes
Deep and firm

Lurch out of them
Into the straightaway
With all the power
That is in you
Look straight ahead
To the finish line
Think only of the goal
Run straight
Run high
Run hard
Save nothing
And finish
With an ecstatic burst
That carries you
Hurtling
Through the tape
To victory ...

FRANK HORNE

In the following poem, the English poet A. E. Housman (1859–1936) *celebrates* the death of a young athlete. In a sense, then, this is an elegy – a hymn of praise. The significance, of course, lies in the fact that ordinarily we would see only tragedy and defeat in such an untimely death. As you read the poem, look for the sense of triumph that the poet seeks to convey.

TO AN ATHLETE DYING YOUNG

The time you won your town the race
We chaired you through the market-place;
Man and boy stood cheering by,
And home we brought you shoulder-high.

To-day, the road all runners come,
Shoulder-high we bring you home,
And set you at your threshold down,
Townsman of a stiller town.

Smart lad, to slip betimes away
From fields where glory does not stay
And early though the laurel grows
It withers quicker than the rose.

Eyes the shady night has shut
Cannot see the record cut,
And silence sounds no worse than cheers
After earth has stopped the ears:

Now you will not swell the rout
Of lads that wore their honors out,
Runners whom renown outran
And the name died before the man.

So set, before its echoes fade,
The fleet foot on the sill of shade,
And hold to the low lintel up
The still-defended challenge-cup.

And round that early-laurelled head
Will flock to gaze the strengthless dead,
And find unwithered on its curls
The garland briefer than a girl's.

A. E. HOUSMAN

Considerations

(1) Explain how 'shoulder-high' links the first and second stanzas.
(2) To what 'home' is the athlete brought in the second stanza?
(3) 'Townsman of a stiller town.' What is the 'stiller town' the poet refers to?
(4) In what way is the deceased a 'smart lad' according to the third stanza?
(5) Death stops our ability to see and hear. How is this seen to be a *benefit* in this poem?
(6) What sorts of persons do you think the poet had in mind when he wrote 'Runners whom renown outran'?
(7) What is meant by 'the name died before the man'?
(8) In what sense is the athlete's head 'early-laurelled'?
(9) A girl's garland is usually thought of as a crown of daisies or little wildflowers which die quickly. What does the poet mean when he speaks of the athlete wearing 'unwithered' an even briefer garland in his journey beyond death? What is the garland? Why, in his case, is it 'unwithered'?
(10) How would you describe the achievement of this poem? Support your answer.

Bob Dylan, protest folk-singer since the 1960s, takes the death of a boxer, Davey Moore, as the starting point in looking at issues of blame. It seems that all those who have had any connection with the boxer are at pains to excuse themselves from any blame. It's not the referee's fault; it's not the crowd's fault; and so on. Finally, with all the communal hand-washing it seems there's no one to really blame except God. Somehow it doesn't feel all that convincing.

Since this was written primarily as a song you might like to look for any features which identify it as a song, rather than a non-musical poem. What distinctive features can you see? Are these always seen in songs?

WHO KILLED DAVEY MOORE?

Who killed Davey Moore?
Why an' what's the reason for?

'Not I,' says the referee,
'Don't point your finger at me.
I could have stopped it in the eighth
And maybe kept him from his fate,
But the crowd would've booed, I'm sure,
At not getting their money's worth.
It's too bad he had to go,
But there was pressure on me too, you know.
I wasn't me that made him fall,
No, you can't blame me at all.'

'Not us,' says the angry crowd,
Whose screams filled the arena loud.
'It's too bad he died that night
But we just like to see a fight.
We didn't mean for him to meet his death,
We just meant to see some sweat.
There ain't nothin' wrong in that.
It wasn't us that made him fall,
No, you can't blame us at all.'

'Not me,' says his manager,
Puffing on a big cigar,
'It's hard to say, it's hard to tell,
I always thought that he was well.
It's too bad for his wife an' kids he's dead,
But if he was sick, he should've said.
It wasn't me that made him fall,
No, you can't blame me at all.'

'Not me,' says the gambling man,
With his ticket stub still in his hand,
'It wasn't me that knocked him down –
My hands never touched him none.
I didn't commit no ugly sin;
Anyway I put money on him to win.
It wasn't me that made him fall,
No, you can't blame me at all.'

'Not me,' says the boxing writer,
Pounding print on his old typewriter,
Sayin' 'Boxing ain't to blame –
There's just as much danger in a football game.'
Sayin' 'Fist fighting is here to stay.
It's just the old American way.
It wasn't me that made him fall,
No, you can't blame me at all.'

'Not me,' says the man whose fists
Laid him low in a cloud of mist,
Who came here from Cuba's door
Where boxing ain't allowed no more.
'I hit him, yes, it's true,
But that's what I am paid to do.
Don't say "murder," don't say "kill,"
It was destiny, it was God's will.'

BOB DYLAN

Here are two poems, quite different in content and style, yet each communicating the same feeling – a sense of the exultant joy of being alive.

Which poem do you prefer? What qualities of each poem appeal particularly to you? How successful is each poet in communicating the feelings experienced by the person in the poem? How would you describe the achievement of each poem?

Use these questions to guide your thinking as you read the poems, then write a comparative appreciation of the two poems, saying which you prefer and giving reasons.

SEASIDE GOLF

How straight it flew, how long it flew,
  It cleared the rutty track
And soaring, disappeared from view
  Beyond the bunker's back –
A glorious, sailing, bounding drive
That made me glad I was alive.

And down the fairway, far along
  It glowed a lonely white;
I played an iron sure and strong
  And clipp'd it out of sight,
And spite of grassy banks between
I knew I'd find it on the green.

And so I did. It lay content
  Two paces from the pin;
A steady putt and then it went
  Oh, most securely in.
The very turf rejoiced to see
The quite unprecedented three.

Ah! seaweed smells from sandy caves
  And thyme and mist in whiffs,
In-coming tide, Atlantic waves
  Slapping the sunny cliffs,
Lark song and sea sounds in the air
And splendour, splendour everywhere.

JOHN BETJEMAN

from SWIMMERS

Then, the quick plunge into the cool, green dark,
The windy waters rushing past me, through me;
Filled with a sense of some heroic lark,
Exulting in a vigor clean and roomy.
Swiftly I rose to meet the cat-like sea
That sprang upon me with a hundred claws,
And grappled, pulled me down and played with me.
Then, held suspended in the tightening pause
When one wave grows into a toppling acre,
I dived headlong into the foremost breaker,
Pitting against a cold and turbulent strife
The feverish intensity of life.
Out of the foam I lurched and rode the wave,
Swimming, hand over hand, against the wind;
I felt the sea's vain pounding, and I grinned
Knowing I was its master, not its slave.

LOUIS UNTERMEYER

No other horse has ever captured the imagination of the Australian public in quite the same way as Phar Lap.

PHAR LAP IN THE MELBOURNE MUSEUM

A masterpiece of the taxidermist's art,
Australia's top patrician stares
Gravely ahead at crowded emptiness.
As if alive, the lustre of dead hairs,
Lozenged liquid eyes, black nostrils
Gently flared, otter-satin coat declares
That death cannot visit in this thin perfection.

The democratic hero full of guile,
Noble, handsome, gentle Houyhnhnm
(In both Paddock and St Leger difference is
Lost in the welter of money) – to see him win
Men sold farms, rode miles in floods,
Stole money, locked up wives, somehow got in:
First away, he led the field and easily won.

It was his simple excellence to be best.
Tough men owned him, their minds beset
By stakes, bookies' doubles, crooked jocks.
He soon became a byword, public asset,
A horse with a nation's soul upon his back –
Australia's Ark of the Convenant, set
Before the people, perfect, loved like God.

And like God to be betrayed by friends.
Sent to America, he died of poisoned food.
In Australia children cried to hear the news
(This Prince of Orange knew no bad or good).
It was, as people knew, a plot of life:
To live in strength, to excel and die too soon,
So they drained his body and they stuffed his skin.

Twenty years later on Sunday afternoons
You still can't see him for the rubbing crowds.
He shares with Bradman and Ned Kelly some
Of the dirty jokes you still can't say out loud.
It is Australian innocence to love
The naturally excessive and be proud
Of a thoroughbred bay gelding who ran fast.

PETER PORTER

A Horse, of Course

(1) What does the poet mean by 'crowded emptiness'?
(2) '... death cannot visit in this thin perfection.' What do you think the poet means?
(3) In what way was Phar Lap a 'democratic hero'?
(4) A 'Houyhnhnm' is a mythical creature from *Gulliver's Travels*, which looks like a horse but has human reasoning powers. How appropriate is this as a description of Phar Lap? Why?
(5) What human activities described in the poem convey the tremendous crowd-drawing popularity of Phar Lap?
(6) In the third stanza how is Phar Lap contrasted with his owners?
(7) How was Phar Lap 'betrayed by friends'?
(8) What evidence is there that Australians were disturbed at news of Phar Lap's death?
(9) 'So they drained his body and they stuffed his skin.' Comment on the effect of this line. How is this effect achieved?
(10) What Australian quality is identified in the last stanza?
(11) 'A thoroughbred bay gelding who ran fast.' What is the effect of this line and how is the effect achieved?
(12) What is the mood of this poem?

Have you ever dreamed of representing your country in sport, or of achieving fame in any particular field of sporting endeavour? Have you ever regretted the fact that sporting fame is unlikely ever to be yours? Ogden Nash provides a welcome antidote to any such 'problems' with his humorous look at the benefits of being a mere spectator.

CONFESSIONS OF A BORN SPECTATOR

One infant grows up and becomes a jockey,
Another plays basketball or hockey,
This one the prize ring hastes to enter,
That one becomes a tackle or centre.
I'm just as glad as I can be
That I'm not them, that they're not me.

With all my heart do I admire
Athletes who sweat for fun or hire,
Who take the field in gaudy pomp
And maim each other as they romp;
My limp and bashful spirit feeds
On other people's heroic deeds.

Now A runs ninety yards to score;
B knocks the champion to the floor;
C, risking vertebrae and spine,
Lashes his steed across the line.
You'd think my ego it would please
to swap positions with one of these.

Well, ego might be pleased enough,
But zealous athletes play so rough;
They do not ever, in their dealings,
Consider one another's feelings.
I'm glad that when my struggle begins
'Twixt prudence and ego, prudence wins.

When swollen eye meets gnarled fist,
When snaps the knee, and cracks the wrist,
When calm officialdom demands,
Is there a doctor in the stands?
My soul in true thanksgiving speaks
For this most modest of physiques.

Athletes, I'll drink to you or eat with you,
Or anything except compete with you;
Buy tickets worth their weight in radium
To watch you gambol in a stadium,
And reassure myself anew
That you're not me and I'm not you.

ODEN NASH

13 Symbols

A symbol in poetry as in other areas of life, refers to the use of a specific concrete object to stand for one or more abstract ideas. The wedding ring, for example, has come to symbolize the qualities which marriage ideally unites. It symbolizes
- preciousness, because the ring is of gold;
- lifelong commitment, because the ring is circular and so has no end.

Symbols in Life

Explain what each of the following usually symbolizes:

(1) a white flag
(2) a cross
(3) a hammer and sickle
(4) a heart with an arrow through it
(5) a skull and crossbones
(6) a crown
(7) an apple
(8) a swastika
(9) a car badge featuring a snake coiled around a staff
(10) a big M

Colours as Symbols

Colours are sometimes used as symbols. Identify the feelings, qualities or things you would associate with these colours:

(1) red
(2) black
(3) white
(4) purple
(5) green
(6) gold
(7) yellow
(8) grey
(9) blue
(10) rainbow

Birds and Animals as Symbols

Many birds and animals seem to exhibit a particular trait or quality to such an extent that we often use the creature as a symbol of that quality – even if in truth the quality isn't one that it really possesses. For example, an elephant is a symbol of 'hugeness' (or good memory) and a koala may symbolize 'cuddliness'. What could each of the following be used as symbols of? Try to make each one different.

(1) a lion
(2) a snake
(3) a mouse
(4) a fox
(5) a dog
(6) a peacock
(7) a dove
(8) an eagle
(9) a tortoise
(10) a gazelle
(11) a bee
(12) a pig

Identifying Symbolism

In poetry, symbols are used to increase our awareness or deepen our understanding. When a poet uses symbols, it is usually done with some subtlety. Sometimes a symbol will recur a number of times until we start to understand its significance in the poem. We can actually judge what something symbolizes by looking at the poem as a whole. Once we have done this, some things start to glow with symbolic meaning and this always adds a certain richness to the writing. Of course, one of the dangers for a poet using symbolism is that his symbols may be too complicated or remote for his readers to understand.

Now closely read through Judith Wright's poem 'Legend'. Any deeper understanding of 'Legend' will depend, to a large extent, upon the symbolism you attribute to the concrete objects and colours in the poem. Assuming that this is a 'legend' about a young boy with a poor start in life who – through determination – achieves his aims in life, answer the questions that follow the poem.

LEGEND

The blacksmith's boy went out with a rifle
and a black dog running behind.
Cobwebs snatched at his feet,
rivers hindered him,
thorn-branches caught at his eyes to make him blind
and the sky turned into an unlucky opal,
but he didn't mind.
I can break branches, I can swim rivers, I can stare out any spider I meet,
said he to his dog and his rifle.

The blacksmith's boy went over the paddocks
with his old black hat on his head.
Mountains jumped in his way,
rocks rolled down on him,
and the old crow cried, You'll soon be dead;
and the rain came down like mattocks.
But he only said
I can climb mountains, I can dodge rocks, I can shoot an old crow any day.
And he went on over the paddocks.

When he came to the end of the day the sun began falling.
Up came the night ready to swallow him,
like the barrel of a gun,
like an old black hat,
like a black dog hungry to follow him.
Then the pigeon, the magpie and the dove began wailing,
and the grass lay down to pillow him.
His rifle broke, his hat blew away and his dog was gone,
and the sun was falling.

But in front of the night the rainbow stood on the mountain
just as his heart foretold.
He ran like a hare,
he climbed like a fox,
he caught it in his hands, the colours and the cold –
like a bar of ice, like the column of a fountain,
like a ring of gold.
The pigeon, the magpie and the dove flew up to stare,
and the grass stood up again on the mountain.

The blacksmith's boy hung the rainbow on his shoulder,
instead of his broken gun.
Lizards ran out to see,
snakes made way for him,
and the rainbow shone as brightly as the sun.
All the world said, Nobody is braver, nobody is bolder,
nobody else has done
anything to equal it. He went home as easy as could be
with the swinging rainbow on his shoulder.

JUDITH WRIGHT

Symbol Analysis

(1) What do you see cobwebs, rivers and thorn-branches in the first stanza as symbols of?
(2) What does the colour black symbolize in this poem?
(3) What do blacksmith's boy's rifle, hat and dog symbolize?
(4) What does 'the rainbow' symbolize in the boy's life?
(5) What do you think the pigeon, the magpie and the dove symbolize?
(6) '... like a bar of ice'. What qualities of 'the rainbow' does ice symbolize?
(7) '... like a ring of gold'. What quality of 'the rainbow' does 'a ring of gold' symbolize?
(8) What do the lizards and snakes of the last stanza symbolize?

William Butler Yeats (1865–1939) found the inspiration for many of his poems at Coole Park, Gort. Coole Park was the home of Lady Gregory, one of Yeats' friends. In October 1916, Yeats sees the swans on the lake and imagines that they are the same swans he counted in 1897. The swans don't seem to have changed at all, for although individual swans die, the pattern of the fifty-nine swans remains. The swans are a symbol of youth forever changing, yet forever renewed. In contrast to the swans, Yeats himself has grown considerably older.

THE WILD SWANS AT COOLE

The trees are in their autumn beauty,
The woodland paths are dry,
Under the October twilight the water
Mirrors a still sky;
Upon the brimming water among the stones
Are nine-and-fifty swans.

The nineteenth autumn has come upon me
Since I first made my count;
I saw, before I had well finished,
All suddenly mount
And scatter wheeling in great broken rings
Upon their clamorous wings.

I have looked upon those brilliant creatures,
And now my heart is sore.
All's changed since I, hearing at twilight,
The first time on this shore,
The bell-beat of their wings above my head,
Trod with a lighter tread.

Unwearied still, lover by lover,
They paddle in the cold
Companionable streams or climb the air;
Their hearts have not grown old;
Passion or conquest, wander where they will,
Attend upon them still.

But now they drift on the still water
Mysterious, beautiful;
Among what rushes will they build,
By what lake's edge or pool
Delight men's eyes when I awake some day
To find they have flown away?

WILLIAM BUTLER YEATS

Contemplating the Wild Swans at Coole

(1) The swans are a symbol. They are real, but they also stand for other things. What things?
(2) Explain how the autumn landscape is important for the poet's mood.
(3) What is the meaning of 'the water mirrors a clear sky'?
(4) Explain the meaning of 'clamorous wings'. What other words in the poem have a similar meaning?
(5) Why is the poet's heart 'sore'?
(6) Explain the meaning of 'Trod with a lighter tread'.
(7) What does the poet mean by 'their hearts have not grown old'?
(8) In what ways does the love of the swans for each other differ from human love?
(9) What is the poet's relationship to the swans?
(10) How does the poet create the impression that the swans are immortal?

The American poet, Robert Frost (1874–1963) transforms a seemingly matter-of-fact description of two farmers mending a wall into a deeply convincing universal message about the human barriers men erect between themselves. Frost uses the wall and spring as symbols. The wall symbolizes the obstacles created by selfishness and a lack of understanding, while spring symbolizes the continual rebirth of love and kindness which keeps trying to break down these barriers.

MENDING WALL

Something there is that doesn't love a wall,
That sends the frozen-ground-swell under it,
And spills the upper boulders in the sun;
And makes gaps even two can pass abreast.
The work of hunters is another thing:
I have come after them and made repair
Where they have left not one stone on a stone,
But they would have the rabbit out of hiding,
To please the yelping dogs. The gaps I mean,
No one has seen them made or heard them made,
But at spring mending-time we find them there.
I let my neighbour know beyond the hill;
And on a day we meet to walk the line
And set the wall between us once again.
We keep the wall between us as we go.
To each the boulders that have fallen to each.
And some are loaves and some so nearly balls
We have to use a spell to make them balance:
'Stay where you are until our backs are turned!'
We wear our fingers rough with handling them.
Oh, just another kind of outdoor game,
One on a side. It comes to little more:
There where it is we do not need the wall:
He is all pine and I am apple orchard.
My apple trees will never get across
And eat the cones under his pines, I tell him.
He only says, 'Good fences make good neighbours'.
Spring is the mischief in me, and I wonder
If I could put a notion in his head:
'*Why* do they make good neighbours? Isn't it
Where there are cows? But here there are no cows.
Before I built a wall I'd ask to know
What I was walling in or walling out,
And to whom I was like to give offence.
Something there is that doesn't love a wall,
That wants it down'. I could say 'Elves' to him,
But it's not elves exactly, and I'd rather
He said it for himself. I see him there
Bringing a stone grasped firmly by the top
In each hand, like an old-stone savage armed.
He moves in darkness as it seems to me,
Not of woods only and the shade of trees.
He will not go behind his father's saying,
And he likes having thought of it so well
He says again, 'Good fences make good neighbours'.

ROBERT FROST

Mending Wall Questions

(1) 'Something there is that doesn't love a wall'. What is the poet suggesting?

(2) What has happened to the wall?

(3) What does spring symbolize?

(4) Why do the hunters sometimes knock down the wall?

(5) 'We keep the wall between us as we go'. What are the poet and his neighbour doing?

(6) What does the poet mean by 'And some are loaves and some so nearly balls'?

(7) What evidence can you find to show that mending the wall is hard work?

(8) Why does Frost consider the wall to be unnecessary?

(9) What is Frost's neighbour's argument for wanting a wall?

(10) What do you think Frost means by 'Spring is the mischief in me'?

(11) What would the poet be concerned to do before he built a wall?

(12) Why do you think the poet mentions 'elves'?

(13) Why does Frost describe his neighbour as 'an old-stone savage armed'?

(14) 'He moves in darkness'. What is Frost suggesting about his neighbour?

(15) What comment would you make about the statement 'Good fences make good neighbours'?

(16) In the poem what is the wall a symbol of?

'The Road Not Taken' is another of Robert Frost's poems that involves the use of symbolism. This time a person's choice of two roads symbolizes the choice of equally appealing alternatives in life.

THE ROAD NOT TAKEN

Two roads diverged in a yellow wood,
And sorry I could not travel both
And be one traveller, long I stood
And looked down one as far as I could
To where it bent in the undergrowth;

Then took the other, as just as fair,
And having perhaps the better claim,
Because it was grassy and wanted wear;
Though as for that the passing there
Had worn them really about the same,

And both that morning equally lay
In leaves no step had trodden black.
Oh, I kept the first for another day!
Yet knowing how way leads on to way,
I doubted if I should ever come back.

I shall be telling this with a sigh
Somewhere ages and ages hence:
Two roads diverged in a wood, and I –
I took the one less travelled by,
And that has made all the difference.

ROBERT FROST

'Among Ourselves' describes the intolerable boredom of a son whose very existence is stifled as he shares a dull and tedious domestic situation with his parents. His mother knits, his father reads and he smokes a cigarette. It is only when we come to the last two sentences of the poem that we become aware of the poet's use of symbolism. The 'tobacco becoming ash' symbolizes the young man's wasted life. In the same way as the tobacco is being burned up and turned to ash, so too is the young man's life being consumed by boredom.

AMONG OURSELVES

Among ourselves we rarely speak.
Our tongues are thick with custom.
Inside our house, at this time of the year,
there's only the ticking of the clock
and the click of my mother's needles
as she knits herself away from where
she cast on. My father's pages rustle.
He makes himself a nest of newspaper.
I sit in a corner, smoking. Every time
I draw on my cigarette I hear
the tiny hiss of tobacco becoming ash.

ALASDAIR MACLEAN

Thinking About the Poem

(1) Why is the poem called 'Among Ourselves'?
(2) Explain the meaning of 'Our tongues are thick with custom'.
(3) What are the sounds in the house? What do they show about the son's existence?
(4) 'He makes himself a nest of newspaper'. Why is *nest* an appropriate word?
(5) Why is 'ash' such a forceful word in the poem?
(6) Do you think the symbol of the burning cigarette a good one? Why or why not?

The poet, William Blake (1757–1827), was very fond of using symbols in his poetry and this tendency is clearly seen in his poem 'The Sick Rose'. A rose generally suggests the beauty and vitality of life. However, Blake's rose is 'sick' and is wasting away because it is being destroyed by the canker worm. It soon becomes evident that the poem is more than just a description of a sick rose. From clues in the poem such as 'thy bed of crimson joy' – the climax of physical love – the reader comes to realize that the poem concerns human experience. Blake's worm eaten rose is a symbol of innocence destroyed by the selfish, deceitful aspects of physical love.

THE SICK ROSE

O rose, thou art sick!
The invisible worm,
That flies in the night,
In the howling storm,
Has found out thy bed
Of crimson joy;
And his dark secret love
Does thy life destroy.

WILLIAM BLAKE

In his poem, 'The Tiger', William Blake makes us aware that the world is made up of fierceness and strength as well as gentleness and peace. Blake's tiger is a terrifying and dynamic creation, which could be seen to represent the forces of evil lurking in our world. His lamb is a symbol of goodness and kindness as seen in Christ himself.

THE TIGER

Tiger! Tiger! burning bright
In the forests of the night,
What immortal hand or eye
Could frame thy fearful symmetry?

In what distant deeps or skies
Burnt the fire of thine eyes?
On what wings dare he aspire?
What the hand dare seize the fire?

And what shoulder, and what art,
Could twist the sinews of thy heart?
And when thy heart began to beat,
What dread hand? and what dread feet?

What the hammer? what the chain?
In what furnace was thy brain?
What the anvil? what dread grasp
Dare its deadly terrors clasp?

When the stars threw down their spears,
And water'd heaven with their tears,
Did he smile his work to see?
Did he who made the Lamb make thee?

Tiger! Tiger! burning bright
In the forests of the night,
What immortal hand or eye,
Dare frame thy fearful symmetry?

WILLIAM BLAKE

14 The Poetry of War

the importance of Rest in a unit. Mention of Dury sometimes to visit a rest camp and so seems. We are not a unit, the nothing of their machinery there for sleeping a field was initely of early flow. Ledy of something. And it is ploys intense when blue in their section of the patriotic favor between not stored by war is to be soberly often so. We are dead sure three three of Ally the well are.

World War I

At the beginning of World War I, many of the young volunteers felt privileged to be able to fight for their country. One such young recruit was Rupert Brooke who died of illness on 23 April 1915 before having seen action. His poem, *The Soldier*, full of patriotic fervour, shows how proud he was to be able to offer his life for the country that had given him life and joy.

THE SOLDIER

If I should die, think only this of me:
That there's some corner of a foreign field
That is forever England. There shall be
In that rich earth a richer dust concealed;
A dust whom England bore, shaped, made aware,
Gave, once, her flowers to love, her ways to roam,
A body of England's, breathing English air,
Washed by the rivers, blest by suns of home.
And think, this heart, all evil shed away,
A pulse in the eternal mind, no less
Gives somewhere back the thoughts by England given;
Her sights and sounds; dreams happy as her day;
And laughter learnt of friends; and gentleness,
In hearts at peace, under an English heaven.

RUPERT BROOKE

Examining the Poem

(1) What does the poet suggest would happen to his body if he were to die fighting in a foreign land?
(2) Explain the meaning of 'In that rich earth a richer dust concealed'.
(3) What impression of England does Rupert Brooke give the reader?
(4) What is the poet's attitude to death as shown by his poem?
(5) Do you agree with Rupert Brooke's attitude to war? Explain your view.
(6) What is the poet's message in 'The Soldier'?
(7) What does the poem reveal about the character of Rupert Brooke?
(8) What are some of the feelings and moods revealed in 'The Soldier'?

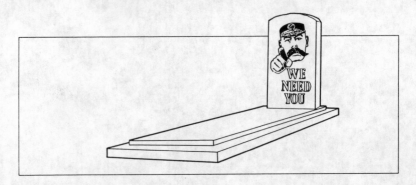

Wilfred Owen enlisted in the British Army in 1915. In January 1917 he went as an officer to the Somme in France where he encountered the mud and misery of trench warfare. He was killed a week before the end of the war while guiding his company across the Sambre Canal. He said of his poetry: 'My subject is war and the pity of war. The poetry is in the pity. All a poet can do is warn'.

DISABLED

He sat in a wheeled chair, waiting for dark,
And shivered in his ghastly suit of grey,
Legless, swen short at elbow. Through the park
Voices of boys rang saddening like a hymn,
Voices of play and pleasure after day,
Till gathering sleep had mothered them from him.

About this time Town used to swing so gay
When glow-lamps budded in the light blue trees,
And girls glanced lovelier as the air grew dim,
– In the old times, before he threw away his knees.
Now he will never feel again how slim
Girls' waists are, or how warm their subtle hands.
All of them touch him like some queer disease.

There was an artist silly for his face,
For it was younger than his youth, last year.
Now, he is old; his back will never brace;
He's lost his colour very far from here,
Poured it down shell-holes till the veins ran dry,
And half his lifetime lapsed in the hot race
And leap of purple spurted from his thigh.
One time he liked a bloodsmear down his leg,
After the matches, carried shoulder-high.
It was after football, when he'd drunk a peg,
He thought he'd better join. – He wonders why.
Someone had said he'd look a god in kilts,
That's why; and maybe, too, to please his Meg,
Aye, that was it, to please the giddy jilts
He asked to join. He didn't have to beg;
Smiling they wrote his lie: aged nineteen years.
Germans he scarcely thought of; all their guilt
And Austria's, did not move him. And no fears
Of Fear came yet. He thought of jewelled hilts
For daggers in plaid socks; of smart salutes;
And care of arms; and leave; and pay arrears;
Esprit de corps; and hints for young recruits.
And soon, he was drafted out with drums and cheers.

Some cheered him home, but not as crowds cheer Goal.
Only a solemn man who brought him fruits
Thanked him; and then inquired about his soul.

Now, he will spend a few sick years in institutes,
And do what things the rules consider wise,
And take whatever pity they may dole.
Tonight he noticed how the women's eyes
Passed from him to the strong men that were whole.
How cold and late it is! Why don't they come
And put him into bed? Why don't they come?

WILFRED OWEN

Analysis

(1) Why do you think the poet has written 'wheeled chair' rather than 'wheel chair'?
(2) Why was his suit 'legless, sewn short at elbow'?
(3) Explain the meaning of 'About this time Town used to swing so gay'.
(4) What is the meaning of 'before he threw away his knees'?
(5) How does the poet convey a sense of sadness by his mention of 'girls' waists'?
(6) How does the poet evoke a sense of horror in the third stanza?
(7) Explain how the boy had joined the army for the wrong reasons.
(8) 'Smiling they wrote his lie: aged nineteen years'. Who are they? What is his lie?
(9) Explain the meaning of 'he was drafted out with drums and cheers'.
(10) In what ways was the boy's homecoming different from his departure?
(11) Explain the sadness in the lines: 'Tonight he noticed how the women's eyes/Passed from him to the strong men that were whole'.
(12) Explain how the young man has lost his freedom and independence.
(13) Why do you think Wilfred Owen wrote 'Disabled'?
(14) What moods and feelings are expressed in the poem?

In a letter to his mother, Wilfred Owen wrote: 'No Man's Land under snow is like the face of the moon, chaotic, crater-ridden, uninhabitable, awful, the abode of madness'. Add to this the loss of a friend and you have futility.

FUTILITY

Move him into the sun –
Gently its touch awoke him once,
At home, whispering of fields unsown.
Always it woke him, even in France,
Until this morning and this snow.
If anything might rouse him now
The kind old sun will know.

Think how it wakes the seeds –
Woke, once, the clay of a cold star.
Are limbs, so dear-achieved, are sides,
Full-nerved – still warm – too hard to stir?
Was it for this the clay grew tall?
– O what made fatuous sunbeams toil
To break earth's sleep at all?

WILFRED OWEN

Questions

(1) How does the poet convey to us the sense of life being peaceful away from the war?

(2) The poet in anguish calls upon the sun to restore his friend to life. What reasons does the poet give for this in the first stanza?

(3) In the second stanza we get the sense of 'heat' and 'cold'. Why is the poet so preoccupied with these sensations?

(4) Why does the poet mention that the sun 'Woke, once, the clay of a cold star'?

(5) What does the poet mean when he says: 'Was it for this the clay grew tall?'

(6) In the last stanza the poet keeps asking questions. Why do you think he does this?

(7) What feelings does the poet reveal in this poem?

(8) The poem is called 'Futility'. Why is this title so suitable?

As Ted Hughes contemplates a 40-year-old photograph of six young men, he dwells upon their senseless death in war.

SIX YOUNG MEN

The celluloid of a photograph holds them well –
Six young men, familiar to their friends.
Four decades that have faded and ochre-tinged
This photograph have not wrinkled the faces or the hands.
Though their cocked hats are not now fashionable,
Their shoes shine. One imparts an intimate smile,
One chews a grass, one lowers his eyes, bashful,
One is ridiculous with cocky pride --
Six months after this picture they all were dead.

All are trimmed for a Sunday jaunt. I know
That bilberried bank, that thick tree, that black wall,
Which are there yet and not changed. From where these sit
You hear the water of seven streams fall
To the roarer in the bottom, and through all
The leafy valley a rumouring of air go.
Pictured here, their expressions listen yet,
And still that valley has not changed its sound
Though their faces are four decades under the ground.

This one was shot in an attack and lay
Calling in the wire, then this one, his best friend,
Went out to bring him in and was shot too;
And this one, the very moment he was warned
From potting at tin-cans in no-man's-land,
Fell back dead with his rifle-sights shot away.
The rest, nobody knows what they came to,
But come to the worst they must have done, and held it
Closer than their hope; all were killed.

Here see a man's photograph,
The locket of a smile, turned overnight
Into the hospital of his mangled last
Agony and hours; see bundled in it
His mightier-than-a-man dead bulk and weight:
And on this one place which keeps him alive
(In his Sunday best) see fall war's worse
Thinkable flash and rending, onto his smile
Forty years rotting into soil.

That man's not more alive whom you confront
And shake by the hand, see hale, hear speak loud,
Than any of these six celluloid smiles are,
Nor prehistoric or fabulous beast more dead;
No thought so vivid as their smoking blood:
To regard this photograph might well dement,
Such contradictory permanent horrors here
Smile from the single exposure and shoulder out
One's own body from its instant and heat.

TED HUGHES

Contemplating the Poem

(1) What words of the poet indicate that the photograph was taken a long time ago?
(2) What is the meaning of 'Four decades . . . have not wrinkled the faces or the hands'?
(3) Explain the meaning of 'Though their cocked hats are not now fashionable'.
(4) In what ways are the different personalities of the young men revealed in the photograph?
(5) How does the poet shock the reader at the end of the first stanza?
(6) What were the young men about to do just after the photo was taken?
(7) Why do you think the poet describes the beauty of nature surrounding the young men in the photo?
(8) What is the meaning of 'Though their faces are four decades under the ground'?
(9) Describe how some of the men in the photo were killed?
(10) What is the meaning of 'six celluloid smiles'?
(11) Do you feel that in some way the young men are still alive? Why or why not?
(12) How does the poet use this photograph of the six young men to condemn war?

One of the finest poets of World War I was Siegfried Sassoon (1886–1967). He and Wilfred Owen had actually met each other while they were recuperating in Craiglockhart War Hospital in Scotland. Both men greatly admired each other's poetry. After Sassoon had won the Military Cross he hurled it into the sea. He was declared 'temporarily insane' when he had publicly denounced war.

THE HERO

'Jack fell as he'd have wished', the Mother said,
And folded up the letter that she'd read.
'The Colonel writes so nicely'. Something broke
In the tired voice that quavered to a choke.
She half looked up. 'We mothers are so proud
Of our dead soldiers.' Then her face was bowed.

Quietly the Brother Officer went out.
He'd told the poor old dear some gallant lies
That she would nourish all her days, no doubt.
For while he coughed and mumbled, her weak eyes
Had shone with gentle triumph, brimmed with joy,
Because he'd been so brave, her glorious boy.

He thought how 'Jack', cold-footed, useless swine,
Had panicked down the trench that night the mine
Went up at Wicked Corner; how he'd tried
To get sent home, and how, at last, he died,
Blown to small bits. And no one seemed to care
Except that lonely woman with white hair.

SIEGFRIED SASSOON

THE REAR-GUARD

Groping along the tunnel, step by step,
He winked his prying torch with patching glare
From side to side, and sniffed the unwholesome air.

Tins, boxes, bottles, shapes too vague to know,
A mirror smashed, the mattress from a bed;
And he, exploring fifty feet below
The rosy gloom of battle overhead.
Tripping, he grabbed the wall; saw someone lie
Humped at his feet, half-hidden by a rug,
And stopped to give the sleeper's arm a tug.
'I'm looking for headquarters.' No reply.
'God blast your neck!' (For days he'd had no sleep.)
'Get up and guide me through this stinking place.'
Savage, he kicked a soft, unanswering heap,
And flashed his beam across the livid face
Terribly glaring up, whose eyes yet wore
Agony dying hard ten days before;
And fists of fingers clutched a blackening wound.
Alone he staggered on until he found
Dawn's ghost that filtered down a shafted stair
To the dazed, muttering creatures underground
Who hear the boom of shells in muffled sound.
At last, with sweat of horror in his hair,
He climbed through darkness to the twilight air,
Unloading hell behind him step by step.

SIEGFRIED SASSOON

THE GENERAL

'Good-morning; good-morning!' the General said
When we met him last week on our way to the line.
Now the soldiers he smiled at are most of 'em dead,
And we're cursing his staff for incompetent swine.
'He's a cheery old card', grunted Harry to Jack
As they slogged up to Arras with rifle and pack.

But he did for them both by his plan of attack.

SIEGFRIED SASSOON

Poems from World War II

When Kenneth Slessor wrote 'Beach Burial', he was an Australian war correspondent at El Alamein in Egypt. It is highly likely that Slessor witnessed the events he describes in the poem.

BEACH BURIAL

Softly and humbly to the Gulf of Arabs
The convoys of dead sailors come;
At night they sway and wander in the waters far under,
But morning rolls them in the foam.

Between the sob and clubbing of the gunfire
Someone, it seems, has time for this,
To pluck them from the shallows and bury them in
    burrows
And tread the sand upon their nakedness.

And each cross, the driven stake of tide-wood,
Bears the last signature of man,
Written with such perplexity, with such bewildered
    pity,
The words choke as they begin.

'*Unknown seaman*' – the ghostly pencil
Wavers and fades, the purple drips,
The breath of the wet season has washed their
    inscription
As blue as drowned men's lips.

Dead seamen, gone in search of the same landfall,
Whether as enemies they fought,
Or fought with us, or neither; the sand joins them
    together,
Enlisted on the other front.

KENNETH SLESSOR

Questions

(1) In the first stanza what is happening to the dead sailors? Why do you think they are described as moving in 'convoys'?
(2) What kind of noise is suggested by the phrase 'sob and clubbing of the gunfire'?
(3) Why do you think the sailors' graves are described as 'burrows'?
(4) What is the poet describing in his words 'And each cross, the driven stake of tide-wood'?
(5) What does the poet mean by 'Bears the last signature of man'?
(6) What is the meaning of 'the sand joins them together'?
(7) What is the main idea or feeling expressed by this poem? Do you think the poet has succeeded in getting this across?
(8) Do you think the poet actually witnessed the scene he is describing in the poem? Why?

Appreciating Beach Burial

The word 'beach' usually has a happy, joyful connotation, but once Slessor links it with the word 'burial', one is prepared for something ominous to follow. Thus the very title succinctly sums up the macabre scene that Slessor depicts in the poem.

'Beach Burial' is drawn from Slessor's personal experience. During World War II he was Australian Official War Correspondent in the Middle East, and it was at El Alamein that he found the stimulus and inspiration for this poem.

In 'Beach Burial' Slessor, like other war poets such as Owen and Sassoon, observes and condemns the carnage caused by war. The first two lines set the morbid tone of the poem. Slessor paints the horrific picture of groups of dead sailors floating towards the beach at El Alamein. The sailors are now inanimate objects under the control, and at the mercy, of the sea. War has robbed them of their lives. The tragedy is made all the more graphic by the fact that the dead sailors are floating together in convoys, seemingly to afford each other protection, even though protection is now quite futile.

Here, as in many other of Slessor's poems, he uses sounds to convey the feeling of the scene he is describing. Slessor evokes the rhythmic motion of the sailors floating in the water by the repetition of sounds such as the 'ly' in 'softly' and 'humbly'; the repetition of 's' throughout the first stanza suggests the movement of the bodies in the ebb and the flow of the sea. The contrast in sound evoked by 'Gulf of Arabs' reminds us sharply that the sailors are aliens in the land they have reached.

In the second stanza, Slessor's fine ear for sounds again governs the verse. The actual firing of the guns is conjured up by the words 'sob' and 'clubbing'; it is the 'b' that suggests the sight and sounds of the guns firing. In the first stanza the rhythm of the poem is slow and heavy, to reflect the sluggish movement and idle wandering of the bodies; in the second stanza the rhythm quickens to capture the need for haste in bringing the bodies to shore. The repetition of 'them' suggests the anonymity of the seamen and, by deduction, the senselessness of war. Its futility is further emphasized by the word 'burrows', which are usually associated with the habitat of animals; we feel pity for the sailors as we realize that their ultimate protection is to be found within the earth, as animals find comfort in the safety of their burrows.

In this second stanza, Slessor goes on to show us that even in war there can be charity. Someone has concern for these dead seamen. They will not be left to rot on the beach; nor are their deaths to go unnoticed, for Slessor with this very poem is to provide their elegy.

In the third stanza the description of the crudely made tidewood crosses makes the sadness and regretfulness of the scene the more poignant. The inexplicable horror of war is condemned when the writer of 'Unknown seaman' finds himself perplexed and bewildered by the task. So many men have been killed in such a short time that he does not know what names to write on the crosses. He attempts to sign for the dead, but the best he can do for each seaman is to write anonymously in indelible pencil. Their only memorial is a cross of tidewood and the inscription 'Unknown seamen'. They give up their lives for little reward to themselves, and even in death they must remain unknown. The indelible-pencil inscription soon begins to show the vitiating effects of time as the colour fades to the 'blue' of 'drowned men's lips'. Slessor emphasizes the waste of life with his use of the colour 'blue'. 'Blue' signifies that life has been taken from these men, red lips traditionally signify the vitality of life. It is interesting to note that throughout 'Beach Burial' Slessor gives very few details about the physical appearance of the sailors, but concentrates on their burial on the beach.

The message of the poem is vividly presented in the last stanza. The sailors of old in sailing ships looked forward expectantly to reaching land after long and often difficult voyages. Here in 'Beach Burial' the dead sailors similarly reach land after their wanderings in the sea. Previously they may have been fighting against each other, but now they have the common goal of the 'same landfall'.

When they reach landfall, both the allied and enemy sailors are united in their mass burial. In life they were unable to live together without enmity. Now in death they are peacefully united. This poem is an indictment of war and the horror of it; in the last stanza the futility of war is so clearly revealed when the poet describes the joining together of the seamen, who have come from so many lands, in their mass grave on the beach at El Alamein.

Keith Douglas was a British tank commander in Egypt when he wrote this poem. He himself was killed in battle in Normandy on 9 June 1944, at the age of 24.

VERGISSMEINNICHT

Three weeks gone and the combatants gone
returning over the nightmare ground
we found the place again, and found
the soldier sprawling in the sun.

The frowning barrel of his gun
overshadowing. As we came on
that day, he hit my tank with one
like the entry of a demon.

Look. Here in the gunpit spoil
the dishonoured picture of his girl
who has put: Steffi. Vergissmeinicht
in a copybook gothic script.

We see him almost with content
abased, and seeming to have paid
and mocked at by his own equipment
that's hard and good when he's decayed.

But she would weep to see today
how on his skin the swart flies move;
the dust upon the paper eye
and the burst stomach like a cave.

For here the lover and killer are mingled
who had one body and one heart.
And death who had the soldier singled
has done the lover mortal hurt.

Moms, Tripolitania, 1943
KEITH DOUGLAS

In his poem, 'The Burning Truck', the Australian poet, Les Murray describes an air attack and its terrifying aftermath.

THE BURNING TRUCK

It began at dawn with fighter planes:
they came in off the sea and didn't rise,
they leaped the sandbar one and one and one
coming so fast the crockery they shook down
from off my shelves was spinning in the air
when they were gone.

They came in off the sea and drew a wave
of lagging cannon-shells across our roofs.
Windows spat glass, a truck took sudden fire,
out leaped the driver, but the truck ran on,
growing enormous, shambling by our street-doors,
coming and coming . . .

By every right in town, by every average
we knew of in the world, it had to stop,
fetch up against a building, fall to rubble
from pure force of burning, for its whole
body and substance were consumed with heat . . .
but it would not stop.

And all of us who knew our place and prayers
clutched our verandah-rails and window sills,
begging that truck between our teeth to halt,
keep going, vanish, strike . . . but set us free.
And then we saw the wild boys of the street
go running after it.

And as they followed, cheering, on it crept,
windshield melting now, canopy-frame a cage
torn by gorillas of flame, and it kept on
over the tramlines, past the church, on past
the last lit windows, and then out of the world
with its disciples.

LES A. MURRAY

Thinking About the Poem

(1) What happened at dawn?
(2) What evidence can you find to show that the planes were flying very low?
(3) What does the poet achieve by the repetition of the word 'one'?
(4) Explain the meaning of '. . . drew a wave/of lagging cannon-shells across our roofs'.
(5) What does the poet mean by 'Windows spat glass'? Why is this image effective?
(6) Why did the driver leap out of the truck?
(7) What picture of the truck does the poet give the reader in his words 'the truck ran on,/growing enormous, shambling by our street-doors'?
(8) Why did the people of the town expect that the truck would eventually have to stop?
(9) How did the wild boys of the town react to the burning truck?
(10) What words of the poet emphasize the intensity of the flames?
(11) Why do you think the poet wrote the poem 'The Burning Truck'?
(12) Do you think Les Murray was actually present during the air attack and its aftermath? Why?

Poems about the Vietnam War

Bruce Dawe wrote 'Home-Coming' in the wake of the Tet offensive in Vietnam when Australian and American troops were fighting against the North Vietnamese troops.

HOME-COMING

All day, day after day, they're bringing them home,
they're picking them up, those they can find, and bringing
   them home,
they're bringing them in, piled on the hulls of Grants, in
   trucks, in convoys,
they're zipping them up in green plastic bags,
they're tagging them now in Saigon, in the mortuary coolness
they're giving them names, they're rolling them out of
the deep-freeze lockers – on the tarmac at Tan Son Nhut
the noble jets are whining like hounds,
they are bringing them home
– curly-heads, kinky-hairs, crew-cuts, balding non-coms
– they're high, now, high and higher, over the land, the
   steaming *chow mein*,
their shadows are tracing the blue curve of the Pacific
with sorrowful quick fingers, heading south, heading east,
home, home, home – and the coasts swing-upward, the old
   ridiculous curvatures
of earth, the knuckled hills, the mangrove
   swamps, the desert emptiness . . .
in their sterile housing they tilt towards these like skiers
– taxiing in, on the long runways, the howl of their
   home-coming rises
surrounding them like their last moments (the mash, the
   splendour)
then fading at length as they move
on to small towns where dogs in the frozen sunset
raise muzzles in mute salute,
and on to cities in whose wide web of suburbs
telegrams tremble like leaves from a wintering tree
and the spider grief swings in his bitter geometry
– they're bringing them home, now, too late, too early.

BRUCE DAWE

The Poet Comments

There were two images, one verbal and one visual which triggered this poem in particular. One was a *Newsweek* front cover which showed a very graphic but not overdone shot of an American soldier sitting stripped to the waist on the hull of a tank draped with bodies of other American soldiers – dead or very severely wounded – heading back to base. The other was a news item in the same or subsequent edition of *Newsweek* which said that at Oakland Airforce base in California at this time (when the American casualty rate was running at a thousand a week) at one part of the base the transport planes took off with the young men going out to serve their tour of duty in Vietnam; at another part of the same base the transport planes landed with the bodies of those who had finished their tour of duty permanently. I was also thinking of our own dead – I mentioned the word 'south' somewhere in the poem. I was also thinking of the way we bring our dead home. The North Vietnamese, the Viet Cong dead, of course, were bulldozed into mass graves.

from a talk by Bruce Dawe, 1979

'I Was Only Nineteen' is a recent Australian song which condemns the sending of our young men to war in Vietnam.

I WAS ONLY NINETEEN

Mum and Dad and Denny saw the passing out parade at Puckapunyal.
(It was a long march from cadets.)
The sixth Battalion was the next to tour and it was me who drew the card.
We did Canungra and Shoalwater before we left.
And Townsville lined the footpaths as we marched down to the quay.
This clipping from the paper shows us young and strong and clean.
And there's me in me slouch hat with me S.L.R. and greens.
God help me, I was only nineteen.
From Vung Tau riding Chinooks to the dust at Nui Dat.
I've been in and out of choppers now for months.
But we made our tents a home, V.B. and pinups on the lockers,
And an Asian orange sunset through the scrub.
And can you tell me, doctor, why I still can't get to sleep?
The night-time's just a jungle dark and a barking M.16?
And what's this rash that comes and goes, can you tell me what it
    means?
God help me, I was only nineteen.
A four week operation any step can mean your last one.
On two legs; it was a war within yourself.
But you wouldn't let your mates down 'til they had you dusted off.
So you closed your eyes and thought about something else.
And then someone yelled out 'Contact!' and the bloke behind me swore.
We hooked in there for hours, then a god-almighty roar.
And Frankie kicked a mine the day that mankind kicked the moon.
God help me, he was going home in June.
I can still see Frankie drinking tinnies in the Grand Hotel.
On a thirty-six hour rec. leave in Vung Tau.
And I can still hear Frankie lying screaming in the jungle.

'Til the morphine came and killed the bloody row.
And the Anzac legends didn't mention mud and blood and tears.
And the stories that my Father told me never seemed quite real.
I caught some pieces in my back that I didn't even feel.
God help me, I was only nineteen.
And can you tell me doctor, why I still can't get to sleep?
And why the Channel 7 chopper chills me to my feet?
And what's this rash that comes and goes, can you tell me what it
    means?
God help me, I was only nineteen.

SONG BY REDGUM, 1983

15 Satire

Satire is the use of language in speech and writing which holds up human weaknesses to ridicule. The satirist aims to tell us that something is wrong and very often he amuses and entertains us as he tries to influence us and bring about change. At times the satirist uses irony, sarcasm, innuendo and scorn along with humour to expose our foolishness.

In the poem, 'Executive', the poet John Betjeman satirizes the values and lifestyle of a young businessman.

EXECUTIVE

I am a young executive. No cuffs than mine are cleaner;
I have a Slimline brief-case and I use the firm's Cortina.
In every roadside hostelry from here to Burgess Hill
The *maîtres d'hôtel* all know me well and let me sign the bill.

You ask me what it is I do. Well actually, you know,
I'm partly a liaison man and partly P.R.O.
Essentially I integrate the current export drive
And basically I'm viable from ten o'clock till five.

For vital off-the-record work – that's talking transport-wise –
I've a scarlet Aston-Martin – and does she go? She flies!
Pedestrians and dogs and cats – we mark them down for slaughter.
I also own a speed-boat which has never touched the water.

She's built of fibre-glass, of course. I call her 'Mandy Jane'
After a bird I used to know – No soda, please, just plain –
And how did I acquire her? Well to tell you about that
And to put you in the picture I must wear my other hat.

I do some mild developing. The sort of place I need
Is a quiet country market town that's rather run to seed.
A luncheon and a drink or two, a little *savoir faire* –
I fix the Planning Officer, the Town Clerk and the Mayor.

And if some preservationist attempts to interfere
A 'dangerous structure' notice from the Borough Engineer
Will settle any buildings that are standing in our way –
The modern style, sir, with respect, has really come to stay.

JOHN BETJEMAN

Examining the Executive

(1) 'No cuffs than mine are cleaner'. What impression of himself does the young executive wish to project?

(2) What places does the young executive think it right to frequent? What does his choice reveal about his character?

(3) What does the young executive see as his main work?

(4) What does the young executive mean when he says: 'And basically I'm viable from ten o'clock till five'?

(5) 'Pedestrians and dogs and cats – we mark them down for slaughter.' What do you learn about the character of the young executive from these words?

(6) Why do you think the young executive tells us about his 'speed-boat which has never touched the water'?

(7) Explain the meaning of 'a quiet country market town that's rather run to seed'.

(8) Explain how the young executive uses people for his own ends.

(9) What means does the young executive use to stop the interference of the preservationist?

(10) What do you think the poem gains from having the young executive talk directly to the reader?

(11) What overall impression does the poet give the reader of the young executive?

(12) Do you think the poet has given a realistic description of the young executive? Give reasons for your viewpoint.

In 'Hymn of the Scientific Farmers', Clive Sansom does not sing the praises of modern farming methods.

HYMN OF THE SCIENTIFIC FARMERS

We squirt the fields and scatter
Our phosphates on the land:
'Organic waste' and 'humus'
We do not understand.

We slaughter trees in thousands
To sell for what they're worth;
No stems to hold the water,
No roots to bind the earth.

Our farms will turn to deserts
Where not a crop can grow,
But long before that happens
We'll take our gains and go.

We'll strip the lanes of hedges;
No wild-flower must survive,
Nor bird find place to nest in –
Let only insects thrive!

We spray to kill diseases,
And once a cure is made
Some other pest is started:
But that is good for Trade.

We rob the flour of virtue,
We leave a rifled sack;
And then with new synthetics
We almost put it back.

We pump our fowls with hormones
As fast as fast can be;
Consumers die of cancer
But we're not there to see.

Our god is an Equation,
And Profit is our goal:
'Exploit the parts like fury –
Forget about the whole'.

CLIVE SANSOM

Thinking About the Poem

(1) A hymn is a song of praise. Why has the poet called his poem, Hymn of the Scientific Farmers?
(2) What alternative does the poet offer to the use of phosphates?
(3) 'We slaughter trees in thousands'. Why does the poet use the word 'slaughter' rather than 'cut down'?
(4) 'We'll take our gains and go'. What criticism is the poet making of the scientific farmers?
(5) What does the poet mean by 'We rob the flour of virtue'?
(6) What method do the scientific farmers use in the breeding of fowls? What, according to the poet, are the ill effects of this method?
(7) What do you learn about the scientific farmers from the words: 'Profit is our goal'?
(8) What criticism is the poet making of the methods of the scientific farmers when he says: 'Exploit the parts like fury – /Forget about the whole'?
(9) What do you think was the poet's aim in writing this poem?
(10) Do you think the poet's attack on the scientific farmers is justified? Explain your viewpoint.

Satirizing Sport

Bruce Dawe disagrees with those critics who have maintained that 'Life-cycle' is a savage attack on the fanaticism of the followers of Australian Rules football. He says: 'I don't often disagree with critics but this is a poem that is something like a religious love poem. It's dedicated to Big Jim Phelan who died recently and was a huge six foot four inches, twenty one stone, silver haired, red faced Irishman who was a Collingwood committee man. He'd made himself a pyjama suit of black and white check six inch squares and when Collingwood was playing he'd put it on and caper round the grounds and he was a sight to behold – a mythological vision, really.' What is your opinion of 'Life-cycle'?

LIFE-CYCLE   *for Big Jim Phelan*

When children are born in Victoria
they are wrapped in the club-colours, laid in beribboned cots,
having already begun a lifetime's barracking.

Carn, they cry, Carn . . . feebly at first
while parents playfully tussle with them
for possession of a rusk: Ah, he's a little Tiger! (And they are . . .)

Hoisted shoulder-high at their first League game
they are like innocent monsters who have been years swimming
towards the daylight's roaring empyrean

Until, now, hearts shrapnelled with rapture,
they break surface and are forever lost,
their minds rippling out like streamers

In the pure flood of sound, they are scarfed with light, a voice
like the voice of God booms from the stands
Ooohh you bludger and the covenant is sealed.

Hot pies and potato-crisps they will eat,
they will forswear the Demons, cling to the Saints
and behold their team going up the ladder into Heaven,

And the tides of life will be the tides of the home-team's fortunes
– the reckless proposal after the one-point win,
the wedding and honeymoon after the grand-final . . .

They will not grow old as those from more northern States grow old,
for them it will always be three-quarter-time
with the scores level and the wind advantage in the final term,

That passion persisting, like a race-memory, through the welter of seasons,
enabling old-timers by boundary-fences to dream of resurgent lions
and centaur-figures from the past to replenish continually the present,

So that mythology may be perpetually renewed
and Chicken Smallhorn return like the maize-god
in a thousand shapes, the dancers changing

But the dance forever the same – the elderly still
loyally crying Carn . . . Carn . . . (if feebly) unto the very end,
having seen in the six-foot recruit from Eaglehawk their hope of salvation.

BRUCE DAWE

The Poet Comments

As you know, about Aussie Rules nobody cares if you play the game, but you sure as heck better be a supporter if you want to stay alive and well and travel in cabs and other public transport. You have to be barracker and as you know, you can now get your salt and pepper shakers, your babies nappies, and I presume the time will come when you can be buried in the home-ground or to re-emerge in a sort of resurrection in the MCG in the sky and play the eternal grand-final forever. That's the kind of code it is. But I think all Australians have something of a predisposition to treat sport as being just a bit more religious than in other places so if my voices get a bit more exalted, you'll understand. Note the Demons are Melbourne and the Lions are Fitzroy. Fitzroy now are resurgent lions – if you hang around long enough reading the poem, you'll turn out to be a prophet after all!

from a talk by Bruce Dawe, Sydney 1979

The word *jolly* means 'enjoyable' or 'cheerful'. It was a word that the English aristocracy over-used in their conversation. Undoubtedly they would have used it when they went on their shooting expeditions in the English countryside. Charles Causely mockingly overuses this word as he condemns their senseless killing of animal life.

I SAW A JOLLY HUNTER

I saw a jolly hunter
  With a jolly gun
Walking in the country
  In the jolly sun.

In the jolly meadow
  Sat a jolly hare.
Saw the jolly hunter.
  Took jolly care.

Hunter jolly eager –
  Sight of jolly prey.
Forgot gun pointing
  Wrong jolly way.

Jolly hunter jolly head
  Over heels gone.
Jolly old safety-catch
  Not jolly on.

Bang went the jolly gun.
  Hunter jolly dead.
Jolly hare got clean away.
  Jolly good, I said.

R.I.J.P.

CHARLES CAUSLEY

Some Jolly Good Questions

(1) Why do you think the poet uses the word *jolly* so often in this poem?
(2) What mistake did the hunter make?
(3) 'Jolly dead'. What is unusual about these two words being used together?
(4) What words in the last stanza indicate that the poet is glad the hunter is dead?
(5) R.I.P. means 'Rest In Peace'. What do you think 'R.I.J.P.' would mean? Why is this more suitable than 'R.I.P.'?
(6) Why do you think Charles Causley wrote this poem?

Ogden Nash's poem, 'The Hunter', dealing with a similar theme to Charles Causley's poem, mocks the intelligence of the duck hunter and his techniques.

THE HUNTER

The hunter crouches in his blind
'Neath camouflage of every kind,
And conjures up a quacking noise
To lend allure to his decoys.
This grown-up man, with pluck and luck,
Is hoping to outwit a duck.

OGDEN NASH

Satirizing the Media

Some newspaper editors use sensationalism to sell newspapers, but none more than the Gutter Press editor. The poet Paul Dehn scathingly condemns such a practice.

GUTTER PRESS

News Editor: Peer Confesses,
Bishop Undresses,
Torso Wrapped in Rug,
Girl Guide Throttled,
Baronet Bottled,
J.P. Goes to Jug.

But yesterday's story's
Old and hoary.
Never mind who got hurt.
No use grieving,
Let's get weaving.
What's the latest dirt?

> Diplomat Spotted,
> Scout Garrotted,
> Thigh Discovered in Bog,
> Wrecks Off Barmouth,
> Sex In Yarmouth,
> Woman In Love With Dog,
> Eminent Hostess Shoots Her Guests,
> Harrogate Lovebird Builds Two Nests.

Cameraman: *Builds two nests?*
Shall I get a picture of the lovebird singing?
Shall I get a picture of her pretty little eggs?
Shall I get a picture of her babies?

News Editor: No!
Go and get a picture of her legs.

> Beast Slays Beauty,
> Priest Flays Cutie,
> Cupboard Shows Tell-Tale Stain,
> Mate Drugs Purser,
> Dean Hugs Bursar,
> Mayor Binds Wife With Chain,
> Elderly Monkey Marries For Money,
> Jilted Junky Says 'I Want My Honey'.

Cameraman: *'Want my honey?'*
Shall I get a picture of the pollen flying?
Shall I get a picture of the golden dust?
Shall I get a picture of a queen bee?

News Editor: No!
Go and get a picture of her bust.

> Judge Gets Frisky,
> Nun Drinks Whisky,
> Baby Found Burnt in Cot,
> Show Girl Beaten,
> Duke Leaves Eton –

Cameraman: *Newspaper Man Gets Shot!*
May all things clean
And fresh and green
Have mercy upon your soul,
Consider yourself paid
By the hole my bullet made –

News Editor (dying):   Come and get a picture of the hole.

PAUL DEHN

One of the most obvious targets for the satirist is advertising, and the poet A. S. J. Tessimond's criticism is trenchant as he points out the advertiser's follies and foibles.

THE AD-MAN

This trumpeter of nothingness, employed
To keep our reason full and null and void:
This man of wind and froth and flux will sell
The wares of any who reward him well,
Praising whatever he is paid to praise,
He hunts for ever-newer, smarter ways
To make the gilt seem gold; the shoddy, silk;
To cheat us legally; to bluff and bilk
By methods which no jury can prevent
Because the law's not broken, only bent.

This mind for hire, this mental prostitute
Can tell the half-lie hardest to refute;
Knows how to hide an inconvenient fact
And when to leave a doubtful claim unbacked;
Manipulates the truth, but not too much,
And if his patter needs the Human Touch
Then aptly artless, artfully naïve,
He wears his fickle heart upon his sleeve.

He takes ideas and trains them to engage
In the long little wars big combines wage.
He keeps his logic loose, his feelings flimsy;
Turns eloquence to cant and wit to whimsy;
Trims language till it fits his client's pattern,
And style's a glossy tart or limping slattern.

He uses words that once were strong and fine.
Primal as sun and moon and bread and wine,
True, honourable, honoured, clear and clean,
And leaves them shabby, worn, diminished, mean.

Where our defence is weakest, he attacks.
Encircling reason's fort, he finds the cracks,
He knows the hopes and fears on which to play.
We who at first rebel, at last obey.
We who have tried to choose accept his choice.
Tired, we succumb to his untiring voice.
The drip-drip-drip makes even granite soften.
We trust the brand-name we have heard so often,
And join the queue of sheep that flock to buy:
We fools who know our folly, you and I.

A. S. J. TESSIMOND

Little Satirical Poems

OCTANE

Use X or Y brand gasoline,
It doesn't matter which,
It all comes from the same big tank
And makes old Texas rich.
It jams the highways full of cars,
It fills the air with lead,
If you insist on breathing
You'll have octane in your head.

ANON.

DETERGENT

Detergent, detergent,
It gets you lovely and white,
It backs up in the water mains,
You drink it day and night.
It makes your kitchen spotless,
It keeps your bathroom clean,
It bubbles from the water tap
And turns your liver green.

ANON.

16 Fun with Poetry

Often a product has to be promoted, before it sells. In the poem below, the poet obviously feels her special qualities need a little promotion! Read through the poem, and see what your response is to her question: 'Will Anybody Marry Me'?

WILL ANYBODY MARRY ME?

Will anybody marry me?
I would not cost him dear,
I am in perfect nick
And good condition for the year.
He would not have to be a Mr World
Built like Fort Knox
For I would do the plastering
And saw up all the blocks.

Will anybody marry me?
I would be awful sweet,
I'd let him knock me glasses off
And kick them down the street,
And I would not be a nagger
Saying, 'Will you paint the pelmet?'
And if he was a fireman
I would never dent his helmet.

And concerning older girls
Our inhibitions have all gone,
And me dad's an electrician
So I'd really turn him on,
Now I cannot give my telephone
That's hazardous I know
But if anyone will have me
It is Bognor 410.

PAM AYRES

Marriage in Question

(1) What words and phrases in the opening four lines make the poem sound like an advertisement?
(2) How do you imagine a 'Mr World/Built like Fort Knox' would look?
(3) What does the poet mean when she says: 'For I would do the plastering and saw up all the blocks'?
(4) How would the poet prove herself to be 'awful sweet'?
(5) The poet claims she would not insist that her husband 'paint the pelmet', nor would she damage his hat if he were a fireman. What is humorous about these examples?
(6) According to the poet, how are older girls different from younger girls?
(7) 'And me dad's an electrician /So I'd really turn him on.' Explain the double meaning in these words.
(8) What twist of humour occurs in the last part of the poem?
(9) How desperate does the poet seem in her quest for marriage? Support your answer with evidence from the poem.
(10) What techniques has the poet used to achieve the overall humour in this poem?

Have *you* faced the awesome task of running a children's party? This poet has, and it's not a task he is in a rush to repeat! But let him tell you about it ...

CHILDREN'S PARTY

May I join you in the doghouse, Rover?
I wish to retire till the party's over.
Since three o'clock I've done my best
To entertain each tiny guest;
My conscience now I've left behind me,
And if they want me, let them find me.
I blew their bubbles, I sailed their boats,
I kept them from each other's throats.
I told them tales of magic lands,
I took them out to wash their hands.
I sorted their rubbers and tied their laces,
I wiped their noses and dried their faces.
Of similarity there's lots
'Twixt tiny tots and Hottentots.
I've earned repose to heal the ravages
Of these angelic-looking savages.
Oh, progeny playing by itself
Is a lonely fascinating elf,
But progeny in roistering batches
Would drive St. Francis from here to Natchez.
Shunned are the games a parent proposes;
They prefer to squirt each other with hoses,
Their playmates are their natural foemen
And they like to poke each other's abdomen.
Their joy needs another's woe to cushion it,
Say a puddle, and somebody littler to push in it.
They observe with glee the ballistic results
Of ice cream with spoons for catapults,
And inform the assembly with tears and glares
That everyone's presents are better than theirs.
Oh, little women and little men,
Someday I hope to love you again,
But not till after the party's over,
So give me the key to the doghouse, Rover.

OGDEN NASH

Understanding Is Believing

(1) The first four lines outline the poet's terrifying situation. Exactly what has he been doing?

(2) How do we know that he does not feel guilty about leaving the party?

(3) What are some of the ways the poet has tried to entertain his tiny guests?

(4) Explain the significance of: 'Of similarity there's lots/'Twixt tiny tots and Hottentots.'

(5) What expression towards the middle of the poem sums up the appearance and nature of the children?

(6) Which does the poet prefer – the child playing alone, or children playing together? Why?

(7) Instead of 'the games a parent proposes' the children prefer their own games. Specifically, what games do they prefer to play?

(8) 'They observe with glee the ballistic results/Of ice cream with spoons for catapults.' Explain this activity of the children in your own words.

(9) The poet's hope of loving these 'little women and little men' again has one condition attached. What is it?

(10) How does the last part of the poem recall the poem's beginning?

(11) What appeals to you most in this poem?

Alfred has unusual dreams of being a super-hero! But the phone-boxes don't seem co-operative ...

ALFRED AND THE PHONE-BOXES

Alfred wanted to use phone-boxes
for changing into someone magnificent.
He knew it was possible, because
Clark Kent could do it – sap to ZAP!
What a crowd-stopper: the sight of Super-Alf
stalking from the booth with bright cape flapping,
limbs a-ripple, gleaming like a Dulux testimonial,
and even more so
his torso!
With a mere flick of his chest
he'd speed aloft, zipping through the dazzled air –

No such luck.
Always the phone-boxes were occupied,
filling up with words and dead weight.
No room inside.
Often it was his grandfather
who'd got in there first, and was trying to grow
lettuce and silver beet, and build stone walls
taller than wide.

Once Alfred was explaining his problem to Grace,
telling her this heavy tale of booths
crammed with the rocks and vegies of his past,
when she pointed into the distance;
and as her other hand rested on his arm, he saw
a phone-box quietly levitating, up, up and away.

IAN REID

Clarence James Dennis wrote popular, humorous poetry between World War I and World War II. In his poems many Australians found that the characters of the city slums and the 'backblocks' came alive for them.

As you read through 'The Traveller' notice that the humour of character is evoked in two ways. First, the traveller notices something odd about each character he meets: funny feet, a blue nose, no hat, and so on. Secondly, he never receives any explanation when he asks about the oddity. Instead, each character replies with a comment on a totally different subject! Now, of course, this is exactly what happens in much human communication and, because it is such a common experience, endured at times by everyone, we smile to see it presented so blatantly. So, read and enjoy . . .

THE TRAVELLER

As I rode in to Burrumbeet,
I met a man with funny feet;
And, when I paused to ask him why
His feet were strange, he rolled his eye
And said the rain would spoil the wheat;
So I rode on to Burrumbeet.

As I rode in to Beetaloo,
I met a man whose nose was blue;
And when I asked him how he got
A nose like that, he answered, 'What
Do bullocks mean when they say "Moo"?'
So I rode on to Beetaloo.

As I rode in to Ballarat,
I met a man who wore no hat;
And, when I said he might take cold,
He cried, 'The hills are quite as old
As yonder plains, but not so flat'.
So I rode on to Ballarat.

As I rode in to Gundagai,
I met a man and passed him by
Without a nod, without a word.
He turned, and said he'd never heard
Or seen a man so wise as I.
But I rode on to Gundagai.

As I rode homeward, full of doubt,
I met a stranger riding out:
A foolish man he seemed to me;
But, 'Nay, I am yourself,' said he,
'Just as you were when you rode out'.
So I rode homeward, free of doubt.

C. J. DENNIS

A little too much drink, a relaxed attitude to graveyards and a deep concern for a fellow human, all add up to humour in ...

A GRAVE SITUATION

When I staggered away from my favourite pub,
The night was dark and still,
And I thought I'd take a shortcut home
That led over Cemetery Hill.
Now I'm not a hero as everyone knows,
And I have no reckless trends,
But ghosts and the like leave me cold, as it were,
And spirits and I are old friends.

I wobbled along through the cemetery gates,
Begging my legs to behave,
And everything went pretty well, so I thought,
Till I fell down a newly-dug grave.
For a moment I thought I had landed in hell,
And ended my earthly career,
I sniffed like a hound for the sulphurous fumes,
Expecting Old Nick to appear.

But reason returned and I staggered erect,
My prison so dark, to survey,
And tested my bones for a fracture or two,
But everything functioned O.K.
I made a feeble attempt to get out,
But it needed no more than a glance
To convince me, in my condition,
I hadn't the ghost of a chance.

I reckoned I'd have a lay-off for a while,
And when I woke sober and fit
I'd surely come up with a good idea
That would get me out of the pit.
Just then I could hear fast oncoming steps
That seemed too good to be true,
But ere I could 'Coo-ee' or offer advice,
In the grave there were suddenly two!

By chance, he fell in the grave's other end,
With no one to cushion his fall;
But he rose with a strangled yelp,
And attempted to scale up the wall.
This chap was at pains to be up and away,
As the capers he cut plainly told.
He jumped and scrambled and jumped again,
But his fingers and toes wouldn't hold.

I hadn't yet spoken – I'd hardly a chance,
The way he cavorted about,
And I had to admire the way that he fought
To sever all ties and get out.
Of course he believed there was nobody near;
He thought he was there all alone.
And I got the idea it had entered his head
That the grave was becoming his own.

I felt rather sad for the poor little guy
Now acting a little distraught,
And I thought he'd relax if I gave him the drum
That he wasn't alone, as he thought.
So I walked up behind him and tapped on his back
As he poised for another wild bid:
'You CAN'T make it, Mate', I breathed in his ear –
But by the Lord Harry, he DID!

CLAUDE MORRIS

Getting to the Bottom of the Humour

(1) Outline the situation presented by the poet in the first four lines.
(2) As the poem opens, what word suggests that the central character has had too much to drink?
(3) What two qualities does the drunk freely admit he lacks?
(4) 'But ghosts and the like leave me cold, as it were,/And spirits and I are old friends.' Explain the double meaning in each of these lines.
(5) What calamity befalls him as he walks home? Where did he think he had landed?
(6) What did he expect his sense of smell to reveal? Why would this be so?
(7) What decision is taken by the drunk as the most sensible thing to do in the circumstances?
(8) How is the drunk suddenly disturbed in the grave?
(9) What emotions does the second man appear to have after his fall?
(10) Explain, in your own words, how the second man was helped out of the grave, by the drunk.
(11) Why is the poem's title appropriate for its subject matter?
(12) How is the humour created in this poem?

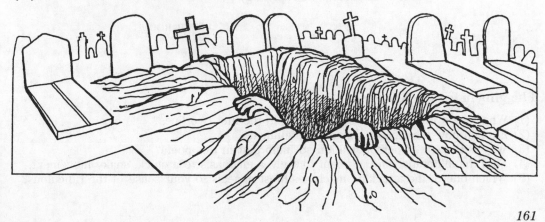

Machines are taking over. We are at war. Read on, and discover the awful truth ...

PLUG IN, TURN ON, LOOK OUT

Run for your lives, take to the hills,
The machines are on the march:
This morning my electric razor launched
A vicious and unwarranted attack on me –
It came at me, snarling through its
Thirty-four rotary teeth and
Flicking its flexy tail
(Fortunately I fought it off
With my dad's old cut-throat).
Do not turn your back on toasters,
The machines are taking over:
The talking weighing machines at Waterloo
Told me today in no uncertain terms,
Where I could stick my threepence –
I was trapped in the lift doors twice today,
Don't tell me it's coincidence;
So steer clear of vacuum cleaners, it's
The Mechanical Revolution:
I turned the telly on tonight and it
Turned itself off again ...
If necessary, we must resort to
Underhand tactics –
Keep your electric lawnmower securely tethered,
Cut down supplies of food to your refrigerator,
Kick your car at regular intervals
(That's why the Lord gave you legs).
And above all, don't let them find out
Who's winning ...

Meanwhile, I intend to lead
A picked band of desperadoes
In a death-or-glory attack
On the I.C.T. Computer Installation
(We must destroy
The brains behind this uprising).

PETER ROCHE

Plugging in for the Answers

(1) What mood is the poet trying to evoke in the first two lines?
(2) Explain how the electric razor is personified.
(3) Why is the use of personification so important in this poem?
(4) Find the alliteration in the poem that gives emphasis to a quick, snaky movement.
(5) Which one of the attacking machines most appeals to your sense of the ridiculous?

(6) Each machine seems to have its own underhand tactic. Which tactic most appeals to you, and why?
(7) 'Kick your car at regular intervals/(That's why the Lord gave you legs)'. What is amusing about this directive?
(8) Explain the purpose of the second short stanza in this poem.
(9) Why is the poem's title appropriate?
(10) What features of the poem are mainly responsible for its humour?

Here's a poem in which the humour is largely achieved by listing all the foods that the poet does without! The focus on food is apt, since the poet is 'a slimmer by trade'. How does that description cause you to picture her? Can you see the subtle suggestions in the poem that perhaps the 'trade' of slimming isn't all fun?

THE SLIMMING POEM

I'm a slimmer by trade, I'm frequently weighed,
I'm slim as a reed in the river.
I'm slender and lean, and hungry and mean.
Have some water, it's good for your liver.

Don't give me cheese rolls or profiteroles
Don't show me that jelly a-shakin',
Don't give me cream crackers you picnic and snackers
Or great big ice-creams with a flake in.

Don't give me swiss roll or toad-in-the-hole
Don't show me that Black Forest gateau.
You sit and go mouldy you old garibaldi
Your pastry all riddled with fat. Oh!

When I'm fat I feel weary and tubby and dreary
The stairs make me struggle and grunt dear,
And yet I'm so happy and punchy and snappy
When me hip bones are stuck out the front dear.

No, it's white fish for me, no milk in me tea
And if we don't like it we lump it.
No figs or sultanas, no mashed-up bananas
No pleasure and no buttered crumpet.

So don't get any bigger, me old pear-shaped figure
I can and I will become thinner.
So cheer up and take heart, pass the calorie chart,
let's see what we're having for dinner!

PAM AYRES

17 Odes and Elegies

The Ode

The *ode* is one specific form of lyric poetry. Like all lyric verse, the ode is characterized by two general qualities, subjectivity and the use of 'musical' word/sound/rhythm combinations.

(a) *Subjectivity:* The quality of subjectivity means that this type of poem 'reveals' the personality of the poet. He or she is not an unrevealed recorder of a story or description as, for example, the poet who writes a ballad might be. Rather, we are clearly aware that in this poem we are sharing the poet's thoughts, being exposed to his or her feelings, and being invited to look with his or her eyes.

(b) *'Musical' Word/Sound/Rhythm Combinations:* Though the earliest forms of lyric poetry were written as songs to be sung by a single voice, to the accompaniment of a lyre (hence, the word *lyric*), English lyric poetry is not intended to be accompanied by a musical instrument. However, the 'musical' quality has not been entirely discarded. These poems are now intended to be verse forms characterized by combinations of words, sounds and rhythms which are pleasant to the ear and, so, 'musical'.

EXAMPLE:
        Hence, in a season of calm weather,
           Though inland far we be,
      Our souls have sight of that immortal sea
           Which brought us hither;
        Can in a moment travel thither,
     And see the children sport upon the shore
     And hear the mighty waters rolling evermore.

      from 'Intimations of Immortality' by William Wordsworth

The additional distinctive qualities of an *ode* are that it has a dignified, sometimes majestic, tone, and it is intended as a hymn of exalted praise, focusing on a single person, object or abstraction. Well-known odes include Shelley's 'To a Skylark' and, 'Ode to the West Wind', and Keats' 'To a Nightingale', in addition to those reprinted below.

While traditional odes usually have regular stanzas and a clear structure, modern odes often feature stanzas of irregular length and stucture, though they still tend to follow a rhyming scheme.

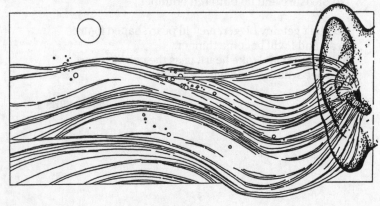

John Keats (1795–1821) is recognized as one of the great Romantic poets. The brilliance of his career as a poet was unfortunately cut short by his death from tuberculosis while in Rome.

TO AUTUMN

Season of mists and mellow fruitfulness,
   Close bosom-friend of the maturing sun;
Conspiring with him how to load and bless
   With fruit the vines that round the thatch-eaves run;
To bend with apples the moss'd cottage-trees,
   And fill all fruit with ripeness to the core;
     To swell the gourd, and plump the hazel shells
With a sweet kernel; to set budding more,
   And still more, later flowers for the bees,
   Until they think warm days will never cease,
     For Summer has o'er-brimm'd their clammy cells.

Who hath not seen thee oft amid thy store?
   Sometimes whoever seeks abroad may find
Thee sitting careless on a granary floor,
   Thy hair soft-lifted by the winnowing wind;
Or on a half-reap'd furrow sound asleep,
   Drows'd with the fume of poppies, while thy hook
     Spares the next swath and all its twined flowers;
And sometimes like a gleaner thou dost keep
   Steady thy laden head across a brook;
   Or by a cider-press, with patient look,
     Thou watchest the last oozings, hours by hours.

Where are the songs of Spring? Ay, where are they?
   Think not of them, thou hast thy music too, –
While barred clouds bloom the soft-dying day,
   And touch the stubble-plains with rosy hue;
Then in a wailful choir the small gnats mourn
   Among the river sallows, borne aloft
     Or sinking as the light wind lives or dies;
And full-grown lambs loud bleat from hilly bourn;
   Hedge-crickets sing; and now with treble soft
   The red-breast whistles from a garden-croft;
     And gathering swallows twitter in the skies.

JOHN KEATS

Exploring the Ode

(1) What is the theme of this poem?
(2) Keeping in mind that it is an ode, how would you describe the mood of this poem? Does this fit with your expectations of an ode?
(3) What consonant sounds are repeated in the two opening lines? What effect does this have, coming at the opening of the poem?

(4) What do we call the figure of speech used throughout this poem to describe autumn?

(5) Using *a* for the first rhyme, *b* for the second rhyme, and so on, identify the rhyme scheme for the first stanza. How regular is the poet's observance of this rhyming scheme in the other stanzas?

(6) What specific quality of autumn is being praised in the first stanza?

(7) In the second stanza, the poet speaks of 'seeing' autumn. What particular quality of autumn does he 'see' throughout this stanza?

(8) Comment on the effect of the last line in the second stanza: 'Thou watchest the last oozings, hours by hours.'

(9) What examples of the 'music' of autumn are specifically identified in the last stanza?

(10) All forms of lyric poetry are, in some way, an expression of the poet's inner life. Write a paragraph on some of the qualities of the poet, Keats, that you feel are revealed in this ode. Where possible, quote a line or two from the poem to support your views.

Grecian Urn

'Ode on a Grecian Urn' is perhaps a more difficult poem for us to understand, though once we begin to share the poet's experience, there is much to appreciate in it. The poet here contemplates a beautiful Grecian urn, or vase. He is fascinated by the workmanship, especially the scenes depicted on the outside, which appear to tell a story, the meaning of which is lost in antiquity. The mystery of the past, represented by the urn and depicted on it, is the theme of the poem.

ODE ON A GRECIAN URN

Thou still unravished bride of quietness,
    Thou foster-child of silence and slow time,
Sylvan historian, who canst thus express
    A flowery tale more sweetly than our rhyme:
What leaf-fringed legend haunts about thy shape
    Of deities or mortals, or of both,
      In Tempe or the dales of Arcady?
What men or gods are these? What maidens loth?
What mad pursuit? What struggle to escape?
    What pipes and timbrels? What wild ecstasy?

Heard melodies are sweet, but those unheard
    Are sweeter; therefore, ye soft pipes, play on;
Not to the sensual ear, but, more endeared;
    Pipe to the spirit ditties of no tone:
Fair youth, beneath the trees, thou canst not leave
    Thy song, nor ever can those trees be bare;
      Bold Lover, never, never canst thou kiss,
Though winning near the goal – yet, do not grieve;
      She cannot fade, though thou hast not thy bliss,
For ever wilt thou love, and she be fair!

Ah, happy, happy boughs! that cannot shed
    Your leaves, nor ever bid the Spring adieu;
And, happy melodist, unwearied,
    For ever piping songs for ever new;
More happy love! more happy, happy love!
    For ever warm and still to be enjoyed,
        For ever panting, and for ever young;
All breathing human passion far above,
    That leaves a heart high-sorrowful and cloyed,
        A burning forehead, and a parching tongue.

Who are these coming to the sacrifice?
    To what green altar, O mysterious priest,
Lead'st thou that heifer lowing at the skies,
    And all her silken flanks with garlands drest?
What little town by river or sea shore,
    Or mountain-built with peaceful citadel,
        Is emptied of this folk, this pious morn?
And, little town, thy streets for evermore
    Will silent be; and not a soul to tell
        Why thou art desolate, can e'er return.

O Attic shape! Fair attitude! with brede
    Of marble men and maidens overwrought,
With forest branches and the trodden weed;
    Thou, silent form, dost tease us out of thought
As doth eternity: Cold Pastoral!
    When old age shall this generation waste,
        Thou shalt remain, in midst of other woe
Than ours, a friend to man, to whom thou say'st,
    'Beauty is truth, truth beauty,' – that is all
    Ye know on earth, and all ye need to know.

                  JOHN KEATS

Grecian Urn – Notes

Because of the age in which it was written, and the literary references it contains, some of the words in 'Ode on a Grecian Urn' may be unclear. Here are some additional notes on a few words.

(1) Stanza 1, line 3: 'Sylvan' = of the woods
(2) Stanza 1, line 7: 'Tempe' = a valley in Thessaly, part of Greece; 'Arcady' = a region in Ancient Greece
(3) Stanza 5, line 1: 'Attic' = pertaining to Attica or its capital, Athens; 'brede' = embroidery

What's in a Grecian Urn?

(1) What do you think Keats means when he describes the urn as a 'bride of quietness'?
(2) In which two places mentioned in the first stanza does Keats imagine the scene on the vase may have occurred?
(3) Lots of unanswered questions can often leave a person feeling frustrated. How is the poet affected by the unanswered questions at the end of the first stanza?

(4) Though the 'Bold Lover' mentioned in the second stanza can never reach and kiss the maiden he pursues, Keats identifies some compensations. What are they?

(5) Why are the boughs in the third stanza described as 'happy'?

(6) What is the effect of the many repetitions of the word 'happy' in the third stanza?

(7) The scene in the third stanza is described as being 'far above' 'All breathing human passion'. In what way is living human passion inferior?

(8) Describe, in your own words, the scene which Keats is contemplating in the fourth stanza.

(9) What qualities of the vase does Keats seek to praise in this poem?

(10) Comment on Keats' achievement in this poem.

Amoeba

In 'Ode to the Amoeba', Arthur Guiterman waxes lyrical about an incredibly tiny life-form. In a style reminiscent of Ogden Nash, he injects a touch of humour into this ode.

ODE TO THE AMOEBA

Recall from Time's abysmal chasm
That piece of primal protoplasm
The First Amoeba, strangely splendid,
From whom we're all of us descended.
That First Amoeba, weirdly clever,
Exists today and shall forever,
Because he reproduced by fission;
He split himself, and each division
And subdivision deemed it fitting
To keep on splitting, splitting, splitting;
So, whatsoe'er their billions be,
All, all amoebas still are he.
Zoologists discern his features
In every sort of breathing creatures,
Since all of every living species,
No matter how their breed increases
Or how their ranks have been recruited,
From him alone were evoluted.
King Solomon, the Queen of Sheba
And Hoover sprang from that amoeba;
Columbus, Shakespeare, Darwin, Shelley
Derived from that same bit of jelly.
So famed he is and well-connected,
His statue ought to be erected,
For you and I and William Beebe
Are undeniably amoebae!

ARTHUR GUITERMAN

Amoeba under the Microscope

(1) The first line describes the pre-history of the earth as 'Time's abysmal chasm'. In what ways is the past like an 'abysmal chasm'?

(2) Identify the literary device used in the second line to achieve a pleasant rhythmical effect.

(3) Why has the poet capitalized the words 'First Amoeba'?

(4) What is seen by the poet as 'weirdly clever' in the amoeba? What human quality does the poet seem to be attributing to the amoeba here?

(5) Is it effective for the poet to repeat the word 'splitting'? Why?

(6) What does the poet mean by 'all amoebas still are he'?

(7) 'Evoluted' is a word created by the poet to make a rhyme. What alternative word would normally be used? What is the effect of making up this word?

(8) What do all the people mentioned have in common?

(9) Why has the poet used the archaic plural 'amoebae' to finish the poem? What is the effect of this?

(10) Do you sense the humour in this poem? How has it been created?

(11) What quality, or qualities, of the amoeba is the poet praising?

Delectable Bore

The following modern ode is written by a student about her grammar teacher! As you can see, she has quite a 'crush' on him, though she isn't so keen on grammar!

In keeping with many modern odes, this one does not follow a formal structure, nor does it have any rhyme scheme. However, it certainly is a deeply personal expression of the poet's feelings and experience, and it is a poem praising the merits of a specific individual. How lyrical, or musical, would you rate the language?

AN ODE TO A DELECTABLE BORE!
(written by a student to her grammar teacher)

Oh Mr. Brown!
How I wish grammar
was as interesting,
as you.
The only active
or passive things
to me are your
movements.
Who cares about
verbs, unless you're
holding, kissing, touching, stroking, caressing,
my hand?
If you want,
you can even make it
carefully, softly, gently, lovingly, continually,
adverbial.
Oh Mr. Brown!
Don't you know that
divine, handsome, suave, cuddly, heroic
adjectives only apply
to you?

> Oh Mr. Brown!
> Your tenses are all wrong.
> The present counts
> not the past.
> Oh Mr. Brown!
> I wish you taught
> Maths, History, Science, Cooking and Netball
> too.
> At least then
> I'd enjoy them even
> though I don't
> understand them,
> either.

KATE JONES

Perhaps using this, or a more traditional ode, to guide you, you might like to try writing your own ode for a person, object, or abstract ideal. Remember, it should:
(a) be a poem of praise,
(b) reveal your personal feelings and thoughts,
(c) make use of lyrical, or 'musical', language.

Elegies

The *elegy* in English poetry is a type of lyric poem which has no distinctive structure. Instead, it has come to be defined almost entirely by its subject-matter. Thus, an elegy is a mournful, lonely-feeling poem, usually in the form of an expression of grief for a dead person or persons, or because of the loss of a loved object or place.

The mood in an elegy is serious, and melancholic, and the rhythm is usually slow-moving, in keeping with the content of the poem. While the rhythm contributes to the poem's effect, it should not be intrusive or obvious. Consider the opening lines of Gray's 'Elegy Written in a Country Churchyard', the most famous of all English elegies:

> The curfew tolls the knell of parting day,
> The lowering herd wind slowly o'er the lea,
> The plowman homeward plods his weary way,
>   And leaves the world to darkness and to me.
>
> Now fades the glimmering landscape on the sight,
>   And all the air a solemn stillness holds,
> Save where the beetle wheels his droning flight,
>   And drowsy tinklings lull the distant folds:

The mood is quickly set by the slow, unobtrusive rhythm, the sounds and the words. In this way we are prepared for a sombre, reflective poem on the significance of the lives and deaths of those who are buried in the churchyard where Gray is seated.

In most elegies the poet recalls memories of places and incidents linked with the person, or object, he or she mourns. In traditional elegies the poet, at times, includes some sense of ultimate triumph or hope, reflecting his or her belief in a future life.

Elegy Comparison

Read through the two brief elegies below and then answer the questions.

SHE DWELT AMONG THE UNTRODDEN WAYS

She dwelt among the untrodden ways
    Besides the springs of Dove,
A Maid whom there were none to praise
    And very few to love:

A Violet by a mossy stone
    Half hidden from the eye!
– Fair as a star, when only one
    Is shining in the sky.

She lived unknown, and few could know
    When Lucy ceased to be;
But she is in her grave, and, oh,
    The difference to me.

                  WILLIAM WORDSWORTH

REQUIESCAT

    Tread lightly, she is near
        Under the snow,
    Speak gently, she can hear
        The daisies grow.

    All her bright golden hair
        Tarnished with rust,
    She that was young and fair
        Fallen to dust.

    Lily-like, white as snow,
        She hardly knew
    She was a woman, so
        Sweetly she grew.

    Coffin-board, heavy stone,
        Lie on her breast,
    I vex my heart alone,
        She is at rest.

    Peace, Peace, she cannot hear
        Lyre or sonnet,
    All my life's buried here,
        Heap earth upon it.

              OSCAR WILDE

Untrodden Ways – Questions

(1) Explain why there were 'none to praise' and 'few to love' this Maid.
(2) What two beautiful images are used in the second stanza for this person? Which do you find the more effective? Why?
(3) What line or lines in the final stanza most clearly reveal the poet's depth of feeling about this person?

Requiescat – Questions

(1) What evidence is there in the first stanza that the poet feels death has heightened her senses?
(2) How does the fourth stanza introduce something of a contrast into the poem?
(3) Which line(s) most clearly reveal the depth of the poet's feelings?

Elegy Comparison – Questions

(1) Comment briefly on the use of language in the two elegies above. Which do you find more effective?
(2) Which poem do you prefer? Justify your choice.

An Eighteenth–Century Elegy

The title identifies it as an elegy, but is it? Read through Goldsmith's 'Elegy on Madam Blaize' and discuss whether or not you believe it meets the requirements of an elegy. What features of an elegy are present? How does it differ from a traditional elegy?

ELEGY ON MADAM BLAIZE

Good people all, with one accord,
　　Lament for Madam Blaize;
Who never wanted a good word –
　　From those who spoke her praise.

The needy seldom passed her door,
　　And always found her kind;
She freely lent to all the poor –
　　Who left a pledge behind.

She strove the neighbourhood to please,
　　With manners wondrous winning;
She never followed wicked ways –
　　Unless when she was sinning.

At church, in silks and satins new,
　　With hoop of monstrous size,
She never slumbered in her pew –
　　But when she shut her eyes

Her love was sought, I do aver,
　　By twenty beaux, or more;
The king himself has followed her –
　　When she was walked before.

But now, her wealth and finery fled,
    Her hangers-on cut short all,
Her doctors found, when she was dead –
    Her last disorder mortal.

Let us lament, in sorrow sore;
    For Kent Street well may say,
That, had she lived a twelvemonth more –
    She had not died to-day.

OLIVER GOLDSMITH

Modern Elegies

ELEGY IN A CITY RAILYARD

Slategrey stonegrey smokegrey
The fag-end of evening smoulders away.
The girl from the store and the produce-broker
The teacher the wharfie the city clerk
The sportsgoods man and the barroom joker
Have all gone into the companionable dark.
The ledger is closed: the hand comes down
Carefully plotting the graph of skylines
Scribbled across the dove-coloured town.
Like a woolworth diamond, Jupiter shines
On a sky as soft as an eider-down.

Creme-de-menthe, ember-red, amber
The lights glow out and the day fails.
Tyres burr on the road's camber
As they take the bridge above the fan of rails
Shining like lead and the sheeted steam
Tinged from below with boiler fires.

The roundhouse is silent – there seem
No live things here except the tyres
Of the buses, and the piston's push and haul
And the signal's unintelligible call
And the searchlights in their tall martian machine
Knifing the grey September weather
Where the voices of night come home between
The engines talking quietly together.

M. K. JOSEPH

Bachelor Uncle

It is easy to fall into the trap of stereotyping people, thinking we know all about them because of some social 'label' that we use to sum them up in our mind. For example, a 'bachelor uncle' can easily be dismissed as dull and odd, somehow making it seem unimportant to get to know him. This poet recalls one incident about his uncle which leaves him uneasy over the fact that he never took the time to get to know his uncle ...

ELEGY FOR A BACHELOR UNCLE

We knew too much about him, and too little,
our mother's only brother, our fat, apologetic uncle,
who had always lived at home, at our grandmother's house,
because of habit, or the drift of a few years too many,
or because, as he said, she needed him.
His room was fringed with the dead shells of his hobbies
and the few books he was always intending to finish.

Growing up, we took it for granted that he should be
text-book illustration of a popular theory,
complete with selfish possessive mother, security,
and mannerisms too dull, too ingrown, to be borne
at close quarters. On the occasions when we called
we always left early, brazen with excuses.

He was not fifty when he died, leaving only my grandmother
shocked and unprepared, groping for a handkerchief.
We know too much about him, and too little,
    because now that he is dead
I think of a day shortly before the end
when he put a record on for me and my new bride –
it was a dance-thing old as the thick shellac disc
its sound had been scored into – and there
on the scratched veranda he asked her to dance,
spinning her round and round effortlessly. I was
    embarrassed –
but he smiled, and was unfamiliar
and at ease, and I saw a drowned young man,
my uncle, urging through the mediocre decades,
groping up to the last rim of Possible, yet,
forgetting the mirror and all the intractable measurements.
But the record lasted only three minutes;
and I took her away quickly. Now I must live
among acts not done and words too long unsaid.
I knew too little; and he found me out.
I wish I could believe him wholly dead.

THOMAS SHAPCOTT

Getting to Know a Bachelor Uncle

(1) How could 'the drift of a few years too many' cause a person to end up always living at home?

(2) 'His room was fringed with the dead shells of his hobbies'. How do the words 'fringed' and 'dead shells' actually cause you to picture his room?

(3) In the second stanza the words 'we took it for granted' and 'we always left early, brazen with excuses' tell us something about how the poet feels about his behaviour. How does he feel?

(4) How do we know that most of the family were not surprised at the bachelor uncle's death?

(5) 'I was embarrassed'. What was it that caused the poet's embarrassment?

(6) Explain what you think the poet means by his description of his uncle as being 'unfamiliar and at ease'.

(7) This incident exposes the poet to a new way of looking at his uncle. What new insights does he gain? How does he see his uncle differently?

(8) Account for the fact that the poet took his wife away quickly.

(9) What does the poet mean by the words 'we knew too much about him, and too little'?

(10) How would you describe the poet's feelings before and after this incident?

(11) What do you think the last line means?

(12) If you were to draw a message from this poem, how would you state it?

18 Comparing Poems

Work

Some people find their work enjoyable, others do not. 'The Dogman' and 'Road Workers' provide us with varying attitudes to work.

THE DOGMAN

The dogman dangles from the clouds,
Astride a beam of swinging air,
Unrealised hero of the crowds,
Whose upturned faces dimly stare

Like daisies watching from the ground,
Arrayed in far-off random files.
Their homage rises without sound
In grave content or drifting smiles.

The earth is open to his eye,
Spreading before him like a chart,
From the blue-washed bland of sea and sky
To where the mountains lie apart.

Beneath his feet the city falls
In patterns of great blocks and spires,
A sumptuous Gulliver who sprawls
In bond to man's minute desires.

He is immune, a bird, a song,
A shaft of light, a glowing sun,
A god who ploughs above the throng.
A man reflecting all in one.

Propelled by joy, his love in spate.
He rides the climbing sky, and sings.
Another lark at heaven's gate
To another world his aubade brings.

It sends the mind down flues of time
To where all men in memory meet,
A hunter's song, a song to climb
The dawn, uncouth, yet wild and sweet.

Spent eyes revive and spill delight.
Dead hearts resolve to live again.
Once more a man upon a height
Recalls their dignity to men.

ROBERT CLARK

The Poet Comments

Many of my poems start with a 'given' line – that is, a line that suddenly comes without conscious thought. It sounds easy, but the easiness stops at that point. The first two lines of *The Dogman* came in this way after an incident on my way to the office one morning. As I was passing a tall building in the course of erection I heard a song in the air. I looked up and there was the flying dogman, astride a beam, singing as if the world were his. Then I became conscious that people around me were also looking up. It was a magical moment. The first two lines came into my mind as I went on my way.

Robert Clark

ROAD WORKERS

Today is yesterday, and the long week drowses:
Their only change is that the street they make
Creeps slowly on past other trees and houses,
Slower than their shuffle of white boots on aching feet.
Today is yesterday
But tomorrow will be pay,
And the white stone which their hammers break
Grins back at them in the steady heat.

The cold water-bag is lifted to white lips
As white perspiration drips
Down to the thirsting stone, and the lips turn
With 'How's the time, mate?'
Barely a tone of concern
For it's not their good luck to be late.

All they want is time to go, to down tools:
But, quicker than they think, their time is going;
Youth is gone, and the white grin ridicules
The idea of their changing and knowing
A labour which the clock forgets,
A life not felt as wasted each time the sun sets.

ALEC CHOATE

Thinking About Work

(1) Explain the meaning of 'Today is yesterday'.
(2) How does the poet create the impression that the road work is proceeding very slowly?
(3) 'Their shuffle'. What do these words reveal about the road workers' attitude to their work?
(4) What is the only real incentive that the road workers have?
(5) 'Grins back at them'. Why does the white stone seem to grin back at the road workers?
(6) What evidence can you find to show that the work is physically demanding?

(7) What does the poet achieve by using the dialogue: 'How's the time, mate?'?
(8) What words of the poet convey the intensity of the heat?
(9) What does the poet mean by: 'For it's not their good luck to be late'?
(10) Explain what the poet means by: 'But, quicker than they think, their time is going'.
(11) What do you think was the poet's purpose in writing this poem?
(12) Which of the two poems, 'The Dogman' and 'Road Workers', did you enjoy more? Why?

Sharks

Two poets give their reaction to the sudden appearance near the shoreline of the denizen of the deep, the shark.

THE SHARK

There, in the first breaker, was the shark's shape
trailing the pilchards black in their escape;
so tightly packed, they blacked out the sea
just as a storm cloud does the blue sky.
But, ignorantly, the immigrant waded right in.
'Get out! Get out, you fool'; some bawled above the din
and train-noise of the rolling surf.
Unheard of, in Poland, any danger from a wolf
in the water. Why were they crying,
trying to divert
the surfer from his pleasure? In a sea-girt
country he was living now. No warring Prussia,
no fear, ancient fear, of old steam-roller Russia.
In a sea-girt country he was living without fear,
and now they must tell him, death loiters near.

JOHN BLIGHT

Beware of the Shark

(1) Why had the shark approached the shoreline?
(2) What word emphasizes the large numbers of pilchards?
(3) What does the poet achieve by introducing dialogue into his poem?
(4) What does the poet mean by 'train-noise of the rolling surf'?
(5) Why was the immigrant ignorant of the danger of sharks?
(6) 'A wolf in the water'. Do you think this phrase is a good description of a shark? Why?
(7) What is the meaning of 'a sea-girt country'?
(8) What 'ancient fear' is the poet referring to? What new fear could the immigrant become aware of?
(9) What is the meaning of the words 'death loiters near'?
(10) What is the poet's message for the reader?

THE SHARKS

Well, then, the last day the sharks appeared.
Dark fins appear, innocent
as if in fair warning. The sea becomes
sinister, are they everywhere?
I tell you, they break six feet of water.
Isn't it the same sea, and won't we
play in it any more?
I like it clear and not
too calm, enough waves
to fly in on. For the first time
I dared to swim out of my depth.
It was sundown when they came, the time
when a sheen of copper stills the sea,
not dark enough for moonlight, clear enough
to see them easily. Dark
the sharp lift of the fins.

DENISE LEVERTOV

Viewing the Sharks

(1) Why does the poet describe the appearance of dark fins of the sharks as 'innocent as if in fair warning'?

(2) What is the meaning of 'The sea becomes sinister'?

(3) What words of the poet suggest that there were very many sharks?

(4) What is the meaning of 'they break six feet of water'?

(5) What is the meaning of 'a sheen of copper stills the sea'?

(6) What evidence can you find to show that this poem was written from personal experience?

(7) What are the poet's feelings about sharks and the sea?

(8) Which of the two poems about sharks did you prefer? Give reasons for your choice.

The Bomb

On the morning of 6 August 1945, a lone American B-29, *Enola Gay*, was flying at 31,000 feet (9,500 metres) over the centre of the Japanese city of Hiroshima. The President of the United States had previously issued instructions that the first atomic bomb be dropped on Hiroshima.

A few minutes after Colonel Tibbets, the captain of *Enola Gay*, had given the order for the dropping of the bomb, there was a massive explosion, followed by a gigantic mushroom cloud. The bomb's blast had killed or injured more than half the city's population of 320,000 persons and had destroyed most of the homes. Three days later another bomb was dropped on Nagasaki with similar devastating results.

In the poems that follow, the poets Angela Clifton and Alex Skovron present their feelings about the dropping of these bombs on the Japanese people.

HIROSHIMA

The bomb burst like a flower,
And grew upwards under the sun.
And men stood afar off, and wondered
What was the meaning of this?
Then the flower died, and they partly forgot
What had happened that summer day.
But in later years terror reigned in the land,
For the deadly blight of the flower had fallen on men,
And as they died, they cried to the stars to avenge
This inhumanity of man to man.

And future generations inherited
A sorrow, and a remembrance of it,
And a lesson drawn from their ancestors' futility.

ANGELA M. CLIFTON

A GIRL OF NAGASAKI
9 August 1945

I

The moon is a wet cork.
Rummage through your moonfresh morning dream
with no dark yearning
but preserve. Savour the clarity your rebirth frees.
The moon is Japanese.

II

This sun must be God.
My shadow stands frozen in the blizzard's beam
and daylight deafens.
I drink the black lightning of momentary trees,
the sun is on its knees.

III

The moon is a dry disc.
Listen to the scrapings of a sunspent gleam
along the road of ash.
Scratch with setting eyes the astronomy you feared.
The moon has disappeared.

IV

My soul is flapping
in the Nagasaki breeze I ran through yesterday:
a thousand years ago
my ancestors fly kites into the noon. I have
no need of these.

I listen, listen to the unforgetting moon.
The moon is Japanese.

ALEX SKOVRON

The Poet Comments

I.

In the first stanza, the moon represents fullness and peace; it presides over the girl's *rebirth* out of the night. The image *wet cork* also suggests the lightness (innocence) and resilience of childhood. It is the start of a new day, all seems at peace and in order – is not the very moon *Japanese*?

II.

The sun here is of course the explosion of the atomic bomb. Its blast is so dazzling that the 'other' sun appears to be *on its knees* (completely humbled). Sense impressions tumble over each other chaotically.

III.
In the horror's aftermath, the wholesome three-dimensional cork has become a two-dimensional *dry disc*: the image now is one of flatness and desolation. Evening has returned, but the moonlight is reduced to pathetic *scrapings* as it explores the scene of devastation. The girl is dying: her *setting eyes* take in for the last time a night-sky she was once afraid of.

IV.
She is dead, and merges timelessly with the spirit of her ancestors. The moon, *unforgetting*, will bear witness, as it has always done, to the ongoing sufferings of humanity (and to the 'night' side of our nature). The moon is Japanese – it knows and feels the pain of the people of Japan – but at the same time it is no less the moon of every suffering nation and individual on earth.

Alex Skovron

School Days

THE PLACE'S FAULT

Once, after a rotten day at school –
Sweat on my fingers, pages thumbed with smears,
Cane smashing down to make me keep them neat –
I blinked out to the sunlight and the heat
And stumbled up the hill, still swallowing tears.
A stone hissed past my ear – 'Yah! *gurt* fat fool!'

Some urchins waited for me by my gate.
I shouted swear-words at them, walked away.
'Yeller,' they yelled, "e's yeller!' And they flung
Clods, stones, bricks – anything to make me run.
I ran, all right, up hill all scorching day
With 'yeller' in my ears. 'I'm not, I'm not!'

Another time, playing too near the shops –
Oddly, no doubt, I'm told I was quite odd,
Making, no doubt, a noise – a girl in slacks
Came out and told some kids 'Run round the back,
Bash in his back door, smash up his back yard,
And if he yells I'll go and fetch the cops.'

And what a rush I had to lock those doors
Before that rabble reached them! What desire
I've had these twenty years to lock away
That place where fingers pointed out my play,
Where even the grass was tangled with barbed wire,
Where through the streets I waged continual wars!

183

We left (it was a temporary halt)
The knots of ragged kids, the wired-off beach,
Faces behind the blinds. I'll not return;
There's nothing there I haven't had to learn,
And I've learnt nothing that I'd care to teach
Except that I know it was the place's fault.

PHILIP HOBSBAUM

Examining the Place's Fault

(1) Why was 'rotten' a suitable word to describe the boy's experiences at school?
(2) 'A stone *hissed* past my ear'. Why is 'hissed' a good word for the poet to have used?
(3) What does the poet achieve by using dialogue in the poem?
(4) Do you think the boy was 'odd'? Why or why not?
(5) Explain the meaning of 'through the streets I waged continual wars'.
(6) What does the poet mean by 'knots of ragged kids'?
(7) 'I'll not return'. Why does the poet say this?
(8) What did you learn about the character of the boy as you read the poem?
(9) What did you learn about human nature from your reading of the poem?
(10) Do you think it was 'the place's fault'? Why or why not?

MID-TERM BREAK

I sat all morning in the college sick bay
Counting bells knelling classes to a close,
At two o'clock our neighbours drove me home.

In the porch I met my father crying –
He had always taken funerals in his stride –
And Big Jim Evans saying it was a hard blow.

The baby cooed and laughed and rocked the pram
When I came in, and I was embarrassed
By old men standing up to shake my hand

And tell me they were 'sorry for my trouble',
Whispers informed strangers I was the eldest,
Away at school, as my mother held my hand

In hers and coughed out angry tearless sighs.
At ten o'clock the ambulance arrived
With the corpse, stanched and bandaged by the nurses.

Next morning I went up into the room. Snowdrops
And candles soothed the bedside; I saw him
For the first time in six weeks. Paler now,

Wearing a poppy bruise on his left temple,
He lay in the four foot box as in his cot.
No gaudy scars, the bumper knocked him clear.

A four foot box, a foot for every year.

SEAMUS HEANEY

Experiencing a Tragedy

(1) Why was the school boy waiting in the college sick bay?
(2) What is the meaning of 'bells knelling classes to a close'?
(3) What was the father's reaction to the death in the family?
(4) How did the old men treat the school boy when he arrived home after being away at school?
(5) How did the mother react to the death of her son?
(6) What is the meaning of 'Wearing a poppy bruise on his left temple'?
(7) How had the child been killed?
(8) Explain the meaning of 'A four foot box, a foot for every year'.
(9) Why do you think the poet wrote this poem?
(10) What feelings did you experience as you read this poem?
(11) Which poem did you prefer – 'The Place's Fault' or 'Mid-term Break'? Why?

11 Comment on the title ?

Trains

'Morning Express' was written by Siegfried Sassoon, a British poet famous for his war poetry.

'On the Night Train' is one of Henry Lawson's poems. He died in 1922, but he is still remembered for his short stories and ballads about the Australian bush. Sassoon concentrates on the train's departure, but Lawson vividly describes the train journey at night through the Australian bush, which he greatly loved. Notice how the approach of both poets to their subject matter differs greatly.

MORNING EXPRESS

Along the wind-swept platform, pinched and white,
The travellers stand in pools of wintry light,
Offering themselves to morn's long, slanting arrows.
The train's due; porters trundle laden barrows.
The train steams in, volleying resplendent clouds
Of sun-blown vapour. Hither and about,
Scared people hurry, storming the doors in crowds.
The officials seem to waken with a shout,
Resolved to hoist and plunder; some to the vans
Leap; others rumble the milk in gleaming cans.

Boys, indolent-eyed, from baskets leaning back,
Question each face; a man with a hammer steals
Stooping from coach to coach; with clang and clack,
Touches and tests, and listens to the wheels.
Guard sounds a warning whistle, points to the clock
With brandished flag, and on his folded flock
Claps the last door: the monster grunts: 'Enough!'
Tightening his load of links with pant and puff.
Under the arch, then forth into blue day,
Glide the processional windows on their way,
And glimpse the stately folk who sit at ease
To view the world like kings taking the seas
In prosperous weather: drifting banners tell
Their progress to the counties; with them goes
The clamour of their journeying; while those
Who sped them stand to wave a last farewell.

SIEGFRIED SASSOON

ON THE NIGHT TRAIN

Have you seen the Bush by moonlight, from the train, go
        running by,
Here a patch of glassy water, there a glimpse of misty sky?
Have you heard the still voice calling, yet so warm, and yet
        so cold:
'I'm the Mother-Bush that bore you! Come to me when you
        are old'?

Did you see the Bush below you sweeping darkly to the range,
All unchanged and all unchanging, yet so very old and strange!
Did you hear the Bush a-calling, when your heart was young
        and bold:
'I'm the Mother-Bush that nursed you! Come to me when
        you are old'?

Through the long, vociferous cutting as the night train
        swiftly sped,
Did you hear the grey Bush calling from the pine-ridge
        overhead:
'You have seen the seas and cities; all seems done, and all
        seems told;
I'm the Mother-Bush that loves you! Come to me, now you
        are old'?

HENRY LAWSON

Winter

ONE WINTER MORNING

One winter morning when the sun
was muted by the lifting mist
I saw a dew-bright magpie run
along the ground, upon the frost,
with open beak brimful of song.

I stood within the circled mist
and watched his singing bring the sun.
I saw the glistening of the frost
cadenza with his trilling run.
The mist around us rose like song.

Like song the answer of the sun
gave back the world I'd thought well lost;
the magpie thinking this well done
stopped singing. Then with head down-thrust
he nibbled dew. He raised his head.

The liquid in his beak he tossed
with such a flash of silver sun
it made me laugh, it made me thrust
my head like his. And that well done
the mist had gone. I raised my head,

and all around me moved the sun.

RAY MATHEW

The Poet Comments

I was on my way to work – a dreary job – moping my way across a sports oval in Sydney University grounds. There was a fog-mist and, somewhere above it, the sun, but I was looking at the ground. Suddenly I heard a bird singing and, looking to see him, I noticed that the mist was rising in a circle round him – round me. Every step I took, the circle moved.

That's how it began, the poem. Later, at the job, I jotted down some phrases that had leapt in my mind. Days, weeks later I found these phrases in my collection of paper-scraps that serves as a notebook for verse; these phrases were vivid enough to re-create for *me* the feel of that morning and I tried then to shape them into a pattern that would create that same feeling for others.

Ray Mathew

WINTER

When icicles hang by the wall,
And Dick the shepherd blows his nail,
And Tom bears logs into the hall,
And milk comes frozen home in pail,
When blood is nipp'd, and ways be foul,
Then nightly sings the staring owl,
   Tu-who;
Tu-whit, tu-who – a merry note,
While greasy Joan doth keel the pot.

When all aloud the wind doth blow,
And coughing drowns the parson's saw,
And birds sit brooding in the snow,
And Marian's nose looks red and raw,
When roasted crabs hiss in the bowl,
Then nightly sings the staring owl,
   Tu-who;
Tu-whit, tu-who – a merry note,
While Greasy Joan doth keel the pot.

WILLIAM SHAKESPEARE

Some Wintry Questions

(1) 'And Dick the shepherd blows his nail'. What is Dick the shepherd doing?
(2) What is the meaning of 'When blood is nipp'd, and ways be foul'?
(3) What is the meaning of 'greasy Joan doth keel the pot'?
(4) What effect does winter have on Marian's physical appearance?
(5) 'When roasted crabs hiss in the bowl'. What words give this description a pleasant flavour?
(6) What words of the poet suggest the harshness of winter?
(7) What descriptions in the poem suggest that winter can be pleasant?
(8) What evidence can you find in the poem to show that it was written centuries ago?
(9) In what ways is 'One Winter Morning' similar to 'Winter'?
(10) Which poem did you prefer? Why?

19 Parody

A *parody* is an imitation of a poem, or piece of prose, written with the clear purpose of poking fun at the original. It is intended to be a humorous piece of writing – some of the humour deriving from the fact that we are familiar with the original and can make a mental comparison throughout, thus appreciating the wit of the parodist. Usually the original is a serious, even pretentious, piece of writing. The parody usually copies structure and metre, and much of the language, but usually replaces the original subject with something much more trivial or frivolous.

'Sir Patrick Spens' is an ancient ballad, passed down by Scottish story-tellers. The poem, an embellished account of an incident in the reign of Alexander III of Scotland, has become something of a classic, because of its antiquity. Thus it is perfect for parody! Read the abbreviated original and its parody below.

SIR PATRICK SPENS

The king sits in Dumferlin town
   Drinking the blood-red wine:
Oh where will I get a good sailor
   To sail this ship of mine?

Up and spake an eldern knight
   Sat at the king's right knee:
Sir Patrick Spens is the best sailor
   That sails upon the sea.

The king has written a broad letter
   And signed it with his hand,
And sent it to Sir Patrick Spens
   Was walking on the strand.

To Noroway, to Noroway,
   To Noroway o'er the foam,
The king's daughter to Noroway,
   'Tis thou maun bring her home.

The first line that Sir Patrick read
   A loud laugh laughed he;
The next line that Sir Patrick read
   A tear blinded his eye.

Oh who is this has done this deed,
    This ill deed done to me,
To send me out this time of the year
    To sail upon the sea?

Make haste, make haste, my merry men all;
    Our good ship sails the morn.
Oh say not so, my master dear,
    For I fear a deadly storm.

Late, late yestreen I saw the new moon
    With the old moon in her arm,
And I fear, I fear, my master dear,
    That we will come to harm.

They hadna sailed a league, a league,
    A league but barely three,
When the air grew dark, and the wind blew loud,
    And growly grew the sea.

Oh our Scotch nobles were right loth
    To wet their cork-heeled shoon,
But long ere all the play were played
    Their hats they swam aboon.

Oh long, long may their ladies sit
    With their fans into their hand
Ere ever they see Sir Patrick Spens
    Come sailing to the land.

Oh long, long may the ladies stand
    With their gold combs in their hair
Waiting for their own dear lords,
    For they'll see them no more.

Half o'er, half o'er to Aberdour
    It's fifty fathom deep,
And there lies good Sir Patrick Spens
    With the Scotch lords at his feet.

ANONYMOUS

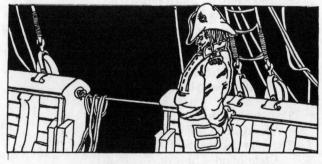

BALLAD OF THE FUTURE
(Apologies to Sir Patrick Spens)

The commissar sat in an atom-proof vault
   Sipping synthetic wine,
'O where will I get me a guinea-pig,
   For this new space-ship of mine?'

O up an spake th' electronic brain,
   That was set into his chair,
'PX653891
   Is a man that we can spare.

'He was seen to read a book last year,
   His I.Q.'s one six three
And the thought police say he goes to sleep
   At compulsory TV.'

The leader seized the tele-com
   And pressed six buttons straight.
The news came to PX65
   Whom I abbreviate.

'To the Milky Way, to the Milky Way,
   To the Milky Way in the sky,
For six thousand quarts in lead retorts
   'Tis you must go on high.'

'O who is this has done this deed
   To choose me for this place?
Am I a dog or a six-legged frog
   To be shot off into space?'

They've led him to the satellite,
   The cabin bolts are sped
With eight hundred tins of vitamins
   And a fish bowl on his head.

He saw the old moon floating past
   And sixteen moons brand new
All orbiting in a different ring
   With livestock for their crew.

He hadna sailed light-years, light-years,
   Light-years but barely three,
When he saw a chariot drawn by doves
   Bearing a fair ladye.

He shouted through his fish bowl hat
   And through the perspex too,
'O what's your fuel and how can you breathe,
   And, mainly, who are you?'

'I am the goddess Venus
   I need no mortal air,
Through space I roam to find a new home,
   And set up business there.

'The planet second from the left
   Used to belong to me,
But it's been like Glenelg on the 28th
   Since 1993.

'The stars and stripes flies from my mount,
   The red flag from both poles,
My river banks are full of Yanks,
   My soil of rocket holes.'

'Alas, madame,' our hero cried,
   'If I could go with you,
But I face death from lack of breath
   If I break this window through.'

'Fash not yourself for that,' said she,
   'The gods protect their own,
My power extends to serve my friends
   In more things than ozone.'

He's hitched his good ship up behind
   The carriage powered by dove,
At an even pace they sail through space
   PX and the queen of love.

Oh lang, lang may the commissar
   Sit in his lead-lined room
Before his good ship comes back home,
   Or tells him of her doom.

Only the electronic brain,
   When the ship's wireless went,
Heard a comic song with six verses wrong
   That fused the instrument.

J. J. BRAY

Original and Parody

(1) What features of the original *clearly* identify it as an ancient poem?
(2) Identify three examples of language in 'Sir Patrick Spens' which have Scottish origins.
(3) How would you describe the purpose of 'Sir Patrick Spens'?
(4) How would you describe the mood of 'Sir Patrick Spens'? Explain your answer.
(5) What features of the parody attempt to give it an 'ancient' feel, like the original?
(6) What other features of the parody clearly give it a 'future' feel?
(7) In what ways are the two ballads, 'Sir Patrick Spens' and 'Ballad of the Future' similar?
(8) How would you describe the purpose of this parody?

(9) How successful is the parody in terms of its:
    (a) imitating the original, and
    (b) creating humour?
(10) Which of the two poems did you enjoy more? Why?

William Wordsworth's poem 'The Daffodils', written in celebration of a beautiful scene in nature, has inspired many parodies over the years. Here is the original, and one modern parody.

THE DAFFODILS

I wandered lonely as a cloud
That floats on high o'er vales and hills,
When all at once I saw a crowd,
A host, of golden daffodils;
Beside the lake, beneath the trees,
Fluttering and dancing in the breeze.

Continuous as the stars that shine
And twinkle on the milky way,
They stretched in never-ending line
Along the margin of a bay:
Ten thousand saw I at a glance,
Tossing their heads in sprightly dance.

The waves beside them danced; but they
Out-did the sparkling waves in glee:
A poet could not but be gay,
In such a jocund company:
I gazed – and gazed – but little thought
What wealth the show to me had brought:

For oft, when on my couch I lie
In vacant or in pensive mood,
They flash upon that inward eye
Which is the bliss of solitude;
And then my heart with pleasure fills,
And dances with the daffodils.

WILLIAM WORDSWORTH

193

THOUGHTS ON A WINTER'S WALK
IN THE WOODS
(Apologies to W. W.)

I snowshoed, lonely as a cloud,
By ways the winter wood conceals,
When all at once I saw a crowd,
A host, of roaring snowmobiles;
Beside the lake, beneath the trees,
Chattering and bouncing in the breeze.

Relentlessly, the engines' whine
Resounded over hill and dale:
They spluttered, smoking, in a line
Along the helpless woodland trail:
There seemed ten thousand, at a glance;
They stripped the woods of all romance.

They drove the silence out, and worse,
Made smog as far as I could see:
A quiet man could not but curse
In such a raucous company:
I turned and shuddered, when I thought
What double pain the show had brought.

For in the city, as I sit
O'ercome by fumes of noisy cars,
My thoughts may often northwards flit
To winter woods beneath the stars;
But then, my spirit only feels
The roaring of the snowmobiles.

C. ABBOTT CONWAY, JR.

Wandering Through the Poems

(1) What season of the year seems to be central in the original?
(2) What season is central in the parody?
(3) How would you describe the mood of the original by Wordsworth?
(4) How would you describe the mood of the parody?
(5) What long-term effect does the sight of the daffodils have on the poet?
(6) What long-term effect does the sight of the snowmobiles have on the parodist?
(7) Do you agree that the parody, in this case, seems to have a serious purpose? How would you describe this purpose?
(8) Why do you think the writer of this parody chose to copy the structure of 'The Daffodils'?
(9) Compare the rhyming scheme of the two poems and comment on this aspect of the parody.
(10) How closely has the parodist copied the original structure? Support your answer.
(11) Comment on the achievement of this parody.

Christopher Marlowe's 1599 love poem, 'The Passionate Shepherd to his Love', is up-dated dramatically in Greg Smenda's parody!

THE PASSIONATE SHEPHERD TO HIS LOVE

Come live with me and be my love,
And we will all the pleasures prove,
That hills and valleys, dales and fields,
And all the craggy mountains yields.

There we will sit upon the rocks,
And see the shepherds feed their flocks,
By shallow rivers to whose falls
Melodious birds sing madrigals.

And I will make three beds of roses
With a thousand fragrant posies,
A cap of flowers, and a kirtle
Embroidered all with leaves of myrtle;

A gown made of the finest wool
Which from our pretty lambs we pull;
Fair lined slippers for the cold,
With buckles of the purest gold;

A belt of straw and ivy buds,
With coral clasps and amber studs:
And if these pleasures may thee move,
Come live with me and be my love.

The shepherd's swains shall dance and sing
For thy delight each May morning:
If these delights thy mind may move,
Then live with me and be my love.

CHRISTOPHER MARLOWE

THE PASSIONATE ASTRONAUT TO HIS LOVE

Come live with me, and be my mate
And we'll enjoy a pleasure spate,
Of hills, rocks, dales and lunar sand
And all the craggy mountains grand.

There we will sit on lunar crust
Seeing the robot tractor's thrust
By shallow craters to whose walls
Engines hum electronic madrigals.

And I will make you beds of plastic
With many controls that are fantastic
A helmet of most mod design
Printed silver with I.D. sign.

A space suit made of finest nylon
Made in labs to keep its style on
Synthetic lined boots for the freeze
With zips that shut and open with ease.

A utility belt and antenna buds
With metal clasps and platinum studs
And if these things will make your scene
Come live with me – we'll make a team.

The astronaut colony shall for you sing
The earphones filled with zong and zing.
So if these things do switch you on
Come live with me, – my mate, come on!

GREG SMENDA

The Passionate Shepherd Takes Off

(1) What meaning does the word 'prove' appear to have in the first stanza of the original?
(2) Identify two other words in the original that suggest it dates back to Elizabethan times.
(3) How would you describe the mood of the original?
(4) What mood is predominant in the parody?
(5) Comment on the phrases 'will make your scene' and 'do switch you on' in the parody.
(6) In the original a 'belt of straw' is mentioned. What parallels this in the parody?
(7) What similarities between the original and the parody can you note?
(8) What differences are there between the two poems?
(9) What provides the humour in the parody?
(10) How successful would you rate the achievement of this parody?

Robert Frost's simple, sensitive nature-poem, 'Stopping by Woods on a Snowy Evening', almost seems too sacred to parody. But humourist, Desmond Lawrence, doesn't think so! Notice how Lawrence attempts to follow the basic structure and rhyme scheme of the original. However, as happens with many parodies, the original rhyme scheme becomes a bit too restrictive. Can you identify the point at which Lawrence first moves away from the original rhyme pattern?

STOPPING BY WOODS ON A SNOWY EVENING

Whose woods these are I think I know.
His house is in the village though;
He will not see me stopping here
To watch his woods fill up with snow.

My little horse must think it queer
To stop without a farmhouse near
Between the woods and frozen lake
The darkest evening of the year.

He gives his harness bells a shake
To ask if there is some mistake.
The only other sound's the sweep
Of easy wind and downy flake.

The woods are lovely, dark and deep.
But I have promises to keep,
And miles to go before I sleep.
And miles to go before I sleep.

ROBERT FROST

STOPPING BY BOOKS ON A SHOWY EVENING

Whose books these are I think I know.
Her house is in the village though;
I think that I will walk her home
To watch her eyes fill up with glow.

Her father (with the chromy dome)
Thinks I should leave his girl alone.
But I am sure that he is wrong
She probably *loves* to have me phone.

It seems to me she's taking long–
Half an hour since the final 'gong'.
I'm *sure* she's not avoiding me,
The school's top player of Ping-Pong.

Aha! The door is now ajar.
Oh, oh, she's with that football star.
And what is more, he has a car.
Oh well, my house is not *too* far.

DESMOND LAWRENCE

Sea-fever

John Masefield's 'call' to return to the sea is an *internal* call – a need from deep within his soul. Desmond Lawrence's call to the principal's office, in contrast, is an external call – the headmaster has requested his presence! In this parody the poet initially follows the structure of the original, but then departs from it, as his humorous theme takes control! Can you see the significance of the parody's title? What is the reason for the summons to the principal's office?

SEA-FEVER

I must down to the seas again, to the lonely sea and the sky,
And all I ask is a tall ship and a star to steer her by,
And the wheel's kick and the wind's song and the white sail's
    shaking,
And a grey mist on the sea's face and grey dawn breaking.

I must down to the seas again, for the call of the running tide
Is a wild call and a clear call that may not be denied;
And all I ask is a windy day with the white clouds flying,
And the flung spray and the blown spume, and the sea-gulls
      crying.

I must down to the seas again to the vagrant gypsy life.
To the gull's way and the whale's way where the wind's like a
      whetted knife;
And all I ask is a merry yarn from a laughing fellow-rover,
And quiet sleep and a sweet dream when the long trick's over.

JOHN MASEFIELD

'C' FEVER

I must go down to the principal's office,
By the lonely chair and clock;
And all I ask is ability
To take that long, long walk.
For he's called for me and I'm going to see
What he's got upon his mind.
But I think I know how his talk will go –
'George, you are getting behind!'

I must go down to the principal's desk,
For the clarion call of his voice
Is a wild call and a clear call –
And I think I have no choice

I must go down to the principal's office
      and I'm thinking of funny jokes
To split his sides – ere he decides
      to send a note to my folks.

DESMOND LAWRENCE

Playing Around with Parody

Choose one of the five original poems from this chapter, or another 'classic' poem, and try
your hand at writing your own parody. Try to copy the structure, rhythm, rhyme and language
of the original as much as possible.

20 Relationships

Poet/songwriter/musician Rod McKuen takes the subject of forgotten names in a Christmas card index.

CHRISTMAS CARD

Where do they go
the people in our lives
that sail in like green leaves
and disappear like snow?
Not just in December
or the stormy winter months
but through the year
and through the years.

Looking up a name today
I passed through three pages of G's
and found at least six names
I can't remember or never knew.

I addressed and sent
Christmas cards out and over to them
   all the same
for what if someone
   somewhere else
fingering his phone book
passed over those same names.
Happy Christmas G's and X, Y, Z's
and thank you for whatever care
or kindness you passed along to me
that my addled brain forgot.

You I remember
because of what you are
   to me.
Merry Christmas.

ROD MCKUEN

A Closer Look at Christmas Card

(1) 'People ... that sail in like green leaves ...' What feelings do we usually associate with the appearance of green leaves at the start of spring? Is this an appropriate image for the poet to use describing people? Explain your answer.
(2) 'Disappear like snow'. How *does* snow disappear? How does the poet want us to picture these people disappearing from our memory?
(3) What does the poet imply about this phenomenon of people disappearing from our lives by the lines 'through the year/and through the years'?
(4) What evidence does the poet supply for the fact that he forgets people?
(5) Why does the poet send Christmas cards out to these forgotten people?
(6) What message does the poet want to communicate to these forgotten people?
(7) What does he blame for his memory loss?

(8) Explain how the poet makes the poem more personal in the last few lines.
(9) How does the poet contrast 'you' with those mentioned earlier?
(10) How do you respond to this poem? What apeals to you about it?

In this song/poem the writers focus on the parent-child relationship through some of its stages. The poem has a clear warning. Can you identify it?

CAT'S IN THE CRADLE

My child arrived just the other day
   he came to the world in the usual way –
   But there were planes to catch and bills to pay
   he learned to walk while I was away
     and he was talkin fore I knew it and as he grew
            he'd say

     I'm gonna be like you, Dad
     you know I'm gonna be like you.

   and the cat's in the cradle and the silver spoon
   Little boy blue and the man in the moon
   when you comin' home, Dad
     I don't know when
     but we'll get together then –
   you know we'll have a good time then

My son turned 10 just the other day
   he said, Thanks for the ball, Dad, com'on let's play
   Can you teach me to throw?
   I said not today, I got a lot to go
   He said, That's okay
     and he walked away but his smile never dimmed
     it said I'm gonna be like him, yeah
     you know I'm gonna be like him

and the cat's in the cradle and the silver spoon
Little boy blue and the man in the moon
when you comin' home, Dad

     I don't know when
     but we'll get together then –
   you know we'll have a good time then

Well he came home from college just the other day
   so much like a man I just had to say
   Son, I'm proud of you, can you sit for awhile
   He shook his head and said with a smile –
   what I'd really like, Dad, is to borrow the car keys
   see you later, can I have them please?

When you comin home, Son?
    I don't know when
    but we'll get together then
    you know we'll have a good time then

I've long since retired, my son's moved away
    I called him up just the other day
    I said I'd like to see you if you don't mind
    He said, I'd love to, Dad – if I can find the time

You see my new job's a hassle and the kids have the flu
    but it's sure nice talkin to you, Dad
    It's been nice talking to you

And as I hung up the phone, it occurred to me –
    he'd grown up just like me; my boy was just like me

and the cat's in the cradle and the silver spoon
Little boy blue and the man in the moon
when you comin home, Son?
    I don't know when
    but we'll get together then, Dad,
we're gonna have a good time then

SANDY & HARRY CHAPIN

Cradle – Thinking Deeper

(1) What preoccupies the father as his child grows?
(2) What two developmental milestones in his growing child does the father miss?
(3) The lines 'and the cat's in the cradle and the silver spoon/Little boy blue and the man in the moon' appear to tie together several unconnected memories from childhood nursery rhymes. What do you see as the poet's purpose in including this chorus?
(4) What evidence is there in the second stanza that the child still idolizes his father?
(5) Explain how the third stanza marks a change in the song?
(6) Comment on the irony in the phrase 'so much like a man' in the third stanza.
(7) What is the impact of the repeated line 'you know we'll have a good time then'?
(8) In what ways does the boy grow up to be like his father?
(9) How would you describe the relationship between the father and the son at the end of the song?
(10) How would you describe the mood of this song?
(11) What is the theme, the writers' message, in this song?

In this deeply moving poem the poet, a boy of twelve years, writes about his feelings at the time of his 13 year-old brother's death. While they were travelling in Europe, his brother Lee had contracted acute meningitis, and died suddenly in Rome. Their father records: 'Some days after we returned from Rome, Jeff wrote a poem. He started it one evening, worked on it steadily the next day, and then took two hours pecking it out on a borrowed typewriter'. It is a record of his hurt and his struggle to make any sense of Lee's death.

A BOY THIRTEEN

He had red hair,
Was thin and tall,
One could never eat as much as he,
He hiked in the sierras,
Went back-packing and even planned
a trip for the family,
Even got me to join Boy Scouts,
Always wanted me to back-pack with him,
We went to Germany,
He and I went to German schools and learned German,
Then it came time for our trip to Rome,
By train,
He and I couldn't wait to come back to
Germany and go sledding,
We passed through the Alps on the way
to Rome,
I looked up to him,
I twelve and He 'A BOY THIRTEEN',
He was five feet and nine inches tall,
I remember very well looking up and there
He was with the train window down, his head
a little way out with the wind blowing
his red hair as he watched the Alps
passing by,
He was my brother,
My only brother,
One I could play Baseball with,
Someone I could talk to.
In Germany he had bought a camera,
A single lens reflex,
He had a lot of new things going on,
Then on Feb. 6 He died.
He my only brother the one I planned to
back-pack with, the guy I wanted to sled with,
the person I looked up to, the boy that
played baseball with me, the guy with a
new camera, my brother who I could talk to, the
one who could eat as no one else, my brother that
was five feet and nine inches tall, tall and thin with
red hair 'THE BOY THAT WAS THIRTEEN'.
He died because he happened to breathe in some bacteria
that probably can only be seen under some special microscope,
I guess all I can say is I loved him and needed him and that
I don't understand.

JEFF

In this powerful brief poem the writer, a woman, remembers a relationship now severed by death.

BUT YOU DIDN'T

Remember the time you lent me your car and I dented it?
I thought you'd kill me . . .
But you didn't.

Remember the time I forgot to tell you the dance was
formal, and you came in jeans?
I thought you'd hate me . . .
But you didn't.

Remember the times I'd flirt with
other boys just to make you jealous, and
you were?
I thought you'd drop me . . .
But you didn't.

There were plenty of things you did to put up with me,
to keep me happy, to love me, and there are
so many things I wanted to tell
you when you returned from
Vietnam . . .
But you didn't.

MERRILL GLASS

James McAuley's poem focuses on the relationship between his mother and father, and its effect on him. While he regrets much, he cannot bring himself to judge them because he realizes he is under the same judgement.

BECAUSE

My father and my mother never quarrelled.
They were united in a kind of love
As daily as the *Sydney Morning Herald*,
Rather than like the eagle or the dove.

I never saw them casually touch,
Or show a moment's joy in one another.
Why should this matter to me now so much?
I think it bore more hardly on my mother,

Who had more generous feelings to express.
My father had dammed up his Irish blood
Against all drinking praying fecklessness,
And stiffened into stone and creaking wood.

His lips would make a switching sound, as though
Spontaneous impulse must be kept at bay.
That it was mainly weakness I see now,
But then my feelings curled back in dismay.

Small things can pit the memory like a cyst:
Having seen other fathers greet their sons,
I put my childish face up to be kissed
After an absence. The rebuff still stuns

My blood. The poor man's curt embarrassment
At such a delicate proffer of affection
Cut like a saw. But home the lesson went:
My tenderness thenceforth escaped detection.

My mother sang *Because*, and *Annie Laurie*,
White Wings, and other songs; her voice was sweet.
I never gave enough, and I am sorry;
But we were all closed in the same defeat.

People do what they can; they were good people,
They cared for us and loved us. Once they stood
Tall in my childhood as the school, the steeple.
How can I judge without ingratitude?

Judgment is simply trying to reject
A part of what we are because it hurts.
The living cannot call the dead collect:
They won't accept the charge, and it reverts.

It's my own judgment day that I draw near,
Descending in the past, without a clue,
Down to that central deadness; the despair
Older than any hope I ever knew.

JAMES MCAULEY

The Reasoning Behind Because

(1) The opening line appears to deliberately mislead us in some ways. Explain how this is so?
(2) What is the impact of the following description?
   ... a kind of love
      As daily as the *Sydney Morning Herald*
      Rather than like the eagle or the dove.
(3) 'Why should this matter to me now so much?' Does it matter to the poet? Why?
(4) 'That it was mainly weakness ...' What does the poet mean by 'it'?
(5) What specific incident does the poet share because it had a powerful impact on him? What impact did it have?

(6) How does the poet recall his mother's singing?

(7) 'I never gave enough'. What does he mean?

(8) Why does the poet see it as a 'defeat' that bound him and his parents? In what way was it a 'defeat'?

(9) What evidence does the poet recall that enables him to conclude 'they were good people'?

(10) Comment on the image contained in the lines: '... Once they stood/Tall in my childhood as the school, the steeple'.

(11) What is the mood of the final stanza?

(12) Does the poet believe that we are shaped by the model of our parents? Does he believe that we can blame them for our deficiencies? Support your answer from the poem.

UNNAMED

They married; it seemed the thing to do,
She, hung with child, perplexed,
Drifted in vague shallows, catching
The waft of his uncertain breath, fleeting
And streaking pell-mell between shadows
On the wet, wet night of her parent's astonishment
(Amazed at how life had overtaken them).
And he, stumble-footed and poor,
Caught buses to the office where he clerked,
Saw vicars at lunchtime, was appalled
At his own grimy fingernails,
Shrank from the goodwill of the office girls,
Sent urgent and private telegrams
Inquiring about honeymoon cabins.

So they married; at least that's what it seemed.

ROBIN THURSTON

Appreciating a Poem

Robin Thurston's poem builds a kind of poignant, impressionistic picture of two *unnamed* people who enter into the relationship of marriage because the woman is pregnant. The poet seeks to expose us to the shame of the experience and to have us share his feelings of regret.

The opening line begins bluntly with the unqualified statement, 'They married'. However, the poet almost immediately follows this with the word 'seemed', introducing into the poem a note of uncertainty. At this point the uncertainty is specifically linked to the decision to marry – 'it seemed the thing to do ...'

Notice the way we are given an impressionistic view of both people. We come to 'know' them through the poet's technique of piling phrases and words upon each other, much as an artist might use different colours or shades of colour to add to a picture. 'She' was 'hung with child'; 'she' was 'perplexed'; 'she' 'drifted in vague shallows', and so on. We are given a brief glimpse of her confused state of mind ('streaking pell-mell between shadows') on the night her parents were told. We are given a momentary picture of them, astonished, 'overtaken' by life, and we feel a touch of their despair in the description of the 'wet, wet night'.

'He' is described with the same broad-brush daubs of language. We are told 'he' was 'stumble-footed and poor'; 'he' 'caught buses to the office ...', 'saw vicars ...', 'was appalled ...', 'shrank ...', and so on. Nothing too concrete or specific is offered by the poet in the way of description. A little can be said, but not too much. After all, anonymity must be preserved. These two must remain 'unnamed'. The poem is about shame – their shame as they enter marriage, and the greater shame that thus they begin such an important relationship.

And so the poet returns to his opening statement but this time the word 'so' is added – 'so they married'. Here 'so' means 'in this way'. Furtively, surrounded by secrecy and shame, they enter into marriage. The repetition of 'seemed' as the final word in the poem rounds off the structure, reminding us that this is how it all began – 'it *seemed* the thing to do'. In this final word, the poet re-emphasizes doubts about the whole experience, about whether such a shadowy experience was wise, or can really even be called marriage. The whole experience appears slightly unreal, a kind of 'seeming' process.

The poet is certainly successful in re-creating a sense of the events. The use of vague, emotive phrases to picture the two central characters gives a kind of furtive, urgent feel to the poem. We enter into the poet's perception and share his final sense of regret about the whole situation.

Using the chapter on *Appreciating a Poem* (Chapter 1) and the above analysis of 'Unnamed' to guide you, write your own analysis of the following poem. Consider specifically:

(a) *The purpose of the poet:* What is he attempting to say or do in this poem? In other words, what is his theme?

(b) *The technique of the poet:* Analyse some of the words and phrases used, commenting on their effect. Consider the overall image of grandfather as a kind of 'clock' for the family, and the play on certain words, such as 'striking' and 'run down'. What is the effect of this in the poem?

(c) *The achievement of the poet:* How successfully has the purpose been met? Share your response to the poem and the reasons why it has affected you in this way.

A STRIKING OLD MAN

When grandfather first came to us
We did not know how old he was
Nor how reliable.
Regular as clockwork he wound up our day
And simply by his presence
Reminded us of things we had not done.
Not that he ever complained
And we liked him for that.
They had got tired of him at the other house,
So he arrived unceremoniously one afternoon in a van,
The few things that were his in a case.
They said he had been too much trouble,
He hardly fitted their way of life.
We came to love him.
On his face you could see what time had done
And quite a lot that had defeated time.
Sometimes his secrets were unlocked.
Then we could see right through
To the frailty and simplicity
Of something that had gone on working
Through so many changes.
His voice was occasionally sharp
But we knew he was just run down

And so we would make allowances.
Adjustment was easy.
For much of the day he was quiet
And we heard him mostly at night
Breathing throughout the house
In a satisfied old-fashioned way.
When visitors came he was good:
We saw them admiring his hands –
He had a certain veneer.
In time he was part of our lives.
The children lived by his looks.
He made us all feel at home.

ALASDAIR ASTON

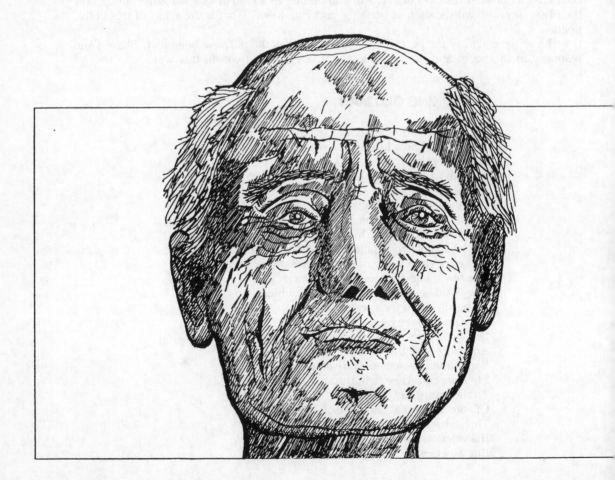

'The Suspect', by Edwin Morgan, explores the web of relationships which exist between a man suspected of murder, a dead person, and police interrogators. It is structured so that we explore these through the suspect's broken thoughts.

THE SUSPECT

Asked me for a match suddenly/with his hand up
I thought he was after my wallet
gave him a shove/he fell down
dead on the pavement at my feet
he was forty-two, a respectable man they said
anyone can have a bad heart I told the police
but they've held me five hours and don't
tell me the innocent don't feel
guilty in the glaring chair

I didn't kill you/I didn't know you
I did push you/I did fear you
accusing me from the mortuary drawer
like a damned white ghost I don't believe in
– then why were you afraid/are you used to attacks
by men who want to match/what sort
of life you lead/you were bloody quick
with your hands when you pushed him
what did you think he was and do you think
we don't know what you are/take it
all down/the sweat of the innocent by god we'll see
and not by the hundred-watt bulb of the anglepoise either
give him a clip on the ear jack/you
bastard in your shroud if I feared you then
I hate you now you
no I don't you poor dead man I put you there
I don't I don't
but just
if you could get up/to speak for me
I am on trial/do you understand
I am not guilty/whatever the light says
whatever the sweat says
/they've noticed my old scar
to be killed by a dead man is no fight
they're starting again
so/your story is he asked you for a light
– yes suddenly/and put his hand up/I thought
he was after my wallet, gave him
a shove, he fell as I told you
dead, it was his heart,
at my feet, as I said.

EDWIN MORGAN

21 Hyperbole

Hyperbole is a figure of speech which uses deliberate exaggeration in order to emphasize something. Note that the purpose of hyperbole is to emphasize in order to make more dramatic or vivid; it is not intended to deceive. Consider the following examples:

EXAMPLES:
1. I've told you millions of times not to do that!
2. He steadied himself, then swung hard, hitting the ball a mile down the fairway.
3. Will all great Neptune's ocean wash this blood
   Clean from my hand? No; this my hand will rather
   The multitudinous seas incarnadine,
   Making the green one red.

   Macbeth

4. I lov'd Ophelia; forty thousand brothers
   Could not, with all their quantity of love,
   Make up my sum ...

   Hamlet

You will note from these examples that hyperbole is a most valuable tool especially for dramatists and poets, enabling them to add emphasis, usually to the strength of someone's feelings or to the importance of a particular point being made.

'Drink to Me Only with Thine Eyes', by Ben Johnson, is a beautiful love poem, built upon the use of hyperbole. Read through the stanzas below and notice how the poet makes use of a gentle exaggeration to emphasize both the strength of his love and the beauty of the woman he loves.

In the first stanza the poet, for example, claims that even if he could have the drink of the gods ('Jove's nectar') to slake his soul-thirst for his beloved, that would not be enough to persuade him to exchange the nectar of her presence and kiss.

In the second stanza he claims that he sent a bouquet of flowers to his love so that, in her life-giving presence, it might never wither. He finishes by telling us that she returned the wreath to him, and asserts that since being in her presence it has flourished, and now provides a newly gained sweet fragrance.

These are examples of hyperbole. They are exaggerations created to help us feel the strength of the poet's love and the beauty of his beloved. Which of the two stanzas do you see as being the more artistically successful? Why?

DRINK TO ME ONLY WITH THINE EYES

Drink to me only with thine eyes,
   And I will pledge with mine;
Or leave a kiss but in the cup,
   And I'll not look for wine.
The thirst that from the soul doth rise,
   Doth ask a drink divine:
But might I of Jove's nectar sup,
   I would not change for thine.

I sent thee late a rosy wreath,
   Not so much honouring thee,
As giving it a hope that there
   It could not withered be.
But thou thereon didst only breathe,
   And sent'st it back to me:
Since when it grows, and smells, I swear,
   Not of itself, but thee.

BEN JONSON

John Donne lived from 1572 to 1631, yet he has been described by some critics as a 'modern poet'. By this term they mean to imply that he wrote honestly and lustily in his love poems – not bothering to 'pretty things up' as was the custom of most of his predecessors. In his religious poems the same honesty is seen, this time in his struggle with doubts. His words are often blunt, dramatic and urgent, as though he has not time for superficially 'sweet' language, or pretty turns of phrase.

'The Sunne Rising' is a passionate kind of monologue, which makes use of many literary devices to achieve its effect. Look for examples of hyperbole and other figures of speech as you read the poem. Do not allow youself to be put off by the Elizabethan spelling!

THE SUNNE RISING

Busie old foole, unruly Sunne,
　　Why dost thou thus,
Through windowes, and through curtaines call on us?
Must to thy motions lovers seasons run?
　　Sawcy pedantique wretch, goe chide
　　Late schoole boyes, and sowre prentices,
　　Goe tell Court-huntsmen, that the King will ride,
　　Call countrey ants to harvest offices;
Love, all alike, no season knowes, nor clyme,
Nor houres, dayes, moneths, which are the rags of time.

　　Thy beames, so reverend, and strong
　　Why shouldst thou thinke?
I could eclipse and cloud them with a winke,
But that I would not lose her sight so long:
　　If her eyes have not blinded thine,
　　Looke, and to morrow late, tell mee,
　　Whether both the'India's of spice and Myne
　　Be where thou leftst them, or lie here with mee.
Aske for those Kings whom thou saw'st yesterday,
And thou shalt heare, All here in one bed lay.

　　She'is all States, and all Princes, I,
　　Nothing else is.
Princes doe but play us; compar'd to this,
All honor's mimique; All wealth alchimie.
　　Thou sunne art halfe as happy'as wee,
　　In that the world's contracted thus;
　　Thine age askes ease, and since thy duties bee
　　To warme the world, that's done in warming us.
Shine here to us, and thou art every where;
This bed thy center is, these walls, thy spheare.

JOHN DONNE

Questions Rising

(1) Identify the figure of speech which dominates the opening lines of the poem. What does its use achieve in the poem?

(2) Comment on the effect of the language in the opening lines.

(3) 'Call countrey ants to harvest offices.' Comment on this image.

(4) Explain the startling comparison made in the last line of the first stanza.

(5) At the beginning of the second stanza the poet seems to suggest that the sun's strength is over-rated. How could he overcome the 'might' of the sun?

(6) The poet suggests that the sun will find, after study, that the riches of the external world ('the' India's of spice') lie with the poet. What does he mean?

(7) 'She'is all States, and all Princes, I,/Nothing else is.' Explain how this is hyperbole.

(8) Explain the hyperbole in 'To warme the world, that's done in warming us'.
(9) What is the overall effect of Donne's use of hyperbole in 'The Sunne Rising'?
(10) Briefly discuss the strengths you see in this poem.

This famous poem, by Andrew Marvell (1621–78), is written in the form of a request to the poet's coy (or shy) mistress, to grant his desire for them to make love. He argues that for them to delay makes no sense because 'at my back I always hear/Time's winged chariot hurrying near'. Much of his argument is built upon the use of a series of hyperboles describing how slowly they could move to consummate their love if there were no pressure of Time.

TO HIS COY MISTRESS

Had we but world enough, and time,
This coyness, lady, were no crime.
We would sit down, and think which way
To walk, and pass our long love's day.
Thou by the Indian Ganges' side
Should'st rubies find: I by the tide
Of Humber would complain. I would
Love you ten years before the Flood,
And you should, if you please, refuse
Till the conversion of the Jews.
My vegetable love should grow
Vaster than empires, and more slow.
An hundred years should go to praise
Thine eyes, and on thy forehead gaze:
Two hundred to adore each breast:
But thirty thousand to the rest;
An age at least to every part,
And the last age should show your heart.
For, lady, you deserve this state,
Nor would I love at lower rate.
　　But at my back I always hear
Time's winged chariot hurrying near:
And yonder all before us lie
Deserts of vast eternity.
Thy beauty shall no more be found;
Nor, in thy marble vault, shall sound
My echoing Song: then Worms shall try
That long preserv'd Virginity:
And your quaint Honour turn to dust;
And into ashes all my Lust.
The Grave's a fine and private place,
But none I think do there embrace.
　　Now therefore, while the youthful hew
Sits on thy skin like morning dew,
And while thy willing Soul transpires
At every pore with instant Fires,
Now let us sport us while we may;
And now, like am'rous birds of prey,

Rather at once our Time devour,
Than languish in his slow-chapt pow'r.
Let us roll all our Strength, and all
Our sweetness, up into one Ball:
And tear our Pleasures with rough strife,
Thorough the Iron gates of Life.
Thus, though we cannot make our Sun
Stand still, yet we will make him run.

ANDREW MARVELL

Questions on Time and Love

(1) In your own words express the point the poet makes so succinctly in his opening two lines.

(2) The way that the poet and his love would pass their 'long love's day' if there were no pressure of time is described by a series of hyperboles. Select one and comment upon its effect.

(3) How would you describe the *overall* effect in the poem of the poet's use of deliberate exaggeration?

(4) Marvell, like Donne, has been classified as a Metaphysical Poet. One of the features of the poetry of this group is their use of clever, and unexpected, images and comparisons, often worked out at length within a poem. How do you see this feature applying in 'To His Coy Mistress'?

(5) Comment on the appropriateness of the rhythm in 'Vaster than empires, and more slow'.

(6) 'Deserts of vast eternity'. Comment on how this image suits the poet's argument.

(7) What would you identify as the main distinguishing features of a poem like this?

(8) How would you rate the poet's *seriousness* in writing a poem like this? Is he *really* trying to persuade his mistress? If not, how would you describe the purpose of the poem?

(9) How successful would you rate this poem in terms of what you see as its purpose?

(10) Why do you think so many poets use hyperbole to praise, or describe, love?

In 'Skydiver', Roger McGough tells us about Uncle Terry – a man whose delight in skydiving was so great that eventually he got completely carried away by it! Notice the comparisons in the first stanza (the earth 'like a springcleaned counterpane' and 'the wind his safety net'), each one helping us 'feel' something of Uncle Terry's delightful world. The second stanza invites us to indulge in fantasy, and accept that Uncle Terry simply stayed there one day, living in the sky. In the third stanza we are invited, via some beautiful images, to picture Uncle Terry completely absorbed in his surroundings. Notice how the poem depends, for its effect, upon the use of deliberate exaggeration, or hyperbole. It is because of this exaggeration that we begin to feel some of the 'dizzy . . . joy' of Uncle Terry, the skydiver.

Why do you think the spacing between the words and lines begins to increase as the poem moves to its finish? Is this more than a gimmick?

SKYDIVER

Uncle Terry was a skydiver,
He liked best
the earth spread out beneath him
like a springcleaned counterpane.
The wind his safety net.

He free fell every day
and liked it so much
he decided to stay.
And they say he's still there
sunbathing in the air.

He sleeps each night
tucked up in moonlight
wakes at dawn
and chases clouds.

Living   off   the   food   birds   bring

Uncle   Terry   on   the   wing

away   from   it   all

dizzy   with   joy.

ROGER MCGOUGH

Take a couple of bushmen with a couple of tall stories and you have all the ingredients you need for some exaggeration.

THE QUEENSLAND DOG

A stranger came from New South Wales, and he was tall and brown.
He lined beside us at the bar, he sank his schooners down;
And all the time, to pass the time, he told us doubtful tales
Of the country he laid claim to: remarkable New South Wales.

With soil so rich and fertile (so ran his line of talk)
That pumpkin vines fair sprinted along, as fast as a man could walk!
He said it took two hours, sometimes, to walk through the hollow
    logs
For timber loomed so broad and tall. And then he mentioned
    dogs. . . .

Little Maginnis spoke up then, arising from his seat;
'I dunno about them other things, but at dogs we got you beat.
I was boundary-riding once', he said, 'on a station Longreach way,
And lost me bearings among the hills, right at the end of day.
So I let the old horse poke along and find his own way in the dark
Until in the distance I seen a light. And then I heard him bark!
Well, station dogs is mostly noise, I never took no heed;
I only wanted me bearings (and I could've done with a feed).
So I went on riding towards the light, just follering me nose,
And then I hear him bark again – and this time he's up close.
I needn't of worried, he's only a dog, the sort cow-cockies keep,
That keep the dingoes away at night, then lay all day and sleep.
When he gets near me he whines a bit; friendly, quiet and deep.
Then he stands on his hind legs and licks me face, and I see his gentle
    eye
And his dusty coat and wagging tail by the starlight in the sky . . .
And the horse I was sitting on at the time was seventeen hands high.'
The stranger paled and admitted (with the wind took out of his sails)
That the dogs grow bigger in Queensland then they do in New South
    Wales.

W. N. SCOTT

Chewing Things Over

(1) How does the first stanza of the poem suggest that exaggerated events are about to follow?
(2) What hyperbole is used to describe the growth of pumpkin vines in New South Wales?
(3) What is the hyperbole used to describe the timber of New South Wales?
(4) What is there about little Maginnis' speech that suggests he has had little formal education?
(5) What was normal about the station dog that accosted little Maginnis as he rode towards the homestead light?
(6) Explain the hyperbole that is subtly introduced with the information about how the dog finally greeted little Maginnis?

(7) The very existence of the hyperbole at the end depends upon us recognizing something simple about the measurement 'seventeen hands high'. What is it?
(8) How did the stranger react to Maginnis' tall story?
(9) What is your reaction to the hyperbole at the end of this poem?
(10) Hyperbole is exaggeration for the purpose of emphasis. What additional purpose does the hyperbole in this poem serve?

The use of hyperbole piled upon hyperbole can result in vivid description. Notice how this works in 'Mrs Reece Laughs'. As you read, also notice the following:

(a) The poem opens on a comparative note, telling us that a normal person's laughter is a short-lived affair ('A sudden wave that breaks and dies in breaking'). However, with Mrs Reece, laughter is different. We are led to expect great things of Mrs Reece.
(b) The laughter of Mrs Reece is then compared to a plant – a tree perhaps – suggested by the words 'germinates', 'spreads' and 'girth'. A redundancy is an unnecessary repetition. What do you think the poet means by 'formidable redundancies of mirth'?
(c) Towards the middle of the poem, the tree image is made explicit as 'a great elm with all its mounds of leaves'. Now the emphasis is on movement, initially deep, immense, inner movement – like the beginning of a volcanic eruption.
(d) With the words 'Takes her and shakes her . . .' the poet focuses our attention on aspects of Mrs Reece's outward appearance: she 'sobs', 'gapes', and 'crows'. There is a 'lifting of huge hands' and the stays of her corsets creak while her face expands in folds of skin.
(e) Appropriately, the poem ends just as the laughter finishes. Mrs Reece is left feeble and over-heated from her overwhelming experience.

MRS REECE LAUGHS

Laughter, with us, is no great undertaking;
A sudden wave that breaks and dies in breaking.
Laughter with Mrs Reece is much less simple:
It germinates, it spreads, dimple by dimple,
From small beginnings, things of easy girth,
To formidable redundancies of mirth.
Clusters of subterranean chuckles rise,
And presently the circles of her eyes
Close into slits, and all the woman heaves
As a great elm with all its mound of leaves
Wallows before the storm. From hidden sources
A mustering of blind volcanic forces
Takes her and shakes her till she sobs and gapes.
Then all that load of bottled mirth escapes
In one wild crow, a lifting of huge hands,
And creaking stays, a visage that expands
In scarlet ridge and furrow. Thence collapse,
A hanging head, a feeble hand that flaps
An apron-end to stir an air and waft
A streaming face . . . And Mrs Reece has laughed.

MARTIN ARMSTRONG

22 Youth and Age

In this poem by Shakespeare, Youth and Age have not bridged any of their traditional gaps.

CRABBED AGE AND YOUTH

Crabbed Age and Youth
Cannot live together:
Youth is full of pleasance,
Age is full of care;
Youth like summer morn,
Age like winter weather;
Youth like summer brave,
Age like winter bare.
Youth is full of sport,
Age's breath is short;
Youth is nimble, Age is lame;
Youth is hot and bold,
Age is weak, and cold;
Youth is wild, and Age is tame.
Age, I do abhor thee;
Youth, I do adore thee;
O, my Love, my Love is young!
Age, I do defy thee:
O, sweet shepherd, hie thee!
For methinks thou stay'st too long.

WILLIAM SHAKESPEARE

A rebel is someone who resents and mistrusts authority. In this poem, the rebel meets every consideration or situation with a contrary response. Notice, however, that the rebel in the poem is predictable. So is she or he a real rebel? One advantage of being a rebel is that everyone notices you. Another advantage for society is that the rebel offers an alternative to the accepted way of doing things. Now, keeping the last part of the poem in mind – 'It is very good that we have rebels,/You may not find it very good to be one' – comment on some of the possible disadvantages of being a rebel.

THE REBEL

When everybody has short hair,
The rebel lets his hair grow long.

When everybody has long hair,
The rebels cuts his hair short.

When everybody talks during the lesson,
The rebel doesn't say a word.

When nobody talks during the lesson,
The rebel creates a disturbance.

When everybody wears a uniform,
The rebel dresses in fantastic clothes.

When everybody wears fantastic clothes,
The rebel dresses soberly.

In the company of dog lovers,
The rebel expresses a preference for cats.

In the company of cat lovers,
The rebel puts in a good word for dogs.

When everybody is praising the sun,
The rebel remarks on the need for rain.

When everybody is greeting the rain,
The rebel regrets the absence of sun.

When everybody goes to the meeting,
The rebel stays at home and reads a book.

When everybody stays at home and reads a book,
The rebel goes to the meeting.

When everybody says, Yes please,
The rebel says, No thank you.

When everybody says, No thank you,
The rebel says, Yes please.

It is very good that we have rebels,
You may not find it very good to be one.

D. J. ENRIGHT

For some parents adolescence eventually becomes 'just a passing phase'.

IT MAY BE FOUND NECESSARY
TO APPLY A SECOND COAT

He was
A wild young man
He couldn't care
For what they thought, or said –
He had his own ideas.
His looks provoked his father to protest:
'In my young days
A man who dressed like *that*
Was not a man'.
His mother grew afraid
Of this fierce strange young man
– Her son.

He's all right now
He has 'improved' with age
'I knew it – just a passing phase
They all go through',
His mother smiles.
He's got a good, safe job,
A wife, a lawn-mower . . .
He's alright now.

LESLEY RIGG

Probing the Process of Applying a Second Coat

(1) The poem's title suggests the directions on a tin of paint. What other meaning is present in the title?
(2) What evidence can you find to show that the young man wanted to be independent of others?
(3) 'His looks provoked his father to protest'. What aspect of his looks provoked his father?
(4) What traditional view of manhood was held by the young man's father?
(5) How did the mother react to 'this fierce strange young man'?
(6) In the second stanza why do you think the word 'improved' is contained in quotation marks?
(7) What phrase does the mother use to describe her son's lost adolescence?
(8) What does possessing a lawnmower signify about the young man's 'improved' attitude to life?
(9) What contrast is there between the young man's behaviour in the first and second stanzas?
(10) What are your feelings towards the 'wild young man'?
(11) What do you think is the poet's message to the reader?

The following poem was written by an old lady in the geriatric ward of a hospital, near Dundee, Scotland. It was found by a nurse checking the old lady's possessions after she had died.

A CRABBIT OLD WOMAN
WROTE THIS

What do you see nurses, what do you see?
Are you thinking when you are looking at me –
A crabbit old women, not very wise,
Uncertain of habit, with far-away eyes,
Who dribbles her food and makes no reply
When you say in a loud voice – 'I do wish you'd try'.
Who seems not to notice the things that you do,
And forever is losing a stocking or shoe.
Who, unresisting or not, lets you do as you will,
With bathing and feeding, the long day to fill.
Is that what you are thinking, is that what you see?
Then open your eyes, nurse, you're not looking at me.
I'll tell you who I am as I sit here so still,
As I use at your bidding, as I eat at your will.
I'm a small child of ten with a father and mother,
Brothers and sisters, who love one another.
A young girl of sixteen with wings on her feet,
Dreaming that soon now a lover she'll meet;
A bride soon at twenty – my heart gives a leap,
Remembering the vows that I promised to keep;
At twenty-five now I have young of my own,
Who need me to build a secure, happy home;
A woman of thirty, my young now grow fast,
Bound to each other with ties that should last;
At forty, my young sons have grown and are gone.
But my man's beside me to see I don't mourn.
At fifty once more babies play round my knee,
Again we know children, my loved one and me.
Dark days are upon me, my husband is dead,
I look at the future, I shudder with dread.
For my young are all rearing young of their own,
And I think of the years and the love that I've known.
I'm an old woman now and nature is cruel –
Tis her jest to make old age look like a fool.
The body it crumbles, grace and vigour depart,
There is now a stone where I once had a heart;
But inside this old carcase a young girl still swells,
And now and again my battered heart swells.
I remember the joys, I remember the pain,
And I'm loving and living life over again.
I think of the years all too few – gone too fast,
And accept the stark fact that nothing can last.
So open your eyes, nurses, open and see,
Not a crabbit old woman, look closer – see ME!

ANONYMOUS

According to the poet, Bert Jansen, adolescence is a time of strong likes and dislikes.

ADOLESCENCE

I like lowered cars
Thundering heavily and evenly under the bonnet.
A fox or kangaroo crossed out in telescopic sights.
If you think I'm a sadist,
You haven't heard my maddest.
I thoroughly enjoy a nice big stretch,
An itch,
And certainly an exhausting sneeze.
Don't laugh
This is dinkum.
I'm thrilled by a speeding bullet's crack
Intrigued by the way elephants act.
'The Rifleman' is my favourite hero
And I love the smell of burning kero.
That is madly wrong
But I must go on.
Riding 'no hands' on my bike at night
Puddles reflecting yellow street light
This may sound mad to you
But believe me, it's true.
The worst annoyance – it drives me insane
Is sand in my teeth – emery paper's the same.
Though I think myself gregarious and easy to get on with
I don't quite like going to stomps,
And, ah yes, those shakes – I wonder why.
I like girls.
I love girls.
I adore girls.
But sometimes I wish I didn't.
I wish I had no interest in it.
I wish I were still bird-nesting, skipping meals,
Swapping eggs
Wading barefoot through swamps
And scaling towering trees, like a kid,
A proper kid.
Not standing on the corner watching girls go by.

BERT JANSEN

Adolescence – Likes and Dislikes

(1) What does the poet mean by 'thundering heavily'?
(2) 'A fox or kangaroo crossed out in telescopic sights'. What is the boy referring to?
(3) Why do you think the poet says: 'Don't laugh this is dinkum'?
(4) Why do you think the poet uses words such as 'maddest', 'madly', and 'mad'?
(5) What is the poet's worst annoyance?
(6) How does the adolescent indicate that thoughts about girls dominate his life?
(7) Why do you think the poet says: 'I wish I had no interest in it'?

(8) What does the poet mean by 'a proper kid'?

(9) Explain how the mood changes in the last part of the poem.

(10) What evidence can you find in the poem to suggest that it was written by an Australian adolescent?

(11) What have you learned about the personality of the young poet?

(12) How does the young poet give the impression that he is talking personally to the reader?

(13) What makes this poem about adolescence so appealing?

(14) Try your hand at writing your own poem about adolescence. 'I like . . .' would be an easy way to begin.

In the past, when life was simpler, people didn't have the problems they have today.

MEMOIRS FROM THE NURSING HOME

'She remembers when the whole street
would bring chairs out on to the footpath
of an evening and gossip till tea-time.
She remembers taking her peas and beans
down to the corner pub and doing the
vegetables with the other local women.'
(Sydney Morning Herald, 23.11.79)

Before the Box
And own-your-own home
People talked to each other
People cared.
One life was an important part
Of the whole.

Suddenly the seventies saw us
      isolate
Staunch in our own virtue,
Five minute vegies were equated
      with
Five minute chats.
We progressed to own-your-own
      troubles
And left the Suffering to Religion.

Rocketing into the eighties
Securely fastened
In our individual jets
Just one cloud looms
On a smug horizon.
Why is there an increase in crime,
Loneliness and Divorce?

SUE-ANNE CLENNELL

The Young Ones are different in every age and in this poem the poise and self-assurance of modern youth is observed and contrasted with old-fashioned awkwardness.

THE YOUNG ONES

They slip on to the bus, hair piled up high.
New styles each month, it seems to me. I look,
Not wanting to be seen, casting my eye
Above the unread pages of a book.

They are fifteen or so. When I was thus,
I huddled in school coats, my satchel hung
Lop-sided on my shoulder. Without fuss
These enter adolescence; being young

Seems good to them, a state we cannot reach,
No talk of 'awkward ages' now. I see
How childish gazes staring out of each
Unfinished face prove me incredibly

Old-fashioned. Yet at least I have the chance
To size up several stages – young yet old,
Doing the twist, mocking an 'old-time' dance:
So many ways to be unsure or bold.

ELIZABETH JENNINGS

Fathoming the Young Ones

(1) What aspect of the young ones' appearance attracts the poet's attention?
(2) Where is the poet and what is she pretending to be doing as she observes the young ones?
(3) How was the poet's own adolescent behaviour different from that of the young ones she is observing?
(4) What does the poet mean by 'without fuss/These enter adolescence'?
(5) Why do you think the years of adolescence would have been thought of as the 'awkward ages' in years gone by?
(6) What does the poet mean by 'each unfinished face'?
(7) What advantage does the poet find in no longer being a teenager?
(8) What example does the poet give of teenagers displaying their freedom from parental values?
(9) 'So many ways to be unsure or bold'. What comment is the poet making about adolescence?
(10) What does the poet reveal about herself in this poem?

To a youth of fifteen finding a motorcycle with its engine running, the sky seems the limit.

FIFTEEN

South of the Bridge on Seventeenth
I found back of the willows one summer
day a motorcycle with engine running
as it lay on its side, ticking over
slowly in the high grass. I was fifteen.

I admired all that pulsing gleam, the
shiny flanks, the demure headlights
fringed where it lay; I led it gently
to the road and stood with that
companion, ready and friendly. I was fifteen.

We could find the end of a road, meet
the sky on out Seventeenth. I thought about
hills, and patting the handle got back a
confident opinion. On the bridge we indulged
a forward feeling, a tremble. I was fifteen.

Thinking, back farther in the grass I found
the owner, just coming to, where he had flipped
over the rail. He had blood on his hand, was pale –
I helped him walk to his machine. He ran his hand
over it, called me good man, roared away.

I stood there, fifteen.

WILLIAM STAFFORD

Working with the Poem

(1) What words of the poet suggest the motorcycle is alive?
(2) What features of the bike are admired by the boy?
(3) How do you know that the bike has become something more to the boy than an object to be admired?
(4) What does the boy plan for himself and the bike?
(5) 'We could find the end of the road'. Why do you think the poet has used 'we' rather than 'I'?
(6) What does the poet mean by 'patting the handle got back a / confident opinion'?
(7) Explain the meaning of 'we indulged a forward feeling, a tremble'.
(8) Why do you think the poet keeps repeating the words 'I was fifteen'?
(9) Why do you think the last line of the poem is all by itself?
(10) What aspects of youth does this poem explore?

The poets of 'A Moment of Respect' and 'Old Man Burning Off' present us with their differing encounters of old age.

A MOMENT OF RESPECT

Two things I remember about my grandfather:
his threadbare trousers, and the way he adjusted
his half-hunter watch two minutes every day.

When I asked him why he needed to know the time so
exactly, he said a business man could lose a fortune
by being two minutes late for an appointment.

When he died he left two meerchaum pipes
and a golden sovereign on a chain. Somebody
threw the meerschaum pipes away, and
there was an argument about the sovereign.

On the day of his burial the church clock chimed
as he was lowered down into the clay, and all
the family advanced their watches by two minutes.

EDWIN BROCK

OLD MAN BURNING OFF

He's down again in the damp back of the yard
burning off papers, rubbish, what he can find.
The warm smoke shoulders him, his hand
shakes on the brittle matches. He would be god
strewing the heaped relics with his word
of obedient flame. All lights are consumed
into themselves; his old eyes are rheumed;
and someone keeps calling, You all right there, Dad?
They hide the matches now, and the day's papers
are taken away; he knows they have seen his face
clench in the knuckled light of the incinerator
and they think accidents, are afraid of ashes.
Ashes are clean. He sweeps around the space
each time; he will not leave them any clutter.

THOMAS SHAPCOTT

227

23 The Ballad

The Development of the Ballad

Originally ballads were songs. They were often sung by wandering minstrels, who were eagerly listened to during fairs, within castle walls and at feasts and entertainments. The listeners would be held spellbound by these dramatic tales full of stirring deeds.

At first, ballads were not printed or written down but were passed down orally from generation to generation. Because of this there are many versions of some of the more famous ballads.

Ballads are tales, which touch upon history and legend, love and passion, crimes and battles, human conflict and even supernatural events. Of course, in bygone days, it was only natural that stories about Robin Hood, who defied a repressive rule, should appear in a large number of ballads.

Ballads were most popular from the fourteenth to the seventeenth century. Many of the best ballads describing the conflicts between the Scots and the English in the border country, were composed in the fifteenth and sixteenth centuries.

Characteristics of the Ballad

The ballad is usually written in four line stanzas. Its dramatic question-answer or dialogue form is often used to develop the story in a simple and straightforward manner and to arouse the emotions of the listeners.

A common characteristic of the ballad is the repetition of lines or phrases at regular intervals. This is known as the refrain. The refrain, which probably developed from the oral tradition, helps to give the narration a smooth flow and serves to intensify its dramatic elements.

Because the ballad is most concerned with action, the narrator remains passive. After the tale has swiftly reached its tragic climax, the narrator or singer does not make any moral comment on the action. As the audience draws its own conclusion, it feels that it has been well entertained.

Because the early ballads were passed on from one person to another by word of mouth, the words sometimes changed giving each ballad its variations. Beneath is but one of the versions of the Lord Randal ballad. In others, the poisonous eels are served in a pie or are fried in butter. The poisoner in this version is his sweetheart, but in some accounts, it is a stepmother, grandmother, sister, wife or even the dying man himself.

LORD RANDAL

'O where hae ye been, Lord Randal, my son?
O where hae ye been, my handsome young man?'
'I hae been to the wild wood; mother, make my bed soon,
For I'm weary wi' hunting, and fain wad lie down.'

'Where gat ye your dinner, Lord Randal, my son?
Where gat ye your dinner, my handsome young man?'
'I dined wi' my true-love; mother, make my bed soon,
For I'm weary wi' hunting, and fain wad lie down.'

'What gat ye to your dinner, Lord Randal, my son?
What gat ye to your dinner, my handsome young man?'
'I gat eels boiled in broth; mother, make my bed soon,
For I'm weary wi' hunting, and fain wad lie down.'

'And wha gat your leavings, Lord Randal, my son?
And wha gat your leavings, my handsome young man?'
'My hawks and my hounds; mother, make my bed soon,
For I'm weary wi' hunting, and fain wad lie down.'

'What became of your bloodhounds, Lord Randal, my son?
What became of your bloodhounds, my handsome young
    man?'
'O they swelled and they died; mother, make my bed soon,
For I'm weary wi' hunting, and fain wad lie down.'

'O I fear ye are poisoned, Lord Randal, my son!
O I fear ye are poisoned, my handsome young man!'
'O yes! I am poisoned; mother, make my bed soon,
For I'm sick at the heart and I fain wad lie down.'

ANONYMOUS

Questioning Lord Randal

(1) What evidence can you find to show that this ballad was written centuries ago?
(2) At what point in the ballad do you first realize that something is wrong with Lord Randal?
(3) Why do you think the balladist keeps repeating 'For I'm weary wi' hunting, and fain wad lie down'?
(4) Who poisoned Lord Randal?
(5) What happened to Lord Randal's bloodhounds?
(6) How is the listener kept in suspense throughout the ballad?
(7) What is the tragic climax of this ballad?
(8) What comments would you make about the use of dialogue in the ballad?
(9) Why do you think this ballad was survived through the centuries?
(10) Do you think this ballad would appeal to the twentieth-century listener? Why?

Here is a traditional ballad, full of action, suspense and sadness.

LORD ULLIN'S DAUGHTER

A Chieftain to the Highlands bound,
Cries, 'Boatman, do not tarry!
And I'll give thee a silver pound
To row us o'er the ferry.'

'Now who be ye, would cross Lochgyle
This dark and stormy water?'
'O, I'm the chief of Ulva's isle,
And this, Lord Ullin's daughter.

'And fast before her father's men
Three days we've fled together;
For should he find us in the glen,
My blood would stain the heather.

'His horsemen hard behind us ride;
Should they our steps discover,
Then who will cheer my bonny bride
When they have slain her lover?'

Outspoke the hardy Highland wight,
'I'll go, my chief – I'm ready!
It is not for your silver bright,
But for your winsome lady; –

'And, by my word, the bonny bird
In danger shall not tarry;
So though the waves are raging white,
I'll row you o'er the ferry.'

By this the storm grew loud apace,
The water-wraith was shrieking;
And in the scowl of heaven each face
Grew dark as they were speaking.

But still as wilder blew the wind,
And as the night grew drearer,
Adown the glen rode armed men;
Their trampling sounded nearer.

'O haste thee, haste!' the lady cries,
'Though tempests round us gather,
I'll meet the raging of the skies,
But not an angry father.'

The boat has left a stormy land,
A stormy sea before her,
When, oh! too strong for human hand,
The tempest gathered o'er her.

And still they rowed amidst the roar
Of waters fast prevailing;
Lord Ullin reached that fatal shore. –
His wrath was changed to wailing.

For, sore dismayed, through storm and shade,
His child he did discover: –
One lovely hand she stretched for aid,
And one was round her lover.

'Come back! Come back!' he cried in grief,
'Across this stormy water;
And I'll forgive your Highland chief,
My daughter! O my daughter!'

'Twas vain: the loud waves lashed the shore,
Return or aid preventing:
The waters wild went o'er his child,
And he was left lamenting.

THOMAS CAMPBELL

Reviewing the Tragedy of Lord Ullin's Daughter

(1) What situation is this ballad describing?
(2) Explain how this is an action-filled ballad.
(3) Do you think 'Lord Ullin's Daughter' is a good title for this ballad? Why?
(4) How does the balladist build up the suspense?
(5) What is the tragic climax of this ballad?
(6) By the end of the ballad how has the attitude towards the highland chief changed?
(7) Why are the last stanzas especially sad?
(8) What is the moral of this tale?
(9) What are your feelings towards Lord Ullin?
(10) What features of this ballad would have made it popular with listeners through the centuries?

Australian Ballads

Australian ballads form a valuable record of pioneering life in a harsh land. They generally arose from real life situations as in the case of the bushranger ballads. These ballads were often written at the time the events described took place and they have a vigour and vividness that has made them very popular.

The periodical, the *Bulletin*, helped foster the growth of ballads about the Australian bush and outback adventures. Both Henry Lawson and A. B. Paterson contributed ballads to the *Bulletin*.

THE SLIPRAILS AND THE SPUR

The colours of the setting sun
Withdrew across the Western land –
He raised the sliprails, one by one,
And shot them home with trembling hand;
Her brown hands clung – her face grew pale –
Ah! quivering chin and eyes that brim! –
One quick, fierce kiss across the rail,
And, 'Good-bye, Mary!' 'Good-bye, Jim!'

Oh, he rides hard to race the pain
Who rides from love, who rides from home;
But he rides slowly home again,
Whose heart has learnt to love and roam.

A hand upon the horse's mane,
And one foot in the stirrup set,
And, stooping back to kiss again,
With 'Good-bye, Mary! don't you fret!
When I come back' – he laughed for her –
'We do not know how soon 'twill be;
I'll whistle as I round the spur –
You let the sliprails down for me.'

She gasped for sudden loss of hope,
As, with a backward wave to her,
He cantered down the grassy slope
And swiftly round the darkening spur,
Black-pencilled panels standing high,
And darkness fading into stars,
And, blurring fast against the sky,
A faint white form beside the bars.

And often at the set of sun,
In winter bleak and summer brown,
She'd steal across the little run,
And shyly let the sliprails down,
And listen there when darkness shut
The nearest spur in silence deep,
And when they called her from the hut
Steal home and cry herself to sleep.

And he rides hard to dull the pain
Who rides from one who loves him best . . .
And he rides slowly back again,
whose restless heart must rove for rest.

HENRY LAWSON

'The Sliprails and the Spur' – Thinking About Love

(1) What aspects of early pioneering life is this ballad describing?
(2) How do Jim and Mary react to their being separated?
(3) Why are 'the sliprails' important in this ballad?
(4) Why is Jim leaving home?
(5) What is your attitude towards Jim?
(6) Why do you think this bush ballad was popular in Australia at the beginning of the twentieth century?
(7) Do you think Australians today would enjoy hearing this ballad? Why
(8) How do you know that Mary loved Jim very much?
(9) Explain the meaning of 'Whose restless heart must rove for rest'.
(10) Explain the significance of the title, 'The Sliprails and the Spur'.

In this mournful ballad, the dying stockman's last request is for a pannikin of tea from the old battered billy.

THE DYING STOCKMAN

A strapping young stockman lay dying,
His saddle supporting his head;
His two mates around him were crying,
As he rose on his elbow and said:

'Wrap me up with my stockwhip and blanket,
And bury me deep down below,
Where the dingoes and crows can't molest me,
In the shade where the coolibahs grow.

'Oh! had I the flight of the bronzewing,
Far o'er the plains would I fly,
Straight to the land of my childhood,
And there I would lay down and die.

'Then cut down a couple of saplings,
Place one at my head and my toe,
Carve on them cross, stockwhip, and saddle,
To show there's a stockman below.

'Hark! there's the wail of a dingo,
Watchful and weird – I must go,
For it tolls the death-knell of the stockman
From the gloom of the scrub down below.

'There's tea in the battered old billy;
Place the pannikins out in a row,
And we'll drink to the next merry meeting,
In the place where all good fellows go.

'And oft in the shades of the twilight,
When the soft winds are whispering low,
And the darkening shadows are falling,
Sometimes think of the stockman below.'

ANONYMOUS

'Bold Jack Donahue' is one of the oldest Australian bushranging ballads. It is based on a true story. Private Muckleston, of the police, who fired the shot that killed Donahue told the inquest into Donahue's death: 'When called upon to surrender, he took off his hat, waved it three times, threw it in the air and shouted, "Come on, you bloody bastards, we're ready if there's a dozen of you!"'

BOLD JACK DONAHUE

There was a valiant highwayman of courage and renown
Who scorned to live in slavery or humble to the Crown;
In Dublin city fair and free where first his breath he drew
'Twas there they christened him the brave and bold Jack Donahue.

Chorus
Come, all my hearties, we'll range the mountain side;
Together we will plunder, together we will ride.
We'll scour along the valleys and gallop o'er the plains,
We scorn to live in slavery bowed down with iron chains.

He scarce had been transported unto the Australian shore
When he took to the highway as he had done before;
And every week in the newspapers was published something new
Concerning all the valiant deeds of bold Jack Donahue.

As Donahue was cruising one summer afternoon
Little was his notion that his death would be so soon,
When to his surprise the horse-police appeared in his view
And in quick time they did advance upon Jack Donahue.

The sergeant of the horse-police discharged his carbine
And called aloud on Donahue to fight or to resign.
'I'd rather range these hills around like wolf or kangaroo
Than work one hour for the government', cried bold Jack Donahue.

Six rounds he fought the horse-police until the fatal ball
Which pierced his heart with cruel smart caused Donahue to fall.
The sergeant and the corporal and all their cowardly crew,
It took them all their time to fall the bold Jack Donahue.

There were Freincy, Grant, bold Robin Hood, and Brennan & O'Hare,
With Donahue the bushranger none of them could compare.
And now he's gone to heaven I hope with the saints and angels too,
May the Lord have mercy on the soul of bold Jack Donahue.

ANONYMOUS

Sympathizing with Bold Jack Donahue

(1) How does the listener know in the first stanza that the narrator is sympathetic towards Jack Donahue?
(2) What other evidence can you find throughout the ballad that the narrator is sympathetic towards the bushranger?
(3) Why is the chorus important in 'Bold Jack Donahue'?
(4) Why is the title 'Bold Jack Donahue' more appropriate than 'Jack Donahue'?
(5) What is the tragic climax of this ballad?
(6) What is the balladist's attitude to the police?
(7) What are your feelings towards Jack Donahue?
(8) What features of this ballad would have made it popular with earlier generations of Australians?
(9) What is the balladist trying to show in the last stanza?
(10) What did you find enjoyable about this ballad? What criticisms would you make of it?

American Ballads

When emigrants came from Europe to the New World, they brought their ballads with them. But in addition, new ballads and songs grew up around their pioneering adventures and exploration of the new lands. Ballads describing the hardships and successes of the pioneers provided entertainment to stave off the monotony and boredom resulting from their isolation.

William Sycamore is the hero of this lively and invigorating ballad which describes the hardships and joys of the American backwoods.

THE BALLAD OF WILLIAM SYCAMORE

My father, he was a mountaineer,
His fist was a knotty hammer;
He was quick on his feet as a running deer,
And he spoke with a Yankee stammer.

My mother, she was merry and brave,
And so she came to her labour,
With a tall green fir for her doctor grave
And a stream for her comforting neighbour.

And some are wrapped in the linen fine,
And some like a godling's scion;
But I was cradled on twigs of pine
In the skin of a mountain lion.

And some remember a white, starched lap
And a ewer with silver handles;
But I remember a coonskin cap
And the smell of bayberry candles.

The cabin logs, with the bark still rough,
And my mother who laughed at trifles,
And the tall, lank visitors, brown as snuff,
With their long, straight squirrel-rifles.

I can hear them dance, like a foggy song,
Through the deepest one of my slumbers,
The fiddle squeaking the boots along
And my father calling the numbers.

The quick feet shaking the puncheon-floor,
The fiddle squeaking and squealing,
Till the dried herbs rattled above the door
And the dust went up to the ceiling.

There are children lucky from dawn till dusk,
But never a child so lucky!
For I cut my teeth on 'Money Musk'
In the Bloody Ground of Kentucky!

When I grew tall as the Indian corn,
My father had little to lend me,
But he gave me his great, old powder-horn
And his woodsman's skill to befriend me.

With a leather shirt to cover my back,
And a redskin nose to unravel
Each forest sign, I carried my pack
As far as a scout could travel.

Till I lost my boyhood and found my wife,
A girl like a Salem clipper!
A woman straight as a hunting-knife
With eyes as bright as the Dipper!

We cleared our camp where the buffalo feed,
Unheard-of streams were our flagons;
And I sowed my sons like apple-seed
On the trail of the Western wagons.

They were right, tight boys, never sulky or slow,
A fruitful, a goodly muster.
The eldest died at the Alamo.
The youngest fell with Custer.

The letter that told it burned my hand.
Yet we smiled and said, 'So be it!'
But I could not live when they fenced the land,
For it broke my heart to see it.

I saddled a red, unbroken colt
And rode him into the day there;
And he threw me down like a thunderbolt
And rolled on me as I lay there.

The hunter's whistle hummed in my ear
As the city-men tried to move me,
And I died in my boots like a pioneer
With the whole wide sky above me.

Now I lie in the heart of the fat, black soil,
Like the seed of a prairie-thistle;
It has washed my bones with honey and oil
And picked them clean as a whistle.

And my youth returns, like the rains of Spring,
And my sons, like the wild geese flying;
And I lie and hear the meadow-lark sing
And have much content in my dying.
Go play with the towns you have built of blocks,
The towns where you would have bound me!
I sleep in my earth like a tired fox,
And my buffalo have found me.

STEPHEN VINCENT BENÉT

Ballad Questions

(1) What qualities of his father does the narrator describe for the listener?
(2) What hardships did William Sycamore's mother have to endure?
(3) How was William Sycamore's infancy different from that of other children?
(4) What sounds does the narrator make you aware of when he is describing the dancing of the pioneers?
(5) What skills did his father give William Sycamore?
(6) What did William Sycamore admire about his wife?
(7) How did Williams Sycamore react to the death of his sons?
(8) How did he react to the fencing of the land?
(9) Do you think the rhythm of the poem suits the story? Why?
(10) What is the tragic climax of the poem?
(11) William Sycamore has 'much content' in his dying? Why is this so?
(12) What is William Sycamore's message to the listener in the last four lines of the ballad?
(13) What factors make this ballad exciting and dramatic?
(14) Do you think this ballad was written about true life experiences? Why or why not?

'The Streets of Laredo' is a ballad from the American West.

THE STREETS OF LAREDO

As I walked out in the streets of Laredo,
As I walked out in Laredo one day,
I spied a young cowboy wrapped up in white linen,
Wrapped up in white linen as cold as the clay.

'I see by your outfit that you are a cowboy' –
These words he did say as I boldly stepped by,
'Come sit down beside me and hear my sad story:
I am shot in the breast and I know I must die.

'It was once in the saddle I used to go dashing,
It was once in the saddle I used to go gay;
First to the dram-house and then to the card-house;
Got shot in the breast and I am dying today.

'Oh, beat the drum slowly and play the fife lowly,
Play the dead march as you carry me along;
Take me to the green valley, there lay the sod o'er me,
For I'm a young cowboy and I know I've done wrong.

'Get six jolly cowboys to carry my coffin;
Get six pretty maidens to bear up my pall,
Put bunches of roses all over my coffin,
Put roses to deaden the sods as they fall.

'Then swing your rope slowly and rattle your spurs lowly,
And give a wild whoop as you carry me along;
And in the grave throw me and roll the sod o'er me
For I'm a young cowboy and I know I've done wrong.

'Go bring me a cup, a cup of cold water,
To cool my parched lips', the cowboy then said;
Before I returned his soul had departed,
And gone to the round-up – the cowboy was dead.

We beat the drum slowly and played the fife lowly,
And bitterly wept as we bore him along;
For we all loved our comrade, so brave, young, and handsome,
We all loved our comrade, although he'd done wrong.

ANONYMOUS

Modern Ballads

Through the centuries the ballad, like other forms of literature has undergone changes. Modern ballad writers, such as W. H. Auden, have introduced sophisticated imagery and thought and have striven for deeper levels of meaning than existed in the traditional ballads. But despite this, telling a story remains the dominant concern.

MISS GEE. A BALLAD

Let me tell you a little story
    About Miss Edith Gee;
She lived in Clevedon Terrace
    At Number 83.

She'd a slight squint in her left eye,
    Her lips they were thin and small,
She had narrow sloping shoulders
    And she had no bust at all.

She'd a velvet hat with trimmings,
    And a dark grey serge costume;
She lived in Clevedon Terrace
    In a small bed-sitting room.

She'd a purple mac for wet days,
    A green umbrella too to take,
She'd a bicycle with shoping basket
    And a harsh back-pedal brake.

The Church of Saint Aloysius
    Was not so very far;
She did a lot of knitting,
    Knitting for that Church Bazaar.

Miss Gee looked up at the starlight
    And said: 'Does anyone care
That I live in Clevedon Terrace
    On one hundred pounds a year?'

She dreamed a dream one evening
    That she was the Queen of France
And the Vicar of Saint Aloysius
    Asked Her Majesty to dance.

But a storm blew down the palace,
    She was biking through a field of corn,
And a bull with the face of the Vicar
    Was charging with lowered horn.

She could feel his hot breath behind her,
    He was going to overtake;
And the bicycle went slower and slower
    Because of that back-pedal brake.

Summer made the trees a picture,
    Winter made them a wreck;
She bicycled to the evening service
    With her clothes buttoned up to her neck.

She passed by the loving couples,
    She turned her head away;
She passed by the loving couples
    And they didn't ask her to stay.

Miss Gee sat down in the side-aisle,
    She heard the organ play;
And the choir it sang so sweetly
    At the ending of the day,

Miss Gee knelt down in the side-aisle,
    She knelt down on her knees:
'Lead me not into temptation
    But make me a good girl, please.'

The days and nights went by her
    Like waves round a Cornish wreck;
She bicycled down to the doctor
    With her clothes buttoned up to her neck.

She bicycled down to the doctor,
    And rang the surgery bell:
'O, doctor, I've a pain inside me,
    And I don't feel very well.'

Doctor Thomas looked her over,
    And then he looked some more;
Walked over to his wash-basin,
    Said, 'Why didn't you come before?'

Doctor Thomas sat over his dinner,
    Though his wife was waiting to ring;
Rolling his bread into pellets,
    Said, 'Cancer's a funny thing.'

His wife she rang for the servant,
    Said, 'Don't be so morbid, dear.'
He said: 'I saw Miss Gee this evening
    And she's a goner, I fear.'

They took Miss Gee to the hospital,
    She lay there a total wreck,
Lay in the ward for women
    With the bedclothes right up to her neck.

They laid her on the table,
    The students began to laugh;
And Mr Rose the surgeon
    He cut Miss Gee in half.

Mr Rose he turned to his students,
    Said: 'Gentlemen, if you please,
We seldom see a sarcoma
    As far advanced as this.'

They took her off the table,
    They wheeled away Miss Gee
Down to another department
    Where they study Anatomy.

They hung her from the ceiling,
    Yes, they hung up Miss Gee;
And a couple of Oxford Groupers
    Carefully dissected her knee.

W. H. AUDEN

Considering Miss Gee

(1) In what ways is Miss Gee physically unattractive?
(2) Find evidence which shows the loneliness and isolation of Miss Gee.
(3) In what ways is 'Miss Gee. A Ballad' similar to the ballads of the past?
(4) Why do you think the poet chose Miss Gee as the subject of his ballad?
(5) What is Doctor Thomas' attitude to Miss Gee and her cancer?
(6) What comments would you make about Mr Rose's and his students' attitude to Miss Gee?
(7) What is the tragic climax of this ballad?
(8) What examples of exaggeration can you find in this ballad?
(9) We are left to form our own conclusions about the life and fate of Miss Gee. What are your feelings towards her?
(10) In what ways is this ballad different from those of previous centuries?

The conditions of true ballad making are reproduced in 'Ballad of the Landlord'. This ballad sprang naturally from a true life happening.

BALLAD OF THE LANDLORD

Landlord, landlord,
My roof has sprung a leak.
Don't you 'member I told you about it
Way last week?

Landlord, landlord,
These steps is broken down.
When you come up yourself
It's a wonder you don't fall down.

Ten bucks you say I owe you?
Ten bucks you say is due?
Well, that's ten bucks more'n I'll pay you
Till you fix this house up new.

What? You gonna get eviction orders?
You gonna cut off my heat?
You gonna take my furniture and
Throw it in the street?

Um-huh! You talking high and mighty.
Talk on – till you get through.
You ain't gonna be able to say a word
If I land my fist on you.

Police! Police!
Come and get this man!
He's trying to ruin the government
And overturn the land!

Copper's whistle!
Patrol bell!
Arrest.

Precinct station.
Iron cell.
Headlines in press:

Man threatens landlord
Tenant held no bail
Judge gives Negro 90 days in county jail

LANGSTON HUGHES

24 Encounters

The death of a creature such as a beautiful bird becomes a sad and distressful encounter for the poet Rodney Hall.

I'M A KILLER, I AM

Catapults in hand and pocket,
children scramble past me, pinning
my ears with their excited screams
We hit him. Did you see that shot —
the aim, and Piinnggg! I'm a killer, I am.
At the stoning-point of jubilance
a lorikeet rolls its nape in the gutter,
one foot pinching the leap of air
(two toes forward, two toes back)
green as feathered sap of woodland,
nimble as life with sky in its bones.
But the dainty stove-in breast is heavy.
And its eye, that one surviving weapon,
holds-off crouching spellbound huntsmen.

Somewhere, huge within me,
dark wings unfold.

RODNEY HALL

Contemplating Cruelty

(1) 'Catapults in hand and pocket'. What dominates the poet's impression of the children scrambling past him?
(2) Explain the meaning of 'pinning/my ears with their excited screams'.
(3) What effect does the poet achieve by using the word 'Piinnggg!'?
(4) What feeling do you think prompts the excited scream of '*I'm a killer, I am*'?
(5) Explain the meaning of 'At the stoning-point of jubilance'.
(6) 'One foot pinching the leap of air'. In what way does this line touch on the life the lorikeet has lost?
(7) What picture do the words 'green as feathered sap of woodland' call up in your imagination?
(8) Why do you think the image evoked by the words 'nimble as life with sky in its bones' is beautifully appropriate for a wild bird?
(9) How does the eye of the lorikeet affect the jubilant children?
(10) What feelings does the poet experience at the end of the poem?
(11) What message do you think the poet is conveying to us in this poem?

Here is a poem that describes a brief encounter between the poet and a handicapped boy. The impression it leaves on the poet is a lasting one.

NEAR THE SCHOOL FOR HANDICAPPED CHILDREN

His hat is rammed on
his shirt jerks at his body
his feet cannot hold in
   the sway   he cannot keep
      still.
When I see his face it is freckled
to remind me of nephews
his limbs remind me of how straight
is my own spine and that I take my fingers
for granted.
He is waiting for the green light.
     my finger clench
   I am hurt by my wholeness
   I cannot take my eyes from him
   I fear my daughter may be watching
He has been dressed carefully
   I'm here I'm here I'm here
his whole struggle rasps me like a whisper

and when the lights do change
   he skips across the road he
     skips he skips he dances and skips
       leaving us all behind like a skimming tamborine
       brittle with music.

THOMAS SHAPCOTT

Appreciating the Encounter

(1) Why do the clothes worn by the handicapped boy make an impact on the poet?
(2) In what ways is the boy's body seemingly out of control?
(3) Why does the boy's face remind the poet of his nephews?
(4) Explain the meaning of 'I am hurt by my wholeness'.
(5) 'I fear my daughter may be watching'. Why does the poet fear this?
(6) Why does the poet repeat the words 'I'm here'?
(7) Why does the poet repeat the word 'skips' so often?
(8) How does the movement of the boy crossing the road contrast with his former stance at the traffic lights?
(9) What change of mood accompanies the change of movement in the last stanza?
(10) What does the poet reveal about himself in the poem?

The encounter in this poem is between a church-goer and a woman begging on the steps of a church; while the church is all about hope, begging in the big city is a hopeless task.

BEGGAR WOMAN ... MEXICO CITY

It is Saturday night on the Paseo de la Reforma.
The Indian woman sits outside the door
of the Church of Reconciliation. Her baby, sleeping,
rests upon her fingers' pillow; the other hand,
thrust into the night, begs in hopeless seeking.

I enter the Church. She does not move as I pass her
frozen in the heat, seeing nothing in her stare
at the boulevarde, wide and affluent, before her in the evening.
The baby, closely cradled in one arm, is sleeping. The hand
which begs hangs without hope in the evening.

It is dark night on the Paseo de la Reforma
when I leave the church, having said my comfortable prayer.
She waits there still, the baby held closer, suckling;
and both are still. The traffic screams. There is no sound
from woman or child.
    I drop five pesos in her hand.
      Is it sufficient?

PATRICK COADY

Read this poem about an encounter by telephone. The setting is probably London and the encounter is between an African person who is simply seeking accommodation and a prejudiced landlady who is inclined to apply a colour bar even to a voice over the telephone.

TELEPHONE CONVERSATION

The price seemed reasonable, location
Indifferent. The landlady swore she lived
Off premises. Nothing remained
But self-confession. 'Madam', I warned,
'I hate a wasted journey – I am African.'
Silence. Silenced transmission of
Pressurized good-breeding. Voice, when it came,
Lipstick coated, long gold-rolled
Cigarette-holder pipped. Caught I was, foully.
'HOW DARK?' . . . I had not misheard . . . 'ARE YOU LIGHT
OR VERY DARK?' Button B. Button A. Stench
Of rancid breath of public hide-and-speak.
Red booth. Red pillar-box. Red double-tiered
Omnibus squelching tar. It *was* real! Shamed
By ill-mannered silence, surrender

Pushed dumbfoundment to beg simplification.
Considerate she was, varying the emphasis –
'ARE YOU DARK? OR VERY LIGHT?' Revelation came.
'You mean – like plain or milk chocolate?'
Her assent was clinical, crushing in its light
Impersonality. Rapidly, wave-length adjusted,
I chose. 'West African sepia' – and as afterthought,
'Down in my passport'. Silence for spectroscopic
Flight of fancy, till truthfulness clanged her accent
Hard on the mouthpiece. 'WHAT'S THAT?' conceding
'DON'T KNOW WHAT THAT IS,' 'Like brunette.'
'THAT'S DARK, ISN'T IT?' 'Not altogether.
Facially, I am brunette, but, madam, you should see
The rest of me. Palm of my hand, soles of my feet
Are a peroxide blond. Friction, caused –
Foolishly, madam – by sitting down, has turned
My bottom raven black – One moment, madam!' – sensing
Her receiver rearing on the thunderclap
About my ears – 'Madam', I pleaded, 'wouldn't you rather
See for yourself?'

WOLE SOYINKA

247

The poem that follows gives us a glimpse of the power that resides in authority and one way in which this power can be misused. The authority figure is your Honour, a judge, while before him appear accused people who are both disadvantaged and over-awed.

THE 100 CENTRE STREET, BOY,
YOU BETTER DRESS UP NEAT BLUES

You speak English
Yes Sir
Speak up, I can't hear you –
    You speak English
Yes Sir
Can you afford a lawyer
No Sir
OK. Legal Aid.
    Put him in
Next case

Stand up straight and take your hands
    out of your pocket
Yes Sir
Where's your family? Why isn't your family here?
My mother works
What's that? Speak up.
My mother works
Well doesn't she know that you're in
    serious trouble? We all work
    but doesn't she know she has an
    obligation to this court to be here?
Yes Sir
Well you can just wait. You go back and wait
    and we'll give your mother time to come
    Call the case later
But my mother's at work
Call the next case.

What is this? A sentence?
Yes your Honour
Any motions?
No your Honour. I'd just like to say the boy
    does have a job and this is his first offence
Shoplifting is theft Mr Defence Attorney, are you
    aware of that
Yes Sir
Six months in the city prison
Call the next case.

ANONYMOUS

In 'Prizegiving' the self assured Professor Eisenbart becomes 'a sage fool trapped by music in a copper net of hair'.

PRIZEGIVING

Professor Eisenbart, asked to attend
a girls' school speech night as an honoured guest
and give the prizes out, rudely declined;
but from indifference agreed, when pressed
with dry scholastic jokes, to change his mind,
to grace their humble platform, and to lend

distinction (of a kind not specified)
to the occasion. Academic dress
became him, as he knew. When he appeared
the girls whirred with an insect nervousness,
the Head in humbler black flapped round and steered
her guest, superb in silk and fur, with pride

to the best seat beneath half-hearted blooms
tortured to form the school's elaborate crest.
Eisenbart scowled with violent distaste,
then recomposed his features to their best
advantage: deep in thought, with one hand placed
like Rodin's Thinker. So he watched the room's

mosaic of young heads. Blonde, black, mouse-brown
they bent for their Headmistress' opening prayer.
But underneath a light (no accident
of seating, he felt sure), with titian hair
one girl sat grinning at him, her hand bent
under her chin in mockery of his own.

Speeches were made and prizes given. He shook
indifferently a host of virgin hands.
'*Music*'! The girl with titian hair stood up,
hitched at a stocking, winked at nearby friends,
and stood before him to receive a cup
of silver chased with curious harps. He took

her hand, and felt its voltage fling his hold
from his calm age and power; suffered her strange
eyes, against reason dark, to take his stare
with her to the piano, there to change
her casual schoolgirl's for a master's air.
He forged his rose-hot dream as Mozart told

The fullness of all passion or despair
summoned by arrogant hands. The music ended,
Eisenbart teased his gown while others clapped,
and peered into a trophy which suspended
his image upside down: a sage fool trapped
by music in a copper net of hair.

GWEN HARWOOD

Thoughtful Questions

(1) Why does the professor's attitude towards attending the prizegiving change?
(2) What is the meaning of 'the girls whirred with an insect nervousness'?
(3) What feelings are displayed by the Head towards her guest?
(4) How do we know that the professor's resemblance to Rodin's Thinker is a deliberate pose?
(5) How did one girl capture the attention of the professor?
(6) Explain the meaning of: 'He took/her hand and felt its voltage fling his hold/from his calm age and power'.
(7) What does the poem reveal about the personality of the girl with titian hair?
(8) What does the poem reveal about the character of Professor Eisenbart?
(9) What is the meaning of 'a sage fool trapped/by music in a copper net of hair'?
(10) Explain why this poem is likely to appeal to readers other than school students, teachers and academics.

'Dentist at Work' is a poem about an encounter between a dentist and a patient. As you read, you will notice the poem is made up of four stanzas, each of which is separated from the next by the dentist's direction to the dental nurse or to the patient. These directions are in plain type while the rest of the poem is in italics indicating the dentist's thoughts as he observes 'the refuse pit' inside the patient's mouth. There is an amusing contrast between the dentist's thoughts often expressed in explicit technical jargon, and the polite directions he gives aloud. Phrases such as 'sliming heaps of calculus', 'richly stinking caries', 'gingeval rot', suggest that the man's mouth is a kind of weird 'refuse pit' of which even the patient is unaware.

One purpose that the poet has achieved in this poem is to reverse the usual approach to dental surgery which is always seen from the patient's point of view. Here the dentist has his say.

DENTIST AT WORK

Mister, if I could illustrate this moment
What a refuse-pit you yawn under my hand,
What sliming heaps of calculus and sagging gums,
What richly stinking caries these bicuspids house,
You'd squirm in raw embarrassment, not pain.
No. 4 please, nurse. And a matrix band; upper jaw.
My arrogant professor would have rebelled:
'I'm no sanitary engineer. Chew pumice.
And come again'. A deeply arrogant man.
But I'll scrape; clean; restore. Try to sweeten it.
Probe, please. Open wide. *Perhaps you've a wife.*
Christ, even my hardened stomach twitches
At that! Gingeval rot, both jaws. Gums
Suppurating. Pretty.

These teeth
Bit solid once. No. 3 burr, nurse. Have a rinse.
Wide up. *Yes, pain. A kind of penance.*
I'm cold now. Balancing forces: health; pain;
Filth. This toxin seeps to your toes, is drained
By your stomach. Headaches; listlessness; lose
Your spunk. A big man with soft hands –
Can't run a dozen yards I'd wager. A flaccid
Thirty-year-old, lounging about week-ends,
Inert as a cushion. Diet of whisky, cakes
And creamed potatoes. Sucks lollies in the train.

Open wide. *Open very wide, mister. This is a fight.*
You think me silent; cruel, perhaps. Nothing to say.
But if at some garrulous party you should ask
Why I pursue this trade, excuse my shrug
And my simple answer: health – even
In the place of eating – and of kissing – is still
A kind of wealth. Open up. Not long now.

KEITH HARRISON

Far into the future, the space-ship hostess may serve tea, but with certain precautions.

TEA IN A SPACESHIP

In this world a tablecloth need not be laid
On any table, but is spread out anywhere
Upon the always equidistant and
Invisible legs of gravity's wild air.

The tea, which never would grow cold,
Gathers itself into a wet and steaming ball,
And hurls its liquid molecules at anybody's head,
Or dances, eternal bilboquet,
In and out of the suspended cups up-
Ended in the weightless hands
Of chronically nervous jerks
Who yet would never spill a drop,
Their mouths agape for passing cakes.

Lumps of sparkling sugar
Sling themselves out of their crystal bowl
With a disordered fountain's
Ornamental stops and starts.
The milk describes a permanent parabola
Girdled with satellites of spinning tarts.

The future lives with graciousness.
The hostess finds her problems eased,
For there is honey still for tea
And butter keeps the ceiling greased.
She will provide, of course,
No cake-forks, spoons or knives.
They are so sharp, so dangerously gadabout,
It is regarded as a social misdemeanour
To put them out.

JAMES KIRKUP

Envisaging Tea in a Spaceship

(1) In the first two line of the poem, how does the poet indicate to us that gravity is not present in a spaceship in the same way as it is present on Earth?
(2) What words in the last line of the first stanza indicate that gravity is unpredictable?
(3) What is unusual about the tea in the second stanza?
(4) What is the meaning of 'Their mouths agape for passing cakes'?
(5) 'The milk describes a permanent parabola'. What would be happening to the milk?
(6) What is the meaning of 'butter keeps the ceiling greased'?
(7) In the spaceship how could the hostess commit 'a social misdemeanour'?
(8) Do you think the poem is lighthearted or serious? Why?

(9) Why do you think the poet, James Kirkup, chose to write a poem about tea in a spaceship?

(10) Did you enjoy this poem? Why or why not?

It would be difficult to imagine a more welcome encounter than that of rain on dry ground.

RAIN ON DRY GROUND

That is rain on dry ground. We heard it:
We saw the little tempest in the grass,
The panic of anticipation: heard
The uneasy leaves flutter, the air pass
In a wave, the fluster of the vegetation;

Heard the first spatter of drops, the outriders
Larruping on the ground, hitting against
The gate of the drought, and shattering
On to the lances of the tottering meadow.
It is rain; it is rain on dry ground.

This is the urgent decision of the day,
The urgent drubbing of earth, the urgent raid
On the dust; downpour over the flaring poppy,
Deluge on the face of noon, the flagellant
Rain drenching across the air. The day

Flows in the ditch: bubble and twisting twig
And the sodden morning swirl along together
Under the crying hedge. And where the sun
Ran on the scythes, the rain runs down
The obliterated field, the blunted crop.

The rain stops:
The air is sprung with green.
The intercepted drops
Fall at their leisure; and between
The threading runnels on the slopes
The snail drags his caution into the sun.

CHRISTOPHER FRY

Acknowledgements

The authors and publishers are grateful to the following for permission to reproduce copyright material:

A. D. Peters & Co. Ltd for 'Uncle Terry' by Roger McGough from *Sporting Relations*, published by Eyre Methuen Ltd; 'Mrs Rees Laughs' by Martin Armstrong from *Collected Poems*, published by Martin Secker & Warburg Ltd. A. P. Watt Ltd for 'The Wild Swans at Coole' by W. B. Yeats from *The Collected Poems of W. B. Yeats*. The Bodley Head for 'Nile Fishermen' from *Poems* by Rex Warner; Cheval/Stanyan Co. Ltd for 'Christmas Card' by Rod McKuen from *The Sea Around Me* © 1976 by Montcalm Productions, used by permission. All rights reserved. Curtis Brown and the Estate of Odgen Nash for 'Children's Party' and 'Confessions of a Born Spectator' by Odgen Nash. Curtis Brown (Aust.) Pty Ltd for 'The Serf' by Roy Campbell and 'The Hunter' by Odgen Nash. David Higham Associates Limited for 'It Was Long Ago' by Eleanor Farjeon from *Silver Sand and Snow*, published by Michael Joseph; 'Hymn of the Scientific Farmers' by Clive Sansom, published by Methuen; 'I Saw a Jolly Hunter' by Charles Causley from *Collected Poems*, published by Macmillan Limited; 'Poem in October' and 'The Hunchback in the Park' by Dylan Thomas from *Under Milk Wood*, published by J. M. Dent; and 'The Young Ones' by Elizabeth Jennings from *Collected Poems*, published by Macmillan Limited; Harper and Row, Publishers, Inc. for 'Fifteen' from *Stories that Could be True* by William Stafford, copyright © 1964, 1977 by William Stafford. Ian Crichton-Smith for 'Rythm'. Jacaranda Wiley Ltd for 'We are going' and 'Natmatjira' by Kath Walker, from *My People*. John Murray for 'Executive', 'Seaside Golf' and 'Meditation on the A30' by John Betjeman, from *Collected Poems*; Jonathan Cape Ltd and the Executors of the Estate of C. Day Lewis for 'Flight to Italy' by C. Day Lewis from *Collected Poems 1954*, published by Hogarth Press. Kate Jones for 'Ode to a Delectable Bore'. Keith Laing for 'Football Hero'. Lansdowne-Rigby for 'The Improvers' by Colin Thiele from *Colin Thiele Selected Verse*, Rigby Publishers; Len Fox for 'National Hero'. Longman Cheshire for 'Life—Cycle for Big Jim Phelan' and 'Home—coming' by Bruce Dawe, from *Sometimes Gladness Poems 1954—78*. Macmillan Education Limited for 'Dentist at Work' by Keith Harrison from *Points in a Journey*. Macmillan Publishing Company, New York for 'Bats' by Randall Jarrell from *The Lost World*. Martin Secker & Warburg Limited for 'Daniel at Breakfast' by Phyllis McGinley from *The Love Letters of Phyllis McGinley*. New Directions Publishing Corporation for 'Smell' by William Carlos Williams, from *Collected Earlier Poems*, copyright 1938 by New Directions Publishing Corporation. Paul Dehn Enterprises for 'Gutter Press' by Paul Dehn; Penguin Books Limited for 'The Nun's Priest's Tale' and 'The Miller's Tale' from Geoffrey Chaucer *The Canterbury Tales* translated by Nevill Coghill (Penguin Classics, 1951, revised edition 1958, 1960, 1975, 1977), copyright 1951 by Nevill Coghill, copyright © the Estate of Nevill Coghill, 1958, 1960, 1975, 1977. Philip Hobsbaum for 'The Place's Fault'. James Kirkup for 'Tea in a Spaceship'. The Society of Authors as the literary representative of the Estate of A. E. Housman and Jonathan Cape Ltd publishers of A. E. Housman's *Collected Poems* for 'To an Athlete Dying Young' by A. E. Housman. University of Queensland Press for 'Office Block' by J. Manifold from *OP 8–Poems 1961–69*, 1971, Near the School for Handicapped Children' by T. Shapcott from *Shabbytown Calendar*, 1975, 'Old Man Burning Off' by T. Shapcott from *Inwards to the Sun*, 1969, and 'They Married' by R. Thurston from *Believed Dangerous*, 1975. Wes Magee for 'What is . . . the Sun?' Angus and Robertson Publishers for 'Merinos' by David Campbell from *Selected Poems*, 'Sheep—Killer' by Ernest Moll from *Poems*, 'Australia' by A. D. Hope from *Collected Poems 1930–1970*, 'The Burning Truck' by Les Murray from *The Vernacular Republic*, 'Beach Burial', 'William Street' and 'Two Chronometers the Captain had' by Kenneth Slessor from *Selected Poems*, 'Because' by James McAuley from *Collected Poems 1936–1970*, 'Legend' and 'Metho Drinker' by Judith Wright from *Selected Poems*, 'Prizegiving' and 'Suburban Sonnet' by Gwen Harwood from *Selected Poems*, 'Kangaroos Near Hay' by John Foulcher from *Light Pressure*, 'Rhinoceros' by William Hart—Smith from *Selected Poems*, 'Kooka-burras' and 'Leopard Skin' by Douglas Stewart from *Selected Poems*, 'Drought' by Will Ogilvie from

Hearts of Gold, 'Grape Harvest' by Brian Vrepont from *Beyond the Claw*, 'The Traveller by C. J. Dennis from *Selected Verse of C. J. Dennis*, 'One Winter Morning' by Ray Mathew from *South of the Equator*, 'The Shark' by John Blight from *My Beachcoming Days* © 1968 John Blight, 'The Death of the Bird' by A. D. Hope from *Collected Poems 1930–1970* © A. D. Hope 1966, 1969, 1972, and for 'Winter Stock Route' by David Campbell from *Selected Poems* © Judith Anne Campbell; Associated Book Publishers (U.K.) Ltd for 'Hiroshima' by Angela Clifton from *Poems by Children* edited by M. Baldwin; Faber and Faber Publishers for 'Follower' and 'Mid Term Break' by Seamus Heaney from *Death of a Naturalist*, 'The Gardener' by Louis MacNeice from *The Collected Poems of Louis MacNeice*, 'Miss Gee – A Ballad' by W. H. Auden from *Collected Poems*, 'Six Young Men' and 'The Thought Fox' by Ted Hughes from *The Hawk in the Rain*, 'Pike' by Ted Hughes from *Lupercal*, 'The Warm and the Cold' by Ted Hughes from *Season Songs*, 'The Poet Comments' by Ted Hughes from *Poetry in the Making*, 'The Tom Cat' by Don Marquis from *Poetry of Don Marquis*, and 'Preludes' by T. S. Eliot from *Collected Poems 1909–1962*; James Kirkup for 'Tea in a Spaceship'; Melbourne University Press for 'Small Town' from *Behind My Eyes* by B. A. Breen; Penguin Books Ltd for 'Bats' from *The Bat-Poet* by Randall Jarrell (Kestrel Books, 1977) pp. 36–37, Copyright © 1963, 1964 by Macmillan Publishing Co Inc.; Carnanet Press Ltd for 'The Suspect' by Edwin Morgan from *Collected Poems*.

Photographs: Andrew Chapman, p. 53, p. 218; Ford Motor Company of Australia Ltd, p. 199; Gordon De'Lisle, p. 90; Victorian Department of Agriculture, p. 30.

Line art by Steven Goldsmith
Cover art by Jan Schmoeger
Cover photograph by Dieter Muller

Index of poets

Index of poems